Kierkegaard for Apologetics

Kierkegaard for Apologetics

Existence, Faith, and Witness

MICHAEL NATHAN STEINMETZ

WIPF & STOCK · Eugene, Oregon

KIERKEGAARD FOR APOLOGETICS
Existence, Faith, and Witness

Wipf & Stock
An Imprint of Wipf and Stock Publishers
199 W. 8th Ave., Suite 3
Eugene, OR 97401

www.wipfandstock.com

PAPERBACK ISBN: 979-8-3852-3714-2
HARDCOVER ISBN: 979-8-3852-3715-9
EBOOK ISBN: 979-8-3852-3716-6

VERSION NUMBER 02/17/26

To Kimberly
My biggest encourager
Without whom this book would not have been completed

Contents

Abbreviations of Søren Kierkegaard's Works | ix

Introduction | 1

1 How Broad Is the Ditch?
Subjectivity, Objectivity, and the Leap to Faith | 13

2 That Doesn't Mean What You Think It Means:
Fear and Trembling, Faith, and Absurdity | 46

3 The Wound and Blessing of Existence:
Selfhood, Sin, Necessity, and Human Freedom | 80

4 Multiple Personalities:
Indirect Communication and Apologetics | 108

5 Time to Be a Gadfly: Critiquing the Present Age | 135

6 This Life of Care and Love | 155

Conclusion | 178

Bibliography | 183

Index | 193

Abbreviations of Søren Kierkegaard's Works

ENGLISH WORKS

BA — *The Book on Adler*. Edited and translated by Howard V. Hong and Edna H. Hong. Kierkegaard's Writings 24. 1998. Reprint, Princeton: Princeton University Press, 2009.

CA — *The Concept of Anxiety*. Edited and translated by Reidar Thomte, in collaboration with Albert B. Anderson. Kierkegaard's Writings 8. Princeton: Princeton University Press, 1980.

CD — *Christian Discourses*. Edited and translated by Howard V. Hong and Edna H. Hong. Kierkegaard's Writings 17. 1997. Reprint, Princeton: Princeton University Press, 2009.

COR — *The Corsair Affair and Articles Related to the Writings*. Edited and translated by Howard V. Hong and Edna H. Hong. Kierkegaard's Writings 13. 1982. Reprint, Princeton: Princeton University Press, 2009.

CUP1 — *Concluding Unscientific Postscript*. Edited and translated by Howard V. Hong and Edna H. Hong. Vol. 1. Kierkegaard's Writings, 12.1. Princeton: Princeton University Press, 1992.

EO1 — *Either/Or, Part I*. Edited and translated by Howard V. Hong and Edna H. Hong. Kierkegaard's Writings 3. Princeton: Princeton University Press, 1987.

EO2 — *Either/Or, Part II*. Edited and translated by Howard V. Hong and Edna H. Hong. Kierkegaard's Writings 4. 1987. Reprint, Princeton: Princeton University Press, 1990.

EUD — *Eighteen Upbuilding Discourses*. Edited and translated by Howard V. Hong and Edna H. Hong. Kierkegaard's Writings 5. 1990. Reprint, Princeton: Princeton University Press, 1992.

FSE	*For Self-Examination.* Edited and translated by Howard V. Hong and Edna H. Hong. Kierkegaard's Writings 21. 1990. Reprint, Princeton: Princeton University Press, 1991.
FT	*Fear and Trembling.* Edited and translated by Howard V. Hong and Edna H. Hong. Kierkegaard's Writings 6. Princeton: Princeton University Press, 1983.
JP	*Søren Kierkegaard's Journals and Papers.* Edited and translated by Howard V. Hong and Edna H. Hong, assisted by Gregor Malantschuk. Vols. 1–6. Bloomington: Indiana University Press, 1967–1978.
KJN	*Kierkegaard's Journals and Notebooks.* Edited and translated by Niels Jørgen Cappelørn, et al. Vols. 1–11. Princeton: Princeton University Press, 2007–2019.
M	*The Moment and Late Writings.* Edited and translated by Howard V. Hong and Edna H. Hong. Kierkegaard's Writings 23. 1998. Reprint, Princeton: Princeton University Press, 2009.
P	*Prefaces.* Edited and translated by Todd W. Nichol. Kierkegaard's Writings 9. 1997. Reprint, Princeton: Princeton University Press, 2009.
PC	*Practice in Christianity.* Edited and translated by Howard V. Hong and Edna H. Hong. Kierkegaard's Writings 20. Princeton: Princeton University Press, 1991.
PF	*Philosophical Fragments.* Edited and translated by Howard V. Hong and Edna H. Hong. Kierkegaard's Writings 7. 1985. Reprint, Princeton: Princeton University Press, 1987.
PV	*The Point of View.* Edited and translated by Howard V. Hong and Edna H. Hong. Kierkegaard's Writings 22. 1998. Reprint, Princeton: Princeton University Press, 2009.
R	*Repetition.* Edited and translated by Howard V. Hong and Edna H. Hong. Kierkegaard's Writings 6. Princeton: Princeton University Press, 1983.
SL	*Stages on Life's Way.* Edited and translated by Howard V. Hong and Edna H. Hong. Kierkegaard's Writings 11. 1988. Reprint, Princeton: Princeton University Press, 1991.
SUD	*The Sickness unto Death.* Edited and translated by Howard V. Hong and Edna H. Hong. Kierkegaard's Writings 19. 1980. Reprint, Princeton: Princeton University Press, 1983.
SUDh	*The Sickness unto Death.* Translated by Alastair Hannay. 1989. Reprint, New York: Penguin, 2004.
SUDk	*The Sickness unto Death.* Translated by Bruce H. Kirmmse. New York: Liveright, 2023.
TA	*Two Ages.* Edited and translated by Howard V. Hong and Edna H. Hong. Kierkegaard's Writings 14. 1978. Reprint, Princeton: Princeton University Press, 2009.

TD *Three Discourses on Imagined Occasions.* Edited and translated by Howard V. Hong and Edna H. Hong. Kierkegaard's Writings 10. 1993. Reprint, Princeton: Princeton University Press, 2009.

UD *Upbuilding Discourses in Various Spirits.* Edited and translated by Howard V. Hong and Edna H. Hong. Kierkegaard's Writings 15. 1993. Reprint, Princeton: Princeton University Press, 2009.

WA *Without Authority.* Edited and translated by Howard V. Hong and Edna H. Hong. Kierkegaard's Writings 18. 1997. Reprint, Princeton: Princeton University Press, 2009.

WL *Works of Love.* Edited and translated by Howard V. Hong and Edna H. Hong. Kierkegaard's Writings 16. 1995. Reprint, Princeton: Princeton University Press, 1998.

DANISH WORKS

Pap. *Søren Kierkegaards Papirer.* Edited by Peter Andreas Heiberg, et al. Vols. I–XI–3. Copenhagen: Gyldendalske Boghandel, Nordisk Forlag, 1909–1948.

SKS *Søren Kierkegaards Skrifter.* Edited by Niels Jørgen Cappelørn, et al. Vols. 1–28 and K1–K28. Copenhagen: Gads Forlag, 1997–2013.

Introduction

When I was in high school, like many teenage Christians raised in church, I started to have questions about my faith. Some friends at school highlighted difficult issues concerning Christianity that I had not considered. The doubts came creeping in, and I was unsure of which way to turn. Providentially, my youth pastor, Dalton, was patient and wise, listening to my anxious thoughts with compassion and concern. He told me that although Christians experience doubt, all truth is God's truth. When we investigate the truth, it will end up verifying the Christian faith rather than diminishing it. Christians need not worry, but rather they should struggle, wrestle, and grapple with their faith.[1] My youth pastor gave me a few apologetics books. I devoured them. I remember thinking for the first time, "Wow, there are Christians out there that actually address these concerns!"

That encounter with doubt, and my leaning into it rather than ignoring it, led me down the path I am on today. I felt a call from God in my life: I wanted to help others like Dalton helped me. I decided to pursue youth ministry, so I enrolled in a Christian college, majoring in philosophy and religion. My newly chosen path was not without turbulence. At age nineteen, I had what some might call an existential crisis. I was serving in a local church, sharing the responsibility of being de facto youth minister with a close friend. Here I was, studying theology, practicing youth ministry, doing all the things I was supposed to do, yet I was filled with unease. My restless heart kept spinning me around, unsure which direction was up or down. One night I drove around town listening to

1. I am indebted to my college professor Dr. James Heath for talking about the Christian's walk as struggling, wrestling, and grappling.

music, confused, wondering what I had gotten myself into, crying out to God for help and guidance.

At this pivotal time in my life, I was introduced to nineteenth-century Danish theologian and philosopher Søren Kierkegaard.[2] In my history of western philosophy class, my beloved professor Dr. Gerry Heard explained the broad strokes of Kierkegaard's thought. I was enamored, but I had read many apologetic works from various philosophers and theologians who viewed Kierkegaard negatively. For example, one of my textbooks during my undergraduate years was James Sire's *The Universe Next Door*, 4th edition. In that work, Sire investigates different worldviews and compares them to the Christian worldview. In the chapter titled "Beyond Nihilism," Sire examines existentialism, breaking down the viewpoint into its theistic and atheistic varieties. He connects Kierkegaard to theistic existentialism and ultimately states, "Theistic existentialism took two steps away from traditional theism. The first step was to begin to distrust the accuracy of recorded history. The second step was to lose interest in its facticity and to emphasize its religious implication or meaning."[3] For one who affirmed (and still affirms) that Jesus rose from the grave within history, my suspicion was in full gear while sitting in my philosophy class; but something about Kierkegaard's thought intrigued me. I then picked up a copy of *Fear and Trembling*. I struggled through the work—I do not suggest making it one's first foray into Kierkegaard! What I did glean from the book was a mind trying to understand what it means to live the Christian life, not a person trying to tear down Christian faith.

After graduating college, I got a job teaching Spanish in a high school, a long shot away from my initial goals of youth ministry. My doubt deepened. In particular, I could not grasp how a loving God would damn someone to hell for all eternity. I knew all of the responses from the apologetic works I had read. I knew about the eternity of God and how sinning against an eternal God had an eternal consequence. I understood the need for atonement for sins and how much God loved me by providing a way through the blood of the Lamb. I knew all the responses—but

2. I purposefully put "theologian" before "philosopher," for I believe Kierkegaard to be primarily a theologian, not a philosopher. Kierkegaard most definitely engages in philosophical discourse, but his purpose is to push people to the religious reality of Christianity. Murray Rae agrees: "For Kierkegaard, theology *is* the main thing. Kierkegaard was, above all, a Christian thinker, and to think Christianly is precisely to do theology" (Rae, *Kierkegaard and Theology*, 1). See also Gouwens, *Kierkegaard as Religious Thinker*, 3, 12; Barrett, "Passion of Kierkegaard's Existential Method," 18.

3. Sire, *Universe Next Door*, 135.

still, something did not sit well with me. I had the "right" answers, but they brought me no comfort.

I was considering throwing in the towel on religion altogether. My godly mother, like Monica for Augustine, prayed for me and encouraged me. She suggested I listen to her favorite preacher, Timothy Keller. One of Keller's sermons caught my eye (or, I guess, my ear). It was titled "The Sickness unto Death," and the passage was Jer 9:21–26. Keller's title comes from Kierkegaard's magisterial *The Sickness unto Death*, and in the sermon, Keller gives a brief summary on Kierkegaard's understanding of sin: "Kierkegaard gives us a definition of sin that is both modern and biblical, and that is not easy. . . . So what is he saying? He is saying this. If you build your identity on any created thing, you have a radically unstable identity."[4] Keller's tying of Kierkegaard's work to living an authentic Christian life in the here-and-now awakened me. I immediately went out and bought a copy of *The Sickness unto Death*.

As I read, I was shocked: Kierkegaard hauntingly explicates the harrowing effects of sin, how all people are in desperate need of forgiveness—even those who do not think they are in peril. Kierkegaard states,

> So much is spoken about wasting one's life. But the only life wasted is the life of the one who so lived it, deceived by life's pleasure or its sorrow, that he never became decisively, eternally, conscious of himself as spirit, as self, or, what is the same, he never became aware—and gained in the deepest sense the impression—that there is a God there and that "he," himself, his self, exists before this God, which infinite gain is never come by except through despair.[5]

This does not sound like someone attempting to uproot Christian belief, or as Francis Schaeffer puts it, someone who wanted to "discard rational thought about [important things of human life] and make a gigantic, nonrational leap of faith."[6] Kierkegaard sounds like a believer exhorting his countrymen to put their faith in Christ. Kierkegaard continues, "The teaching about sin—that you and I are sinners—a teaching that unconditionally splits up 'the crowd,' confirms that qualitative difference between

4. Keller, "Sickness unto Death," 13:20–13:40.

5. *SUDh*, 57 / *SKS* 11, 142–43. Kierkegaard uses numerous pseudonyms across many of his works. Such leads many scholars to not cite "Kierkegaard" but rather cite the name of his pseudonym. I will address this concern more closely in chapter 4, but suffice it to say, I believe there is a clear voice of Kierkegaard throughout all of his works.

6. Schaeffer, *God Who Is There*, 1:16.

God and Man . . . sin is indeed: *before* God. . . . As sinner, man is separated from God by the most chasmic qualitative abyss."[7] This passage hit me like a ton of bricks. Although I read numerous biblical passages about how God's ways are not my ways, I had always assumed God thought how I thought in some way, shape, or form. I received this impression not from the Bible but from many of the philosophical and theological texts I encountered in my undergraduate studies. Kierkegaard stresses the otherness of God and, at the same moment, explains how sin is a disintegration of the self. He deftly demonstrates the gravity of sin, and for the first time, I understood why eternal judgment happens: sin is *that* serious. God is not some school principal who enforces silly rules because he does not want humanity to have fun. Sin destroys our "selves" and our world. Humans are separated from God, in desperate need of salvation. How does Kierkegaard respond to our plight as humans? The answer is faith in Christ: "Faith is: that the self in being itself and in willing to be itself rests transparently in God."[8] As the old hymn goes, one must *decide* to follow Jesus—to put his or her faith in Christ, the God-man. Kierkegaard's discourse in *The Sickness unto Death* is not "the decision to believe . . . a criterionless choice, a leap of faith into the dark," as William Lane Craig puts it.[9] Kierkegaard claims,

> Truth is precisely the daring venture of choosing the objective uncertainty with the passion of the infinite. I observe nature in order to find God, and I do indeed see omnipotence and wisdom, but I also see much that troubles and disturbs. The *summa summarum* [sum total] is an objective uncertainty, but the inwardness is so very great, precisely because it grasps this objective uncertainty with all the passion of the infinite.[10]

What I encountered when first reading *The Sickness unto Death* was a Christian demonstrating that all is not right—all people are sick unto death, even if they do not realize it. The evangelistic vigor of Kierkegaard's works speaks to his specific context. Kierkegaard saw a culture with all the "right" answers, but with no inwardness, no desire to actually *live* for God.

7. *SUD*, 121–22 / *SKS* 11, 233.
8. *SUD*, 82 / *SKS* 11, 196.
9. Craig, *Reasonable Faith*, 70.
10. *CUP1*, 203–4 / *SKS* 7, 186.

In Kierkegaard, I sensed a kindred spirit. He, too, had all of the right answers—he received his formal training in theology and almost went into the pastorate—yet, Kierkegaard felt something was rotten in the state of Denmark. My own existential crisis—as maudlin as it sounds to my present self—led me to Kierkegaard, and Kierkegaard led me to deepen my faith. Kierkegaard's focus on the existential side of Christianity—that is, the emphasis on internalizing theology and *living* the Christian life—spoke to me out of a slew of voices emphasizing merely correct dogma. Ironically, many paint Kierkegaard as an opponent to Christianity, but he is on my team. As Mark Tietjen comments, "Suffice it to say there is no reason to think [Kierkegaard's] personal Christian beliefs were outside the parameters of classic Reformed, Lutheran orthodoxy."[11] Kierkegaard is a part of my tradition, a tradition that seeks to deal with "the issue: becoming a Christian, with direct and indirect polemical aim at that enormous illusion, Christendom, or the illusion that in such a country all are Christians of sorts."[12] It saddens me that Kierkegaard has such a negative reputation in apologetic circles. He offers a fresh perspective and helpful illustrations for understanding culture and the shortfalls of our modern (and postmodern) age. Kierkegaard is an asset, not a hindrance, for apologetics.

The astute student of apologetics—and many Kierkegaardian scholars—may challenge that Kierkegaard is useful for apologetics. William Lane Craig defines apologetics as

> that branch of Christian theology which seeks to provide a *rational justification* for the truth claims of Christian faith. . . . Apologetics specifically serves to show to unbelievers the truth of the Christian faith, to confirm that faith to believers, and to reveal and explore the connections between Christian doctrine and other truths. . . . Apologetics, to repeat, is a theoretical discipline that tries to answer the question, *What rational warrant can be given for the Christian faith?*[13]

Does not Kierkegaard eschew rationality and proofs of God's existence? Search any book on apologetics and the discussion on fideism almost always mentions Søren Kierkegaard. James Dew and Paul Gould define fideism: "One does not base belief in God on rational argument or

11. Tietjen, *Kierkegaard*, 36.

12. *PV*, 23 / *SKS* 16, 11.

13. Craig, *Reasonable Faith*, 15 (my emphasis).

scientific evidence. Rather one *simply has faith*, and this is what is pleasing to God."[14] For a discipline that seeks a "rational justification," why would apologetics entertain a fideist? Brian Morley also lumps Kierkegaard in the fideist camp, declaring that "fideism is thus a denial of apologetics."[15] In *Christian Apologetics*, Douglas Groothuis has an interesting comment about Kierkegaard:

> While Kierkegaard gave no place to natural theology or evidences for the Bible or Christ, he presents an insightful kind of psychological apologetic in many of his works, particularly *Sickness unto Death*—a work that helped me become a Christian in 1976. Despite his brilliance and insights, I will not follow his lead in commending the Christian faith.[16]

Groothuis, a titan in apologetics, shows how Kierkegaard helped lead him to authentic faith, yet he does not consider him a helpful tool for apologetics because of Kierkegaard's "fideist" position. We will discuss Kierkegaard and the fideist charge in chapter 2, but in short, I think it to be a mischaracterization of Kierkegaard's view. Groothuis mentions Kierkegaard's "psychological apologetic," and it is precisely this perspective that is missing from typical apologetic discourse.[17] Although Kierkegaard does not approach apologetics in the way we contemporarily do, I believe he has much to teach us.

But still, one may protest, did not Kierkegaard hate apologetics? He says as much in *The Sickness unto Death*:

> Now we see how extraordinarily stupid . . . it is to defend Christianity, how little knowledge of human nature it manifests, how it connives even if unconsciously, with offense by making Christianity out to be some poor, miserable thing that in the end has to be rescued by a champion. Therefore, it is certain and true that the first one to come up with the idea of defending Christianity in Christendom is *de facto* a Judas No. 2: he, too, betrays with a kiss, except that his treason is the treason of stupidity. To defend something is always to disparage it.[18]

14. Dew and Gould, *Philosophy*, 64–65 (my emphasis).

15. Morley, *Mapping Apologetics*, 8.

16. Groothuis, *Christian Apologetics*, 52.

17. I prefer the term "existential apologetic" to "psychological apologetic," for "existential" implies the entire person rather than just the mind.

18. *SUD*, 87 / *SKS* 11, 200.

Kierkegaard is abundantly clear: he wants no part in "defending" Christianity. Why include a thinker who insults apologetics as a whole? I argue that Kierkegaard does not oppose apologetics per se. He is deeply concerned with defending Christianity from what he calls Christendom—the social and religious fusion of the state church of nineteenth-century Denmark, deeply influenced by Hegelian philosophy. For example, in *The Moment*, Kierkegaard states, "But it is the case with the existence of these 1000 [Danish church] officials that if one holds the New Testament alongside it is easy to see that, Christianly, their whole existence is malpractice."[19] Kierkegaard's impetus in much of his writing is that a grand illusion has deceived the masses: philosophy is parading as orthodoxy. In *The Point of View*, Kierkegaard shares his heart concerning his writing:

> Humble before God, also before people, I know very well what offenses I *personally* may have committed. But I also know with God that precisely my work as an author was the prompting of an irresistible inner need, the only possibility for a depressed person, an honest indemnifying attempt by one deeply humbled, a penitent, *to make up, if possible, for something by means of ever sacrifice and effort in the service of the truth.*[20]

Kierkegaard, throughout his entire authorship, was committed to the truth of Christianity—not just a Christianity that is true but that it is true *for us*, so true that it *changes us*. This is why Kierkegaard was not satisfied with "defending" Christianity in Christendom: it was all the "right" answers with no inward appropriation. Anyone can memorize formulas and proofs; and what good is a rationally defended faith if we do not believe it to be true? It is as if we have allowed the ghost of Descartes to deceive us that the root issue with non-believers is a simple lack of knowledge. That is why we rationally prove Christianity! Show it to be logical and coherent, and then people will accept it! James K. A. Smith paints a different picture: "What makes us who we are, the kind of people we are—is what we love. More specifically, our identity is shaped by what we ultimately love or what we love *as* ultimate."[21] The heart, more often than not, drives the bus rather than the mind. And does not the Bible teach such? In the parable of the rich man and Lazarus, the rich man, in

19. *M*, 95 / *SKS* 13, 133.

20. *PV*, 24 / *SKS* 16, 12 (my emphasis).

21. Smith, *Desiring the Kingdom*, 26–27.

the torment of Hades, calls out to Father Abraham, begging Abraham to send him back to warn his brothers about the reality of the afterlife. Abraham has a sobering response: "If they do not hear Moses and the Prophets, neither will they be convinced if someone should rise from the dead."[22] What more proof could one ask for?! Surely, seeing one's dead relative will cause one to believe! Yet, "The heart is deceitful above all things, and desperately sick; who can understand it?"[23] This is not to say that truth, knowledge, and rationality do not matter, but rather, the focus on a *purely* rationalistic presentation and defense of our faith leaves out the reality that God made us rational, emotional, and experiential.

While Kierkegaard hated the formal apologetics of his day, I believe he is a needed counterweight to how we currently approach apologetics.[24] There does not have to be an either/or between a rationally justifiable apologetics and existentially livable apologetics. *Kierkegaard even admits as much in his personal journals:*

> What I really need is to be clear about *what I am to do*, not what I must know, except in the way knowledge must proceed all action. It is a question of understanding my own destiny, of seeing what the Deity really wants me to do; the thing is to find a truth which is truth *for me*, to find *the idea for which I am willing to live and die.*[25]

Kierkegaard admits that *knowledge precedes action.*[26] I cannot live the truth if I do not know what the truth is. Conversely, knowing the truth is useless without performing the truth. The two go together, and Kierkegaard is an excellent resource for the oft-neglected side of our apologetic vigor.

This current work is not an introduction to Kierkegaard's thought per se. There are many excellent introductions to Kierkegaard's religious and philosophical thought. My writing is a labor of love, a desire to illuminate some of Kierkegaard's thoughts that helped me personally and

22. Luke 16:19–31.

23. Jer 17:9.

24. There have been some recent positive views of Kierkegaard's role in apologetics. An excellent example is Turchin and Kettering, "Søren Kierkegaard," 410–28.

25. *KJN* 1, 19 / *SKS* 17, 24, AA:12.

26. The above quote from Kierkegaard's journal uses "proceed" rather than "precede": "except in the way knowledge must *proceed* all action." The difference between "proceed" and "precede" is minute in English, but using "proceed" may cause potential confusion, implying that "knowledge" comes after (literally pro-ceeds) action. The Danish says knowledge "must go before" action: *uden forsaavidt en Erkjenden maa gaae forud for enhver Handlen.*

are helpful to apologetics in general, whether the apologist is a professor, professional, pastor, or parishioner. The following chapters are aspects of Kierkegaard's thought that can aid us in our quest to "always being prepared to make a defense to anyone who asks [us] for a reason for the hope that is in [us]."[27]

Chapter 1 deals with the nature of truth, focusing on subjectivity, objectivity, and the relationship of faith and history. This topic may be one of the most contested and, unfortunately, misunderstood across Kierkegaard's various works. When Kierkegaard uses the phrase "subjective truth," he is not talking about the *nature* of truth—meaning Kierkegaard is not declaring that we *create* the truth. Kierkegaard uses "subjectivity" in the most literal sense: relating to the subject. Inward appropriation of the truth is what Kierkegaard is after—meaning the primary importance is that we "walk the walk" rather than "[cheating] by copying and reeling off the results and answers."[28] The ensuing discussion leads us to the famous Kierkegaardian leap. What does Kierkegaard actually mean by "the leap"? Why would we have to leap at all? Does he mean that we shut our eyes to the world and leap without using our minds, or does he mean something else?

Chapter 2 investigates faith, absurdity, and paradox. Kierkegaard states, "[Abraham] had faith by virtue of the absurd,"[29] and numerous Christians take umbrage with faith being labeled "absurd." Calling faith "absurd" is usually where Kierkegaard catches the "fideist" charge, but the quotation comes from *Fear and Trembling*—probably Kierkegaard's most read work—out of the mouth of pseudonym Johannes de Silentio. *Fear and Trembling* may be one of the most misunderstood in the entire Kierkegaardian corpus. Its analysis is often divorced from Kierkegaard's theory of the stages of human existence. Kierkegaard posits three life-spheres—three general ways people live their lives. By examining how people respond to personal events, we can catch a glimpse of where they are in the stages on life's way. Each stage has different goals and desires, and understanding the stages is the key to seeing the brilliance, and personally convicting, "dialectical lyric" of *Fear and Trembling*. Once properly understood, we see Kierkegaard is not a fideist, and *Fear and Trembling* is both a shockingly salient critique of Kierkegaard's cultural

27. 1 Pet 3:15.

28. *CUP1*, 73 / *SKS* 7, 73.

29. *FT*, 35 / *SKS* 4, 131.

moment and a demonstration of the difficulty of living authentically before God.

Chapter 3 discusses the problem of evil, one of apologetic's most challenging topics. Why does God permit evil at all? If I am born sinful, then why am I damned for something I cannot change? Why does God allow us a choice if he knows we will choose to sin? Why did he make the Tree of Knowledge in the Garden of Eden? The questions are endless, and the answers are potentially foreboding. Christians must face the relationship between individual culpability and the necessity that "all have sinned and fall short of the glory of God" while also declaring God to be good.[30] Kierkegaard wrote *The Concept of Anxiety: A Simple Psychologically Orienting Deliberation on the Dogmatic Issue of Hereditary Sin*, where he examines the issue between the sin of Adam and his progeny. While Kierkegaard's book is not an explicit defense of Christianity, his ideas concerning human nature, sin, and culpability are a fantastic resource for addressing the problem of evil. Not only does Kierkegaard argue that sin is an inevitable but not necessary condition of humanity but he offers a positive response to why it is good for humans to exist at all.

We dive into Kierkegaard's method and style of writing in chapter 4. Kierkegaard wrote many works under various pseudonyms. This was no mere artistic flair, for Kierkegaard believes the presentation of the message is just as important as the content. If we directly attack a set of beliefs, then our argument "only strengthens a person in the illusion and also infuriates him."[31] Conversely, if we speak indirectly, we engage as equals, softening the guard of the other person.[32] Kierkegaard's Copenhagen was replete with cultural Christianity—everyone was a "Christian," since he or she, by law, was baptized as an infant. For Kierkegaard, the problem lies in convincing people that they are not authentic Christians. At times, we need direct conversation, but often, argues Kierkegaard, the indirect method is best. Kierkegaard writes "[portraying] the esthetic with all its bewitching charm," yet he displays that such perspectives are ultimately bankrupt.[33] Kierkegaard performs an indirect apologetic, demonstrating how the life of a non-believer is not a satisfying existence. After examining Kierkegaard's method of communication, we will analyze two works—"The Seducer's Diary" and *Prefaces*—to demonstrate

30. Rom 3:23.

31. *PV*, 43 / *SKS* 16, 25–26.

32. We can look to Groothuis's personal experience cited above as an example.

33. *PV*, 46 / *SKS* 16, 28.

how the indirect method shows the superiority of the life of Christian faith. Apologists would do well to take Kierkegaard's method and think creatively about engaging the culture.

Kierkegaard wrote the oft-overlooked *The Two Ages*, a literary review of a novel of the same name. The review is more than a critique of the book's plot; Kierkegaard uses the work to discuss the cultural clime of Copenhagen. Kierkegaard lived during what modern scholars call Golden Age Denmark, an era of immense cultural output for a comparatively small nation. Kierkegaard participated in his age, yet he critiqued what he saw as its troubling trends. A cultural consensus replaced a vibrant, individual faith. Public opinion trumped the truth, and when Kierkegaard spoke up, the public—including the state church—sought to squash him. The parallels to our modern context are uncanny, and in chapter 5 we see that Kierkegaard's assessment of his cultural moment aids us when we speak to our context.

Not every argument against Christian faith is couched in rationalistic defenses or proofs. *This Life* by Martin Hägglund presents a strong existential case for atheism. He notes that any form of religious faith focuses on eternal life/heaven/nirvana. An eternal life makes any sort of present life meaningless, for the current life is simply expectation or preparation for the next. We only care about something if it can truly be lost. Ultimately, Hägglund argues, secular faith is what is needed to have a life well-lived, for secular faith focuses on the here-and-now with a possibility of true loss. In chapter 6, I use Kierkegaard's thought to offer an apologetic for Christian faith in the here-and-now. Kierkegaard wrote a discourse titled "The Care of the Pagans," where he demonstrates how the concerns of non-Christians lead to an unstable life. When we misplace our care, we undercut living in the present. Also, Kierkegaard's *Works of Love* focuses on living a life of love in this present world. Kierkegaard explains that true Christian love is greater than preferential love, but Christian love does not shut its eyes to its current plight. I use the insights from these two works to respond to Hägglund's thesis.

Lastly, I conclude with some general comments on Kierkegaard and suggestions for further reading. Kierkegaard has a steep barrier of entry, and I hope this book exhorts readers to pick up Kierkegaard as a resource for *doing* apologetics—and I mean this in the literal sense: living out what we believe. Kierkegaard is an untapped resource for many, and leaping into his thought is beneficial in our contemporary context. Reading Kierkegaard is somewhat like climbing a mountain. At times, it is strenuous. At times, we wonder why we are still trying to get to the top of the mountain, contemplating if we should just give up and plummet to our deaths; but to those who persevere and reach the top, they will achieve a great reward. Before we start our journey, I want to share a word from Kierkegaard: "For a person to be a Christian, it certainly is required that what he believes is a *definite* something, but then with equal certainty it is also required that it be *entirely definite* that *he* believes."[34] The point of this work, and Kierkegaard's own writing, is not to add more information about an object but to become *subjects*, to become invested in living what we believe as creations of the Creator. As the preacher says at the end of *Either/Or*, "For only the truth that builds up is truth for you."[35] May this work build us up to *live*, for true living is living for God.

34. *CD*, 244 / *SKS* 10, 250.

35. *EO2*, 354 / *SKS* 3, 332.

1

How Broad Is the Ditch?

Subjectivity, Objectivity, and the Leap to Faith

I WAS RAISED IN church: whenever the doors were open, my mother made sure I was present. Every Bible study, ministry outreach, revival meeting, and church camp—I was there. When I was eight years old, a revival preacher came to our congregation. In the Baptist church I attended, it was normal to schedule a revival—because, you know, that's how they happened historically—therefore, I was present at every meeting. I do not remember the evangelist's name, but I remember vividly what happened to me. He preached on choices: do we want to choose our own way, or do we want to choose to be with Jesus? I remember feeling the call of the Holy Spirit, and I responded to follow Jesus. Not long after, I was baptized.

The summer before my junior year of high school, I had another profound religious experience. God spoke to me so clearly at a church camp, and I sensed him asking me, "When are you *really* going to start living like I am the most important thing in your life?" I started to see, even at the young age of sixteen, how easily I adopted behaviors expected of me without reflecting on *why* I was doing them. I was a good kid. I went to church and read my Bible. I didn't cuss, drink, dance, or chew and didn't go with girls who do. Yet, in that moment, I realized I behaved not because I wanted to serve God but simply because I was supposed to behave. I realized that God was not the center of my life, the ground of my being—he was a task to complete among other tasks so my parents would not hassle me. From the outside perspective, I was a paragon of Christian virtue: all boxes checked! On the inside, however, my heart, so to speak, was not in it. At this church camp, I understood I needed to radically reorient my priorities and, in turn, my entire life, around the truth of God.

In *The God Who Is There*, Francis Schaeffer attempts to illuminate what he sees as "*the* most *crucial problem . . . facing Christianity today*": truth.[1] He argues that Søren Kierkegaard is "the father of modern secular thinking," and as such, a danger to the church in its contemporary context. He explains, "Kierkegaard came to the conclusion that you could not arrive at synthesis by reason. Instead, you achieved everything of real importance by a *leap of faith*. So he separated absolutely the rational and logical from faith."[2] Schaeffer sees Kierkegaard as an opponent to truth, since he does not ground faith in the logically objective. In fact, Kierkegaard has an entire chapter in *Concluding Scientific Postscript* titled "Truth is Subjectivity." In that chapter, he states,

> Truth is precisely the daring venture of choosing the objective uncertainty with the passion of the infinite. . . . The inwardness is so very great, precisely because it grasps this objective uncertainty with all the passion of the infinite. . . . But the definition of truth stated above is a paraphrasing of faith. Without risk, no faith. Faith is the contradiction between the infinite passion of inwardness and the objective uncertainty.[3]

Is not Kierkegaard belittling the truth of who God is by stating that faith is a leap into the dark?

Such a reading misunderstands Kierkegaard's primary concern with truth. The question, for Kierkegaard, is not necessarily "do I have the truth?" but rather "do I exist in truth?" As Kierkegaard's pseudonym Johannes Climacus puts it, "The subjective issue is about the individual's relation to Christianity. Simply stated: How can I, Johannes Climacus, share in the happiness that Christianity promises?"[4] My personal faith journey illustrates the issue. I knew the *objective* truth at age eight—that I was a sinner in need of a savior—but it took many years for me to *enact* said truth in my *subjective* existence. Authentic faith is more than correct information,

1. Schaeffer, *God Who Is There*, 1:13.
2. Schaeffer, *God Who Is There*, 1:21 (my emphasis).
3. *CUP1*, 203–4 / *SKS* 7, 186.
4. *CUP1*, 17 / *SKS* 7, 26.

as the apostle James reminds us: "Be doers of the word, and not hearers only, deceiving yourselves."[5] What is the deception? Sadly, we easily "hear" the word—that is, understand it at a cognitive level—but hearing only takes us so far, so much so that we may deceive ourselves into thinking that all is right in our world. If apologetics is simply about having the rational answers to questions, then are we not potentially deceiving ourselves—and others—that the task of Christianity is the accrual of data?

The individual's relationship to the truth is what Kierkegaard is passionate about, and he has been woefully misunderstood (and misappropriated by twentieth century existential philosophers) concerning his use of truth. Schaeffer is a prime example of overlooking Kierkegaard's purpose, method, and historical context. Mark Tietjen explains, "Kierkegaard is highly critical of reason—not generally speaking, but when it takes the form of hubris or ethical and religious evasion, when it fails to recognize its *limits*."[6] Since apologetics is "that branch of Christian theology which seeks to provide a rational justification for the truth claims of Christian faith," then why should it entertain someone who is critical of reason?[7] I argue that Kierkegaard's focus on the limits of reason is a healthy course corrective in how we view truth in our apologetic endeavors.

In this chapter, we investigate Kierkegaard's view of truth. Kierkegaard argues that "subjectivity, inwardness, is truth" as opposed to objectivity, which "assists all humanity to cheat by copying and reeling off the results and answers."[8] In fact, Kierkegaard states that one only comes to faith in Christ through a leap, "because the leap is the category of decision."[9] A cursory reading of these statements leads us to surmise that Kierkegaard affirms some form of relativism—that truth is in the eye of the beholder. As one Kierkegaard commentator puts it,

> Kierkegaard explains truth in his own way. According to him, *truth is within man and cannot be sought objectively*. . . . It is difficult to derive a precise meaning from Kierkegaard's application of the term 'subjectivity.' However, the core meaning of the term emphasizes the thesis that the springs of action and knowledge *lie deep within a person*.[10]

5. Jas 1:22.
6. Tietjen, *Kierkegaard*, 44 (my emphasis).
7. Craig, *Reasonable Faith*, 15.
8. *CUP1*, 278, 73 / *SKS* 7, 254, 73.
9. *CUP1*, 99 / *SKS* 7, 97.
10. Gabriel, *Subjectivity and Religious Truth*, 90–91 (my emphasis).

Does this not sound contradictory to the gospel? Paul explicitly states that "If Christ has not been raised, then our preaching is in vain and your faith is in vain."[11] If it is not an objective truth that Jesus rose from the dead, then have we not turned Christianity into humanity's own fancy, like Schaeffer fears?

I understand the concerns of relativism, but the roots of these fears are in misapplying Kierkegaard's terms "subjective" and "objective." The first purpose of this chapter is to clear up some common misconceptions regarding Kierkegaard's relationship to truth and the leap *to* faith. Much of the misunderstanding derives from ignoring Kierkegaard's historical context. Kierkegaard responds to his cultural moment, to the problem posed by Enlightenment thinker Gotthold Lessing and the potential solution of philosopher G. W. F. Hegel. Reading Kierkegaard within his historical context clears up many misreadings.

Second, Kierkegaard acts as a course corrective to our tendency to make God an object. As one of my seminary professors Jeffrey Riley put it, we never want to treat God like a cadaver to be studied. Turning Christianity into a list of "correct" answers to memorize turns God into an *object* of inquiry rather than a personal *subject* who desires a relationship with his creation. I know this will sound like a shocking statement, but God is not a human being. His ways are not our ways.[12] God lovingly reveals himself to us through his word. We can stand on his written revelation as trustworthy and true, but there is an utter difference between him and me. I have often found in my own life that I reverse this: God's ways are my ways. The way I understand him is the way he is. My logical proofs and deductions accurately depict everything about God. Kierkegaard says, "Not so fast." We are temporal creatures attempting to understand an eternal God, so we should think carefully when predicating attributes to him.

Lastly, Kierkegaard serves as a constant reminder that knowledge of God that does not lead to worship of God is a fruitless endeavor. Anyone can learn Bible trivia. Anyone can memorize the Roman Road. Anyone can get baptized and have his name on the roll of a church. If I study the Bible just to have the right answers—or to appease my parents or to win arguments—I am not bearing fruit as a Christian. If I have the truth but do not actually live it out, then I am like "a noisy gong or a clanging

11. 1 Cor 15:14.

12. Isa 55:8–9.

cymbal," not serving my proper end.[13] God wants us to *actualize* our beliefs, meaning he wants us to live out our beliefs, changing us from the inside-out. Kierkegaard stresses such thinking with his concept of truth as subjectivity, and we do well to heed his call.

To achieve our goals, we will walk through Kierkegaard's posing of the problem of finite creatures knowing an infinite God in *Philosophical Fragments* and its sequel *Concluding Unscientific Postscript to Philosophical Fragments*. We start with the Enlightenment thinker Gotthold Lessing's influential essay "On the Proof of the Spirit and of Power." Therein, Lessing poses the issue of knowing the eternal through historical inquiry. Lessing affirms that only through reason can we truly know God. Second, we examine G. W. F. Hegel's philosophical system of coming to know the truth of Spirit (*Geist*) through a logical system. Although I do not want to bog us down with esoteric philosophical speculations, understanding Lessing and Hegel is key to understanding what Kierkegaard is raving against in *Concluding Unscientific Postscript*. Lastly, we walk through Kierkegaard's dismantling of Hegel and Kierkegaard's praise (which is also an ironic, backhanded critique) of Lessing. Kierkegaard goes to great lengths to explain the dynamics between objective and subjective truth. Since God is personal and not some impersonal force, the goal of the knowledge of God is a relationship with him. The problem is, "How can a contingent creature come to know an eternal God?" Kierkegaard's answer is that we *leap* to God in faith.

1. ON CROSSING A DITCH

Gotthold Ephraim Lessing (1729–1781) was a scholar trained in theology. Lessing wrote during the Enlightenment, a time in history where logic reigned supreme, and reason was "not hampered by undue deference to authority, custom or religious revelation."[14] Philosophers and scholars questioned everything and rejected anything they could not verify through the exercise of autonomous reason. Lessing was not afraid to go against the status quo of Christian orthodoxy, "[identifying] himself with progressive Enlightenment thought."[15] Lessing wrote a short but influential letter to Johann Schumann titled "On the Proof of the Spirit

13. 1 Cor 13:1.

14. Byrne, *Religion and the Enlightenment*, 6.

15. Nisbet, "Introduction," 1.

and of Power." The title is an allusion to the early church father Origen of Alexandria, and Lessing uses Origen's work as a springboard for his theological musings.

Origen wrote *Against Celsus* as a defense of the Christian faith against Celsus, an early attacker of Christianity. Although the name of Origen's work is not very original, he deftly dismantles Celsus's critiques of Christianity. One of Origen's most intriguing rebuttals—to us modern readers as well as Lessing—is how Origen offered proof that Christianity is true. Origen writes,

> We have to say, moreover, that the Gospel has a demonstration of its own, more divine than any established by Grecian dialectics. And this diviner method is called by the apostle the "manifestation of the Spirit and of power:" of "the Spirit," on account of the prophecies, which are sufficient to produce faith in any one who reads them, especially in those things which relate to Christ; and of "power," because of the signs and wonders which we must believe to have been performed, both on many other grounds, and on this, *that traces of them are still preserved among those who regulate their lives by the precepts of the Gospel.*[16]

Did you catch that? Origen says to Celsus, "I have two proofs: the Spirit and power." The proof of the Spirit is in reading the Scriptures—we see the fulfillment of Israel's Messiah and the hope of our future resurrection through the death, burial, and resurrection of Jesus Christ. The second proof is *the power of miracles*. These miracles are obviously referring to the miracles of Jesus and the apostles in the biblical accounts, *but Origen claims they are still happening in his present time*. Origen essentially says to Celsus, "You want proof? Look outside! Find a Christian and she will show you the proof of power!" Origen's argument on the power of God was not unique to him; it was a common argument among early apologists of Christianity. As Ramsay MacMullen comments,

> Jesus' authority (εξουσια) over the fiercest infestations of satanic power, making them do whatever he wished by a mere word of command, he passed on to his disciples, with instructions to use it. They did. . . . The manhandling of demons—humiliating them, making them howl, beg for mercy, tell their secrets, and depart in a hurry—served a purpose quite essential to the Christian definition of monotheism.[17]

16. Origen, *Against Celsus* 1.2 (my emphasis).

17. MacMullen, *Christianizing the Roman Empire*, 27–28.

The early church displayed its proof by the power of God.

Such a quote from Origen leaves Lessing, and contemporary Christians, with a question: When is the last time we saw the proof of power? If we do not see such power, then does the proof not exist? Lessing explains his struggle with the lack of proof:

> Fulfilled prophecies which I myself experience are one thing; fulfilled prophecies of which I have only historical knowledge that others claim to have experienced them are another. Miracles which I see with my own eyes, and have an opportunity to assess, are one thing; miracles of which I know only from history that others claim to have seen and assessed them are another.[18]

Lessing is a child of the Enlightenment, observing everything through reason. He sees an insurmountable problem with historical evidence: he did not experience these reported events. All Lessing has is a report of a report of an event. Lessing bluntly states, "It is because this proof of the spirit and of power no longer has either spirit or power, but has sunk to the level of *human testimonies of spirit and power*."[19] Lessing does not deny that these displays of Spirit and power happened, but he argues that since he has not observed them, they should not be binding on his beliefs. Lessing, then, delivers his famous dictum: "*Contingent truths of history can never become the proof of necessary truths of reason*."[20] Historical events cannot get us to an accurate understanding of the truth.

Let me illustrate why Lessing is harping on history and reason. In *Star Wars, Episode IV: A New Hope*, the character Han Solo is sitting in the Mos Eisley Cantina. Solo is a rogue, someone who rides the line between good and bad. He got into some trouble with Jabba the Hutt, and Jabba sent a bounty hunter after Solo to get his money back. The unfortunate bounty hunter Greedo corners Solo in the Cantina at gunpoint, demanding money. Unbeknownst to Greedo, Solo has his blaster under the table pointed at Greedo. What happens next is a problem of history. In the original cut of the movie (1977), Han shot Greedo first, killing Greedo before he had the chance to fire.[21] In the *Special Edition* (1997), Greedo shot at Han first and missed, and then Han shot and killed Greedo.[22] In

18. Lessing, "On the Proof," 83–84.
19. Lessing, "On the Proof," 84 (my emphasis).
20. Lessing, "On the Proof," 85 (emphasis original).
21. Lucas, *Star Wars.*
22. Lucas, *Star Wars: Episode IV.*

the 2011 cut of the movie, both Greedo and Han shoot almost simultaneously, but Greedo misses and Han does not. Which is the correct cut? Did director George Lucas originally want Greedo to shoot first but was unable to due to the limits of special effects, or did Lucas change his mind down the line, wanting to make Han Solo more of an honorable character that only responds to violence after being attacked? The facts of history are *contingent*, meaning we rely on reported evidence of the past and our experience of said reports. I was not in George Lucas's mind, so I cannot know with certainty what the original intention was. All I can do is present an argument for what I *think* happened. Such is the nature of historical truth: I do not have absolute certainty because I was not there. What Lessing says is that *we should never radically reorient our beliefs on the basis of a historical truth because of the dynamics at play with the reporting of history and our historical distance from the events.* I do not change my entire worldview because I affirm that Han shot first.[23]

Lessing does not want to affirm something unless he proves it through reason. A historical event cannot be proven true in this sense. All we can say is that we have no reason to doubt a historical account, but that is not enough for Lessing when it comes to miracles. Herein lies the heart of the Enlightenment: I do not accept anything I cannot prove without *my* use of reason. As René Descartes put it, "For since God has endowed each of us with some light of reason by which to distinguish truth from error, I could not have believed that I ought for a single moment to rest satisfied with the opinions of another, *unless I resolved to exercise my own judgment in examining these* whenever I should be duly qualified for the task."[24] The Enlightenment makes *me* the center of reality in the sense that all of reality must pass through my mind in order for me to accept it as true. Such thinking leads to Lessing's famous object lesson: "This is *the broad and ugly ditch* which I cannot get across, no matter how often and earnestly *I have tried to make the leap*. If anyone can help me over it, I beg and implore him to do so. He will earn a divine reward for this service."[25]

Lessing says there is a broad, ugly ditch between the contingency of history and the eternity of truth. We cannot get to an accurate knowledge of God through historical methodology, for we cannot know with certainty that a historical event took place the way it was reported. Because

23. Which, of course, is the correct interpretation of the events!

24. Descartes, *Discourse on Method and Meditations on the First Philosophy*, 25 (my emphasis).

25. Lessing, "On the Proof," 87 (my emphasis).

contemporary society has advanced technologically, we may think we accurately record history; Lessing's problem is solved. Such sentiment ignores that all history is *edited* by someone. If all history is edited by someone, then, says Lessing, we cannot use it to get to an accurate understanding of the eternal truth, of God. According to Lessing, though, our reason *can* bridge the gap because reason is not something contingent upon the reports of others. Reason is eternal: 2 + 2 always equals 4, whether recorded in history or a child learning her mathematics. Lessing offers a serious challenge to Christianity, a religion based upon a historical event. For Lessing, we have to prove by use of reason that our faith is reasonable. In Kierkegaard's time, there was one main philosopher who attempted to do such a task.[26]

1.1 You Got That Spirit? G. W. F. Hegel

German philosopher Georg Wilhelm Friedrich Hegel (1770–1831) arrived a generation after Lessing. Hegel wrote during the Romantic period, a rebellion against the Enlightenment's overreliance on reason to explain all of reality. The zeitgeist of the Romantic movement was the intangible nature of the human spirit, which we cannot predicate to the rigid, cold laws of reason. Paintings, music, walking through nature—all of these tap into something deep within us, not explainable by logic. As W. T. Jones puts it, "[The Romantics] were impressed by the largeness of reality, an immensity that baffled the methods of science and that made the whole human enterprise, on which the preceding age had set such store, petty and trivial."[27] At an intuitive level, we sense that there is something *more* to reality than simply being a cog in the machine of a mechanistic world.

We see the Romantic infatuation with emotion and the downplaying of reason in the theological work of Hegel's contemporary Friedrich Schleiermacher (1768–1834). For Schleiermacher, religion is not founded upon reason but rather upon our *feeling*. Such feeling is not fleeting sentiment, but it is the "*feeling of Dependence*."[28] Schleiermacher states that we know

26. In particular, there were Danish theologians who adopted Hegel's philosophy to the teachings of the Danish Lutheran Church. Three of Kierkegaard's teachers, Heiberg, Møller, and Sibbern, were influenced by Hegel. See Stewart, "Kierkegaard and Hegelianism," 145.

27. Jones, *History of Western Philosophy*, 105.

28. Schleiermacher, *Christian Faith*, 13.

God not because someone proved it to us; we know God because we have felt him and still feel a need for him. Schleiermacher explains,

> God is given to us in feeling in an original way; and if we speak of an original revelation of God to man or in man, the meaning will always be just this, that, along with the absolute dependence which characterizes not only man but all temporal existence, there is given to man also the *immediate self-consciousness of it*, which becomes a consciousness of God.[29]

We know God at an *intuitive* level through our experience, not through logical proof. What a world of difference a single generation can make! Lessing says we only know through reason, while Schleiermacher says we can only know through feeling!

Hegel was a colleague of Schleiermacher, serving with him on the faculty of the University of Berlin. Hegel, too, was influenced by the Romantics, but he did not throw out reason altogether. In fact, Hegel thought the Romantics went too far in their assessment of feeling and reason. As Kipton Jenson comments, "Hegel considered the theology of feeling, of contingency, and of the arbitrary will of subjective feeling to be the malady of his time."[30] Hegel did not want to return to the pure reason of the Enlightenment, but he also did not want to leap headlong into the waters of Schleiermacher's God-consciousness. Instead, Hegel attempts a *via media* between the two extremes. Philosophy can unite the disparate parts of thought and feeling "by running together what thought has put asunder, by suppressing the differentiations of the Notion [of the Absolute] and restoring the *feeling* of essential being: in short, by providing edification rather than insight."[31]

Hegel places a high significance on logic. In fact, one can only know "the True in the form of the True" when one uses "*Logic* or *speculative philosophy*."[32] Hegel's conception of logic is not exactly like Lessing's. Lessing sees logic as outside of time, not based on our historical situation. Hegel, being influenced by the Romantic period, reorients the movement of Spirit *into our world*. Hegel refers to Absolute Spirit (*Geist*) as active in all that we do: "Spirit has broken with the world it has hitherto inhabited and imagined. . . . Spirit is indeed never at rest but always engaged in

29. Schleiermacher, *Christian Faith*, 17–18 (my emphasis).

30. Jensen, "Principle of Protestantism," 412.

31. Hegel, *Phenomenology of Spirit*, 5.

32. Hegel, *Phenomenology of Spirit*, 22.

moving forward."[33] We should not equate Hegel's use of "Spirit" as the orthodox Christian understanding of God or the Holy Spirit. For Hegel, Spirit is the *means* of coming to know the truth: Spirit is working in the world to achieve its end.[34]

How do we come to know anything by Spirit? For Hegel, we must become reflective subjects, meaning we have to *think* about our existence. In our everyday lives, we typically live without pondering our existence. For example, on my drive to work, my mind is usually focused on something: music, a podcast, my upcoming responsibilities, etc. Sometimes, I arrive at work without realizing that I made all the necessary turns into the parking lot. Although I was not *thinking about* driving my car, I drove it successfully. Such a dynamic is what Hegel is focusing on—he wants humans to be more reflective (focused on what it means to be driving the car) rather than merely reactive (going about my commute without thinking about my existence). Hegel uses the terms "substance" and "subject" to differentiate between the two types of existing. "Substance" is something which merely exists, while a "subject" has properly reflected on her surroundings. Hegel states that "this Substance is, as Subject, pure, *simple negativity*."[35] By "negative," Hegel does not mean bad or evil; he simply means that it does not have a positive form. We are *missing something*; we need to *reflect* in order to become true subjects, in order to truly be who we ought to be.

How does such reflection work? Hegel states that an individual becomes a subject "only in so far as it is the movement of positing itself, or is the mediation of its self-othering with itself."[36] What Hegel is saying (in a rather obtuse way) is that an individual must *posit* something in order to become a true self. In fact, all understanding of the True can only come through a process of dialectical mediation. This has famously (or infamously, depending on one's perspective) been labeled Hegelian dialectic, a pattern of thesis-antithesis-synthesis.[37] We start with the self,

33. Hegel, *Phenomenology of Spirit*, 6.

34. Notice I use "its" rather than "his." For Hegel, Spirit is more like a force rather than a personality. Hegel's followers split into "Right-wing" and "Left-wing" Hegelians. The "Right-wing" saw Spirit as the divine working in the world, while the "Left-wing" saw Spirit as a naturalistic force operating in the world. For more on this and how it particularly relates to Kierkegaard's context, see Stewart, "Kierkegaard's View of Hegel," 50–65.

35. Hegel, *Phenomenology of Spirit*, 10.

36. Hegel, *Phenomenology of Spirit*, 10.

37. Some Hegelian scholars do not approve of these terms because they originated

which is a *negativity*, lacking what it needs to be complete; this is the *thesis*. We then *posit* something to spur on our reflection; this something is *positive*, an addition, called the *antithesis*. We now have two opposites: what I am and what I want to be. How do the two come together? We use logic to *mediate* the two, to join them together; this is the *synthesis*. Only through this process can we come to know the truth: "Only this self-*restoring* sameness, or this reflection in otherness within itself . . . is the True."[38]

Let me use an example to help clear the muddy waters of Hegel's terminology. If I need to build a table, I will start with some basic knowledge, like thinking the table should be 5 feet long (thesis). Upon further reflection, I say to myself "5 feet is too short. I think 10 feet would be better for the space" (antithesis). Well now I am in a conundrum: Is it 5 feet or 10 feet? I have to *mediate* the two pieces of knowledge in some way; otherwise I will just stand here all day with scraps of wood rather than a table. I then say, "7 feet is actually the sweet-spot" (synthesis). I then move forward with my knowledge of the True. Spirit working in the world makes the above process possible, but I have a stake in it through my reflection. Because humans are negativities—that is, they lack something—"the single individual is incomplete Spirit."[39] Spirit is what allows the individual to take the two opposites (thesis and antithesis) and put them together as a new understanding (synthesis).

We see with Hegel a middle path between The Enlightenment (Lessing) and Romanticism (Schleiermacher). We use logic/reasoning, but we experience logic in the real world: "Reason is, therefore, misunderstood when reflection is excluded from the True."[40] The Enlightenment divorced reason from reality, while Romanticism throws reason out the window. As Jon Stewart correctly states, for Hegel "speculative philosophy removes concepts from the isolation of abstraction and puts them in their appropriate systematic context where they can be properly analyzed."[41] Hegel

---

with the philosopher Johann Gottlieb Fichte rather than Hegel. Hegel does use these three terms but not exclusively. To me, it is a moot point because Hegel affirms a particular process of knowing in his works, even if he does not use the specific terms in every situation in his writing. Also, Hegel's followers use the terms, so I will continue using them because they are a part of the common zeitgeist. For more on this discussion, see Findlay, *Hegel*, 70; Adorno, *Hegel*, 11.

38. Hegel, *Phenomenology of Spirit*, 10.

39. Hegel, *Phenomenology of Spirit*, 16.

40. Hegel, *Phenomenology of Spirit*, 11.

41. Stewart, "Hegel's *Phenomenology* as a Systematic Fragment," 80.

is attempting to unite the eternal with the temporal, logic with actual living. In fact, the process of logic, of becoming in existence guided by Spirit, continues over and over again. Whenever I reflect through Hegel's process, I end in a synthesis. This synthesis becomes a new thesis, and the new thesis begs for another antithesis. With Hegel we experience Spirit, whether that is God or some impersonal force, *in the world through reason*. We do not abstract out to an immaterial, eternal realm, but rather reasoning is tied to Spirit working within the universe. Another side effect of Hegel's view is that we cannot know the end/purpose of Spirit until the process finishes at the end of history. As Hegel puts it, "The True is the whole. But the whole is nothing other than the essence consummating itself through its development. Of the Absolute it must be said that it is essentially a *result*, that only in the *end* is it what it truly is."[42] Humans are a part of the process of Spirit operating in the world. If we want to see Spirit moving, then we look at humans reflecting on their existence, creating culture, and progressing forward.

For Lessing, history is a problem, a ditch we cannot cross. Reason is eternal, outside of the realm of history. Any interference with the messiness of history leads to a potential distortion of reason. Schleiermacher points to the sentimentality of religion—being a human is not simply exercising autonomous reason. Humans are *feelers*, and we know God at an intuitive level through our feeling of God-consciousness. For Schleiermacher, the issue of history is a moot point because we can intuit our way to God. Hegel tries to walk between the extremes. Logic is important, and we have to understand reality through a system. The system, though, is not abstract, outside of human existence. We all experience Spirit in the here and now, through our dialectical process of mediation. By now you may be wondering why I am spending so much time on these thinkers rather than diving into Kierkegaard. The issue is that Kierkegaard responds to all of these points in *Philosophical Fragments* and *Concluding Unscientific Postscript*. Without understanding the background, *Postscript* is extremely easy to misinterpret, and we can miss the genius of what Kierkegaard does in his work. Although we can say much more on the history of philosophy from Lessing to Kierkegaard, this brief introduction primes us to leap into the nature of truth.

42. Hegel, *Phenomenology of Spirit*, 11.

1.2 You Cannot Get There from Here

Søren Kierkegaard wrote *Philosophical Fragments*, "only a pamphlet," in 1844 under the pseudonym Johannes Climacus, wherein Kierkegaard constructs a "thought-project," asking, "Can the truth be learned?"[43] Climacus breaks down two options for learning the truth. The first option is the Socratic method. For Socrates, people already have the truth within themselves; they have simply forgotten it. Their preexisting souls had perfect knowledge, but when their soul was attached to their bodies at birth, the knowledge was forgotten but not lost. The task of a learner is to recollect the forgotten knowledge, and "thus the ignorant person merely needs to be reminded."[44] A teacher, then, acts as a midwife, aiding the student to remember what she forgot. Kierkegaard remarks, "In the Socratic view, every human being is himself the midpoint, and the whole world focuses only on him because his self-knowledge is God-knowledge."[45] For the Socratic teacher, the *moment* of learning is accidental. A midwife assists with birth, but she does not *cause* the birth. The Socratic midwife aids but does not bring any new information to the learner.

Does not the Socratic theory of learning seem counterintuitive? How many times have we learned something about which we had no idea? Knowledge does not seem to be hidden within us—it more accurately seems like a teacher brings us information we do not have. Our intuition tells us the *moment* of learning, of coming to know something outside of ourselves, is of "decisive significance."[46] If I need to know the truth, then I am obviously in a state of untruth, and "the teacher must bring [the truth] to [me] . . . [and] he must provide [me] with the condition for understanding it."[47] None of Climacus's thought-project is scandalous. In fact, it seems like common sense. Let me use this current book as an example. You, the reader of this book, are in a state of untruth regarding Kierkegaard and his relation to apologetics. I, as teacher, have this knowledge, and I want you to know it. I offer the condition for you to know it: I am trying my hardest to make the concepts digestible and pertinent to your life. The moment is right now as you are reading. You

43. *PF*, 5, 9 / *SKS* 4, 215, 218.
44. *PF*, 9 / *SKS* 4, 218
45. *PF*, 11 / *SKS* 4, 220.
46. *PF*, 13 / *SKS* 4, 222.
47. *PF*, 14 / *SKS* 4, 223.

have the opportunity to learn something you do not know on your own. Why is Kierkegaard focusing on the painfully obvious?

The issue is that knowledge of the finite is one thing while knowledge of the eternal is another. How can a human teacher, someone who is not eternal, teach about the eternal within history? Is it God's fault that we cannot come to know him? Kierkegaard eschews such thinking: "Inasmuch as the learner exists, he is indeed created, and, accordingly, God must have given him the condition for understanding the truth." Unlike Socratic ignorance, humanity has *rejected* the eternal, or as Kierkegaard puts it, the learner "is *polemical against the truth*, which is expressed by saying that he himself has forfeited and is forfeiting the condition."[48] Humans *forfeit* the condition of knowing the eternal truth of God. How, then, can humanity know God? For Kierkegaard God must be the teacher: "The teacher, then, is the god himself, who, acting as the occasion, prompts the learner to be reminded that he is untruth and is that through his own fault."[49] The teacher, then, rescues the learner from his plight, and becomes the learner's savior, deliverer, and reconciler.[50]

We have a serious problem, says Kierkegaard. We *forfeit* our understanding of God, yet we need to know God. Only God can teach us about himself, for we have shut our eyes to the truth.[51] Knowledge of the eternal is possible, but we cannot achieve it through our own means of logic (contra Lessing or Hegel). We also cannot come to knowledge of God through immediate feeling (contra Schleiermacher).[52] Lessing, Hegel, and Schleiermacher are simply *repackaging Socratic reasoning*, for the truth is contingent on me *realizing* it rather than someone *revealing* it to me. As M. G. Piety explicates,

> This account [the Socratic understanding of knowledge] represents for Climacus the traditional *philosophical* interpretation of the relation of the individual to the truth. . . . The traditional philosophical position is that *all that is required in order for one to come to know the truth is the possession of the faculty of reason*. Insofar as one possesses this faculty, one may be said to be in the possession

48. *PF*, 15 / *SKS* 4, 224 (my emphasis).

49. *PF*, 15 / *SKS* 4, 224.

50. *PF*, 17 / *SKS* 4, 226.

51. See Rom 1:18–23.

52. *PF*, 68 / *SKS* 4, 269.

> of the truth. That is, reason, on the traditional philosophical view, represents the condition for understanding the truth.[53]

If Socrates is incorrect—and our intuitive interactions with learning the truth tells us he is—then *we cannot know God through our autonomous use of reason*. As Piety succinctly summarizes, "The individual, on this latter view [that learning the truth is not Socratic], loses his autonomy with respect to his relation to the truth and becomes entirely dependent, in this relation, upon another who would be his teacher."[54] The Enlightenment praises the autonomous use of reason, yet Kierkegaard shows how such autonomy leads to humanity being the center of the learning process *rather than the content being the primary focus*.

God must be the teacher, but we still have another issue: how can an eternal God speak to a temporal creation? Kierkegaard calls such a conundrum the absolute paradox: "To want to discover something that thought itself cannot think."[55] In my own reasoning, I would never come to the conclusion that an eternal God would interact in history. A fish in water does not know it is wet: its existence is water. Only when a human takes the fish out of the water does it realize what "wet" is. Such is our existence as humans. We forfeit the condition of knowing God, so we can no longer come to know him on our own; yet, at our core, we *want* to know him. As Augustine puts it, "You [God] made us for yourself and our hearts find no peace until they rest in you."[56] We want to know God—we desire at some deep level the wholeness that only God provides—but we cannot. Kierkegaard has a sobering word: "If a human being is to come to truly know something about the unknown (the god), he must first come to know that it is different from him, *absolutely different from him*. The understanding cannot come to know this by itself. . . . If it is going to come to know this, it must come to know this from the god."[57] God, being in a different existence category, is *foreign* to us, so foreign that he has to reveal to us how foreign he is!

Christianity, says Kierkegaard, is different from other religions because of the eternal entering history in a profound way. God, the eternal, must encounter the individual in history for the individual to know him,

53. Piety, "Little Light Music," 57 (my emphasis).

54. Piety, "Little Light Music," 50.

55. *PF*, 37 / *SKS* 4, 243.

56. Augustine, *Confessions*, 1.1.

57. *PF*, 46 / *SKS* 4, 251 (my emphasis).

yet his interaction causes multitudinous problems. If God raises us up to his status, we would forever treat God as *other* rather than *Father*. God *loves* the learner, and love implies a personal relationship. To have said relationship, God becomes both teacher and savior. The point of such an education is not merely knowledge but proper sonship. The only way the eternal can teach the temporal is by a *descent*—a divine condescension, "the god will appear in the form of a *servant*."[58] How in the world can the eternal be a servant? As Kierkegaard states, "Christianity is the only historical phenomenon that despite the historical . . . has wanted to be the single individual's point of departure for his eternal consciousness, has wanted to interest him otherwise than merely historically, has wanted to base his happiness on his relation to something historical."[59] *You cannot get there from here*: Lessing's ditch is too broad, and nothing within unaided humanity can propel us over the ditch. *God must come here from there*. As Kierkegaard emphasizes in *Concluding Unscientific Postscript*, "The thesis that God has existed in human form, was born, grew up, etc. is certainly the paradox *sensu strictissimo*, the absolute paradox."[60] The God-man is paradoxical because we have both God and man in history, yet we need such revelation in order to know who God is. As the apostle Paul says, "[Christ] is the image of the invisible God, the firstborn of all creation."[61] The Incarnation is paradoxical not because it is false but because it is true, and we hold on to our belief with passion. As Kierkegaard comments about paradoxes, "One must not think ill of the paradox, for the paradox is the passion of thought, and the thinker without the paradox is like a lover without passion: a mediocre fellow."[62] Christianity is not simply a religion about written revelation or some form of esoteric gnosis from on-high, available only to the most sophisticated of thinkers. Christianity declares that God took on flesh *in history*, not in myth, and this very God was crucified, buried, and raised from the dead. This truly is "something that thought itself cannot think."[63]

58. *PF*, 31 / *SKS* 4, 238.

59. *PF*, 109 / *SKS* 4, 305.

60. *CUP1*, 217 / *SKS* 7, 198.

61. Col 1:15.

62. *PF*, 37 / *SKS* 4, 243–44.

63. *PF*, 37 / *SKS* 4, 244.

1.3 The Problem of Objectivity

Kierkegaard wrote *Concluding Unscientific Postscript to Philosophical Fragments* in 1846, and it is ironically close to five hundred pages longer than its predecessor *Philosophical Fragments*. Kierkegaard, again under pseudonym Johannes Climacus, explains the purpose of *Postscript*. *Fragments* poses the question of how we know the truth, asking if a historical event is enough upon which to build our eternal happiness. *Postscript* deals with the individual's relation to Christianity. As Climacus says in the introduction, "The objective issue, then, would be about the truth of Christianity. The subjective issue is about the individual's relation to Christianity. Simply stated: how can I, Johannes Climacus, share in the happiness that Christianity promises?"[64]

Climacus ingeniously highlights a glaring issue when we try to construct a purely objective vision of Christianity. Climacus starts by taking the values of the Enlightenment—and thinkers such as Lessing—to construct a historical religion only using objective means. In usual apologetic discourse, "objective truth" refers to the foundation of truth. As Peter Kreft and Ronal Tacelli define, objective truth means "independent of the knower and his consciousness."[65] The truth is the truth whether we agree with it or not. Subjective truth usually refers to truth being "dependent on the knower."[66] The individual *creates* or *constructs* the truth. In this sense, apologetics champions the objective truth of Christianity, seeking to show the rational basis for the Christian faith. Jesus is Lord of all: this proposition is objectively true. The danger of constructing our own, subjective truth is an ever-shifting world with no standards, an unlivable life view.

When Kierkegaard discusses objective and subjective truth, he refers to the relation *of the individual to the truth*. Kierkegaard is primarily concerned with the teleology of truth rather than the ontology of truth. As Piety correctly explains,

> Knowledge is objective if it is not essentially related to the existence of the individual knower as is the case, for example, with knowledge of the natural sciences, or with any sort of knowledge that is purely descriptive. Knowledge is subjective if it is essentially related to the existence of the individual knower as is

64. *CUP1*, 17 / *SKS* 7, 26.

65. Kreeft and Tacelli, *Handbook of Christian Apologetics*, 363–64.

66. Kreeft and Tacelli, *Handbook of Christian Apologetics*, 367.

> the case, for example, with ethical and religious knowledge, or with any sort of knowledge that has a prescriptive dimension.[67]

Objective truth, for Kierkegaard, is the truth we find as an *object of study* in the natural world. I can use reason to find answers concerning the natural world, but these issues are not related to my existential state. Kierkegaard expresses his frustration in his journals:

> What I really need is to be clear about *what I am to do*, not what I must know, except in the way knowledge must proceed all action. It is a question of understanding my own destiny, of seeing what the Deity really wants me to do; the thing is to find a truth which is truth *for me*, to find *the idea for which I am willing to live and die.*[68]

Subjective truth is truth relating to a *subject*, meaning I *appropriate* the truth into my life so that it affects my existential state as a living *subject*. Kierkegaard's use of "objective" and "subjective" places the impetus on our *relationship to the truth*.

If we attempt to construct a purely objective Christianity, we run into problems. God decisively acted *in history* with the Incarnation, so an objective Christianity treats such as a historical fact *like any other fact*. We use the same methods to verify both the historicity of Christianity and if Han shot Greedo first. The issue, as Kierkegaard points out, is that "to the historical the greatest certainty is only an *approximation*, and an approximation is too little to build [one's] happiness on."[69] History is an approximation for two reasons. First, as Lessing points out, we are operating on reports of reports. As Piety explains, "No matter how much data one might be able to collect that would support a particular interpretation of the past, there would always remain *the formal possibility, which is to say the possibility for thought, that the interpretation was false*."[70] The person writing the original report had to leave out some events. In this sense, all of history is edited by the historians. Likewise, historians may be mistaken, overlooking important factors. Second, Kierkegaard is channeling Hegelian dialectics. If Spirit operates in the world by directing our process of reflection, then we, as individual thinkers, cannot know when we arrive at the final conclusion. In fact, we only know the complete truth at the end of history when Spirit

67. Piety, *Ways of Knowing*, 3.

68. *KJN* 1, 19 / *SKS* 17, 24, AA:12.

69. *CUP1*, 23 / *SKS* 7, 30.

70. Piety, *Ways of Knowing*, 51 (my emphasis).

finishes its work in the world. The synthesis derived from mediation turns into a new thesis, waiting for a new antithesis to continue the process of history directed by Spirit. An objective Christianity, *based upon the presuppositions of Kierkegaard's time*, only leads to approximations—informed guessing without bedrock certainty.

Kierkegaard illustrates the objective process with the nature of Scripture: "If Scripture is viewed as the secure stronghold that decides what is Christian and what is not, the important thing is to secure Scripture historically-critically."[71] We investigate with all of our historical-critical methods to get at *the* text of the Bible. We cannot posit a doctrine of inspiration—that God himself inspired the text, making the text trustworthy and true—for inspiration is an issue of subjectivity, a doctrine we believe. We simply have to prove that the Bible is correct. Here is where approximation rears its ugly head. Let us say that we find a copy of Paul's lost letter to the Corinthians. What does the church do? Insert it into the canon? Try to disprove its Pauline authorship? *Building a religion off humanity's deliberation leads to a constant state of flux whenever a new issue arises.* As Kierkegaard puts it, "the dialectical development walks in danger everywhere, walks in danger of slipping into a parenthesis."[72] Any new data, according to Hegel, *must be mediated*, inserting a parenthesis, stopping our normal process to consider the antithesis, using logic and science to determine the truth or falsity of the new phenomenon. If we accept Hegelian dialectics, then there is no firm foundation in a purely objective Christianity. We contort the beloved hymn to "On mind, the solid rock I stand, faith in Christ is sinking sand." Kierkegaard gives a scathing assessment of a Hegelian objective Christianity: "The great secret of the [Hegelian] system . . . is close to Protagoras's sophism 'Everything is relative,' except that here everything is relative in the continuous progress."[73] The constant process of Hegelianism means that we never arrive at the truth—it is always an antithesis away, like a ghost ship on the horizon. Hegelianism leads to a functional relativism: *we construct the truth via mediation*. Kierkegaard cannot abide such a system of relativism.

A purely objective religion leaves individuals to never *decide* to believe, always waiting for the next bit of information. With objectivity, there is no "choose you this day whom ye will serve."[74] Instead, we have

71. *CUP1*, 24 / *SKS* 7, 31.

72. *CUP1*, 28 / *SKS* 7, 35.

73. *CUP1*, 33 / *SKS* 7, 40.

74. Josh 24:15, KJV.

"mediate this day what ye observe." An objective religion puts the individual in the driver's seat: he calls the shots and determines, through his autonomous reason, what is true. As theologian Emil Brunner puts it, a modern, objective Christianity constructs "a God who does not speak *to* me so much as *out of* me—a God who is nothing other than the depth of my own spirit; therefore a God who is neither personal nor the creator."[75] Objectivity gives us Socrates, not God speaking to us. The push of the Enlightenment turns an individual into "a solitary thinker, engaged in a monologue," as Brunner puts it.[76] Descartes's "I think therefore I am" makes our use of reason the point of departure of knowledge rather than a God who speaks to us. The above dynamic is why Kierkegaard states, "Christianity cannot be observed objectively, precisely because it wants to lead the subject to the ultimate point of his subjectivity, and when the subject is thus properly positioned, he cannot tie his eternal happiness to speculative thought."[77] Christianity is about *subjectivity*.

1.4 Subjectivity Is Truth

Climacus has a curt word for objectivity: "Objective thinking invests everything in the result and assists all humankind to cheat by copying and reeling off the results and answers." Objectivity has its *approximate answers* to truth, and the individual can easily memorize such information and spit it back out. Subjectivity is the opposite: "Subjective thinking invests everything in the process of becoming and omits the result."[78] Gathering more and more "correct" answers does not relate someone properly to Christianity. One has to *decide* to follow Jesus, to will to believe. Reciting a sinner's prayer does not automatically save, for Christianity is an issue of the *heart* as well as the mind. As the apostle Paul states, humans "by their unrighteousness *suppress the truth*."[79] We have to truly repent and put faith in Christ to become a Christian, and this is more than mental assent. Kierkegaard declares Lessing to be a help in understanding the dynamic, for "Lessing opposes what I would call *quantifying* oneself

75. Brunner, *God and Man*, 53–54.
76. Brunner, *God and Man*, 53.
77. *CUP1*, 57 / *SKS* 7, 60.
78. *CUP1*, 73 / *SKS* 7, 73.
79. Rom 1:18 (my emphasis).

into a *qualitative* decision."[80] Learning more facts does not *cause* one to submit to Christ. Submission is an act of will, not an act of knowledge. I can bring a horse to water, but I cannot make it drink.

Kierkegaard actually *praises* Lessing in *Postscript*: "[Lessing] closed himself off in the isolation of subjectivity . . . that the religious pertained to Lessing and Lessing alone, just as it pertains to every human being in the same way."[81] Praise of Lessing seems odd to Christians who believe in the historical truth of the Incarnation. In fact, we almost see Lessing as a villain, someone seeking to undermine our faith in a historical resurrection. Kierkegaard brilliantly displays the irony of Lessing's attempt: "Lessing's issue gains a different significance."[82] Alastair Hannay demonstrates that "Climacus presents Lessing's words about the leap [across the ditch] as essentially comical."[83] Why is Lessing comical? *Lessing's argument is self-defeating.* Lessing cannot achieve what he thinks he can achieve. Lessing states objective history cannot get us across the broad, ugly ditch toward God. Kierkegaard gives a hearty, "Amen." Lessing then says our use of autonomous reason *can* get us across the ditch to God. Kierkegaard gives a hearty, "By no means!" Autonomous reason operates *within history*. The irony is that Lessing is attempting an impossible task. It is as comical as someone driving east to go west: *you cannot get there from here*. The comic is also tragic: Lessing is *convinced* he can get across by reason. If someone—anyone—just proves it to him, he will believe. The Bible declares a resounding, "No!" Adam and Eve knew God existed. The Israelites saw the proof of God through the miraculous. Peter knew that Jesus was the Christ and swore he would be faithful to Him. The Bible bears witness that knowing the truth is *not* the primary issue.

For all the many issues with Hegelian philosophy, it rightly points out our historical contingency. We are not disembodied minds stuck in a meat-suit: we are active agents in the world, thinking, processing, and *existing*. As J. Heywood Thomas notes, "Kierkegaard feels that . . . the error of rationalism was its failure to recognize that reason too had its *interests*."[84] All reason, or any knowledge contingent upon humanity, is

80. *CUP1*, 95 / *SKS* 7, 94 (my emphasis).

81. *CUP1*, 65 / *SKS* 7, 67.

82. *CUP1*, 97 / *SKS* 7, 96.

83. Hannay, "Having Lessing on One's Side," 219.

84. Thomas, "Revelation, Knowledge, and Proof," 167. Immanuel Kant (1697–1731) was an Enlightenment philosopher who posed a serious issue with Enlightenment presuppositions. Reason passes through the categories of the mind, meaning my

an *approximation*, and there is no assurance that an approximation can propel one over Lessing's ditch. I do not want to cross a bridge based on approximate math! I want assurance that I can safely cross. *The problem is that we cannot construct a proof to get us across*; we *have to trust God*. In fact, the only way to achieve what Lessing wants to achieve is to take the leap to faith. Hannay brings home the comical analysis: "Enlightenment goals can only be secured by a relationship to God—in other words through a radical break with [the] Enlightenment."[85] Such a dependence upon God and not our autonomous use of reason is not Kierkegaard denying that truth exists. Kierkegaard clearly speaks to the importance of truth: "[Subjectivity] does not deny the reality of the world-historical development, which, reserved for God and eternity, has both its time and its place."[86] Kierkegaard underlines that God must act in our lives for us to believe. God is the starting point of salvation, not humanity. Or to put it another way, we are saved *by grace, not works*.

1.5 Taking the Leap

We become subjective by taking the leap *toward* faith. Humanity's inability to cross Lessing's ditch leaves us without hope on our own. We cannot come to know God unless he teaches us about himself. Once we encounter the Gospel, we must make a choice: "whether [we] will believe or [we] will be offended."[87] To believe, one must leap toward faith "because the leap is the category of decision."[88] Such a leap is *not based on* historical proof, because the best historical proof can give us is an approximation. As Kierkegaard states, "*An objective uncertainty, held fast through appropriation with the most passionate inwardness, is the truth*, the highest truth there is for an *existing* person. . . . And truth is precisely the daring venture of choosing the objective uncertainty with the passion of the infinite."[89] The leap is *informed* by objective truth, but there

conceptual practices *interpret* the data I see. Because of this, Kant claimed that we could not know the thing in itself (*ding ang sich*), but rather we can only know our *perception* of the thing. For an excellent analysis of Kant's thought on religion in the Enlightenment, see Byrne, *Religion and the Enlightenment*, 203–28.

85. Hannay, "Having Lessing on One's Side," 223.

86. *CUP1*, 159 / *SKS* 7, 148.

87. *PC*, 96 / *SKS* 12, 104.

88. *CUP1*, 99 / *SKS* 7, 97.

89. *CUP1*, 203 / *SKS* 7, 186 (emphasis original).

is always a modicum of uncertainty. We have to take the leap, which is a movement of our passion and will rather than objective formulations.

The Kierkegaardian "leap" is the object of ire of many apologists. Francis Schaeffer is a prime example. He writes, "If rationalistic man [according to Kierkegaard] wants to deal with the really important things of human life . . . he must discard rational thought about them and make a gigantic, nonrational leap of faith."[90] A leap of faith is dangerous, turning Christianity into fideism! While I will address the fideist charge in depth in chapter 2, I will give a few words of clarification on Kierkegaard and the leap. If Kierkegaard proposes a leap *of* faith, meaning a leap only consisting in a blind faith that closes its eyes to reality, then I agree that the concept is dangerous. Relegating truth to a postmodern relativity is problematic for numerous reasons. In reality Kierkegaard never uses the term "leap *of* faith" in his writings. Kierkegaard also never says that historical investigation is a *bad* thing.[91] As M. Jamie Ferreira clarifies,

> The popular association of the leap with Kierkegaard is often couched in terms of the leap *of* faith. It is worthwhile to be reminded, however, and interesting to note, that Kierkegaard never uses any Danish equivalent of the English phrase 'leap of faith,' a phrase that involves circularity insofar as it seems to imply that the leap is made *by* faith. He does, however, clearly and often refer to the concept of a leap (*Spring*) and to the concept of a transition (*Overgang*) that is qualitative (*qvalitativ*) or, alternatively, a *meta-basis eis allo genos* (transition from one genus to another). . . . The concept of a leap *to* faith remains central to his writings.[92]

The leap, according to Kierkegaard, is a *transition to a new existence state*. We *either* believe *or* we do not. If we choose to believe, to take the leap, we now enter a new *sphere of existence*.[93] The leap does not consist of blind faith, but rather it is an objective uncertainty. The following passage from *Practice in Christianity* exemplifies Kierkegaard's insistence on subjectivity:

> It is indeed eighteen hundred years since Jesus Christ walked here on earth, but this is certainly not an event just like other events, which once they are over pass into history and then, as the distant

90. Schaeffer, *God Who Is There*, 1:16.

91. For example, see *PC* no. 1.

92. Ferreira, "Faith and the Kierkegaardian Leap," 207–8.

93. See chapter 2 on an explanation of Kierkegaard's stages of existence.

> past, pass into oblivion. No, his presence here on earth never becomes a thing of the past, thus does not become more and more distant—that is, if faith is at all to be found upon the earth; if not, well, then in that very instant it is a long time since he lived. But as long as there is a believer, this person, in order to have become that, must have been and as a believer must be just as contemporary with Christ's presence as his contemporaries were. This contemporaneity is the condition of faith.[94]

God, the teacher, has reached down into our lives—in our real present moment—to forgive us and open our eyes to the truth. As Kierkegaard explains in *The Sickness unto Death*, "There must be a revelation from God to teach man what sin is and how deeply it is rooted."[95] God must speak for us to know him: the problem of history and our inability to reason properly blinds us from the truth. Kierkegaard defines faith in *Sickness* as "the self in being itself and willing to be itself rests transparently in God."[96] Faith is a state of being, not a system of doctrines, and this state of being is resting in the goodness of God. To put it another way, we become new creations in Christ Jesus.

The leap to faith does not mean we cannot explain our faith in doctrinal terms. Kierkegaard is merely stressing the importance of *being* a Christian. As Kierkegaard explicitly states in *Upbuilding Discourses in Various Spirits*, "[Christ] judges the others, judges that their confession is an untruth—not that what they say is an untruth, since they say what is true, *but that the true statement has no truth in them*."[97] There is a world of difference between saying "Jesus is Lord" and living "Jesus is Lord." We can learn all the facts about God on our own, but we cannot *be* a Christian on our own. All we can do is leap when God presents the condition of the gospel to us.[98]

94. *PC*, 9 / *SKS* 12, 17.

95. *SUD*, 96 / *SKS* 11, 208.

96. *SUD*, 82 / *SKS* 11, 196.

97. *UD*, 325 / *SKS* 8, 416 (my emphasis).

98. This type of language always brings up the age-old free-will vs. determinism debate. Whether one is more Calvinistic or more Arminian, I think it is a moot point in regard to what Kierkegaard is teaching here.

2. THE WHOLLY OTHER

Kierkegaard's emphasis on subjectivity is not simply rooted in his rejection of Hegel's philosophy or the problems of the Enlightenment. Kierkegaard has a high view of God's transcendence, of him being different than us in every way, of him being wholly other. Christianity confesses that God is transcendent: "God is separate from and independent of nature and humanity."[99] When Job comes before God to plead his case, God replies, "Who is this that darkens counsel by words without knowledge? Dress for action like a man; I will question you, and you make it known to me. Where were you when I laid the foundation of the earth? Tell me, if you have understanding."[100] God then unrelentingly questions Job for four chapters. God teaches Job that God, indeed, is not a man. God is creator, and Job is creation. After God questions Job, Job replies in humility: "I know that you can do all things, and that no purpose of yours can be thwarted. 'Who is this that hides counsel without knowledge?' Therefore I have uttered what I did not understand, things too wonderful for me, which I did not know."[101] Job admits his finiteness: God is in heaven, and he is on earth. God's transcendence is on display throughout the Bible, and God's transcendence is more than saying God is separate from his creation. His transcendence is tied to his ways, to the executing of his will. We can think of a classic text in Isaiah: "For my thoughts are not your thoughts, neither are your ways my ways, declares the LORD. For as the heavens are higher than the earth, so are my ways higher than your ways and my thoughts than your thoughts."[102] In the New Testament, Paul calls the gospel a mystery, not in the sense of unknowable but in the sense of it being hard to fathom that God would bring together Jews and Gentiles into one family: "This mystery is that the Gentiles are fellow heirs, members of the same body, and partakers of the promise in Christ Jesus through the gospel."[103]

The otherness of God has always been a point of contention among theologians. We want to understand God, but we will never grasp all that he is. As Charles Hodge explains, "It is included in what has been said, that our knowledge of God is partial and inadequate. There is infinitely

99. Erickson, *Christian Theology*, 282.

100. Job 38:2–4

101. Job 42:2–3.

102. Isa 55:8–9.

103. Eph 3:6.

more in God than we have any idea of; and what we do know, we know imperfectly. We know that God knows; but there is much in his mode of knowing, and in its relation to its objects, which we cannot understand."[104] Our finite situation limits our knowledge of God, and the Bible is chock-full of the confusion of the faithful attempting to understand his ways. Consider Habakkuk; he sees injustice and violence in Israel, and he wonders, "Where is God?" God replies, "Look among the nations, and see; wonder and be astounded. For *I am doing a work in your days that you would not believe if told*. For behold, I am raising up the Chaldeans, that bitter and hasty nation, who march through the breadth of the earth, to seize dwellings not their own."[105] God declares to Habakkuk that he is raising up the pagan, wicked Babylonians to exact his divine justice on an adulterous Israel. Habakkuk is not pleased by this oracle of judgment; it is not something he would have thought God would do. Our finiteness makes it intrinsically difficult for us to fathom God and his will on our own. Our limitations are not a problem but rather a part of God's design. He is the potter; we are the clay.

In *Fragments*, Climacus comments "that if a human being is to come to truly know something about the unknown (the god), he must first come to know that it is different from him, absolutely different from him."[106] Kierkegaard stresses God's otherness as a course-corrective to the modernist enterprise of centering reality on the individual. As Charles Taylor notes, the development of modern philosophy, rooted in Descartes's "I think therefore I am," declares that "the only minds in the cosmos are those of humans . . . and minds are bounded, so that these thoughts, feelings, etc. are situated 'within' them."[107] We see such an erasure of transcendence with Lessing, Schleiermacher, and Hegel. Kierkegaard comments that his philosophical climate attempts to "pantheistically abolish" the concept of the qualitative difference between God and humanity.[108] Louis Berkhof agrees with Kierkegaard's assessment:

> Under the influence of the pantheizing theology of immanence, inspired by Hegel and Schleiermacher, a change came about. The transcendence of God is soft-pedaled, ignored, or explicitly denied. God is brought down to the level of the world, is made

104. Hodge, *Systematic Theology*, 1:337.
105. Hab 1:5–6 (my emphasis).
106. *PF*, 46 / *SKS* 4, 251.
107. Taylor, *Secular Age*, 30.
108. *SUD*, 117 / *SKS* 11, 229.

> continuous with it, and is therefore regarded as less incomprehensible, though still shrouded in mystery.[109]

The Enlightenment changed the rules, and philosophers and theologians followed suit. Kierkegaard sees the theological surrender to autonomous reason as *dangerous and idolatrous*, for it elevates man to be the arbiter of truth rather than God himself. Are we praising God or our man-made system of belief? There is a great temptation to move God into our categories rather than letting God's revelation of himself—his special revelation in Christ and the Scriptures—dictate the conversation.

I will give a contemporary example. Numerous philosophers and theologians are looking to philosophy—analytic philosophy in particular—to help "in the work of constructive Christian theology."[110] Analytic philosophy, the reasoning goes, can help clarify concepts within Christian dogmatics. As Thomas Morris argues, "If God is infinite Mind and has brought into existence minded creatures in his image, then it might be expected that those creatures' minds could grasp something of his existence and nature."[111] My issue with such an enterprise is not that philosophy should be barred from theological discourse. I am not going so far as to say, "What hath Athens to do with Jerusalem?" Philosophy—both continental and analytic—*is* a tool we can and should use when doing theology. Clarity about our faith is something for which we ought to strive, particularly when answering tough questions about Christianity. My concern is in the *functional* removal of the Creator/creature distinction. Notice that Morris assumes that God has a mind like my mind, and it is the point of contact between me and God. *This is what concerns me, a univocal understanding of how our reason accurately depicts God.* It rests on a faulty assumption that my reasoning can get me across Lessing's ditch, that my reasoning is the essence of the divine. It treats divine mystery as a problem to be solved or a cop-out for the weak-minded. Thomas McCall openly admits such: "Perhaps there is a general sense in which it is true that analytic theologians are naïve about religious language. *Perhaps* they are. . . . But the concern itself . . . is, at best, a red herring."[112] I do not think this is a red herring, for it cuts to the foundation of the apologetic enterprise. As Brunner puts it, does God

109. Berkhof, *Systematic Theology*, 29–30.

110. McCall, *Invitation to Analytic Christian Theology*, 16.

111. Morris, *Our Idea of God*, 25.

112. McCall, *Invitation to Analytic Christian Theology*, 26.

speak to me, or does God speak out of me? Or as Kierkegaard puts it, are we pantheistically abolishing God as subject by deferring to an eternal, all-permeating rationality?

German philosopher Rudolph Otto (1869–1937) can aid us in considering the relationship between rationality and God. In his magisterial *The Idea of the Holy*, he investigates the "non-rational" aspects of God. I think Otto has a good word for us: "In our idea of God is the non-rational overborne, even perhaps wholly excluded, by the rational? Or conversely, does the non-rational itself preponderate over the rational?"[113] Are we quick to pass everything through our exercise of reason (Lessing), or do we write off reasoning as superfluous (Schleiermacher)? Kierkegaard aids us in grounding the non-rational in the *otherness of God* rather than the immanence of my personal experience. Otto calls God the wholly other, "that which is quite beyond the sphere of the usual, the intelligible, and the familiar, which therefore falls quite outside the limits of the 'canny,' and is contrasted with it, filling the mind with blank wonder and astonishment."[114] When people encounter the living God, they realize he is wholly other, absolutely different from themselves. Such an encounter with God is both "the daunting and the fascinating," a fear and an awe.[115] What happened when Isaiah encountered God? It was not an experience of divine bliss, but rather he declared, "Woe is me! For I am lost; for I am a man of unclean lips, and I dwell in the midst of a people of unclean lips; for my eyes have seen the King, the LORD of hosts!"[116] As Kierkegaard states in *The Book on Adler*, "*Between God and a human being there is an eternal essential qualitative difference*."[117] God is not a glorified human, like us but to a quantitatively higher degree. He is the "One who is high and lifted up, who inhabits eternity, whose name is Holy."[118] Our rationality, our unaided use of reason, our *works*, cannot get us to God. We need God to reveal himself to us. Kierkegaard acts as a course-corrective, forever reminding us that God is absolutely different from us. It is all too easy to theologically construct a god in our own image. We need to constantly recall our limitations. We humbly seek out God, knowing our own frailty.

113. Otto, *Idea of the Holy*, 3.

114. Otto, *Idea of the Holy*, 26.

115. Otto, *Idea of the Holy*, 31.

116. Isa 6:5.

117. *BA*, 181 / *SKS* 11, 104 (emphasis original).

118. Isa 57:15.

3. LIVING THE LIFE

Kierkegaard's focus on subjectivity is a frequent reminder that we must live what we believe. As he states in *Christian Discourses*, "What is honesty before God? It is that your life expresses what you say."[119] When we limit apologetics to only objective statements, we run the risk of having a nominal faith. If we distill Christianity down to "dos and don'ts," then we replace a religion concerned with relating properly to God with a religion concerned with knowing facts about God. The Bible warns against our pernicious slip into a mental assent rather than a vibrant faith. As James puts it,

> But be doers of the word, and not hearers only, deceiving yourselves. For if anyone is a hearer of the word and not a doer, he is like a man who looks intently at his natural face in a mirror. For he looks at himself and goes away and at once forgets what he was like. But the one who looks into the perfect law, the law of liberty, and perseveres, being no hearer who forgets but a doer who acts, he will be blessed in his doing.[120]

If we are new creations, then we should *be* different. Christians often struggle with this concept. We either go to the extreme of legalism, listing off every holy or sinful action; or we go to the extreme of libertinism, not addressing sanctification out of some fear of works-based righteousness. Both of these are real possibilities we ought to avoid. We should be what we say we are.

Kierkegaard has a humorous parable in *Postscript* showing the ludicrousness of an objective faith. A mental patient springs an escape from the asylum, but he realizes that people will discover he is a lunatic and send him right back. He comes up with an idea: if he spouts out the objective truth, people will not view him as crazy. To remind himself to say true statements, he hides a ball in his coattail, and every time it hits him on the rear-end, he shouts, "Boom! The earth is round!" His statements will demonstrate that he, in fact, is not crazy, for he is speaking the truth. We all know this scheme will fool no one, for although he is saying a true statement, he is acting like a lunatic.[121] We can say the right things, but our actions betray our true beliefs. One of the most frightening sayings of Jesus is Matt 7:21–23:

119. *CD*, 167 / *SKS* 10, 179.

120. Jas 1:22–25.

121. *CUP1*, 195 / *SKS* 7, 178–79.

> Not everyone who says to me, "Lord, Lord," will enter the kingdom of heaven, but the one who does the will of my Father who is in heaven. On that day many will say to me, "Lord, Lord, did we not prophesy in your name, and cast out demons in your name, and do many mighty works in your name?" And then will I declare to them, "I never knew you; depart from me, you workers of lawlessness."

Even demons know the truth, but they are still demons.[122] Knowing the truth is not enough. The tree shows the fruit.

Kierkegaard gives another poignant example of the misplaced nature of an objective faith. We know an earthly king by his presence. Sure, he lives in a palace and has royal garb, but what really sets a king apart is how people *live* around him. His subjects submit to him, showing reverence and respect in his presence. How silly would it be to prove a king exists objectively, to use logic and philosophy to demonstrate that there is a king! One proves someone is a king by submission to his kingship. A true king does not go around telling people he is king. He lives his kingliness. Kierkegaard cuts to the core: "And thus one also demonstrates the existence of God by worship—not by demonstrations."[123] The tree shows the fruit. How does objectivity cause "all humankind to cheat by copying and reeling off the results and answers"?[124] Objectivity can deceive people into thinking they are believers because they have correct dogma. Objectivity can also deceive believers into thinking certain people are Christians when they are in fact not. Charlatans are smooth talkers, and it is high time the church looks to deeds over words, to actions over doctrine, to subjectivity over objectivity. Kierkegaard gives us a fresh word on the *point* of Christian truth: to change us to be the people we are supposed to be, "to walk in a manner worthy of the calling to which you have been called."[125]

4. CONCLUSION

Our starting point when doing theology and apologetics matters. We ought to have an attitude of fear and trembling before God, not a cocksure disposition, believing we posses an Archimedean perspective on

122. Jas 2:19.

123. *CUP1*, 546 / *SKS* 7, 469.

124. *CUP1*, 73 / *SKS* 7, 73.

125. Eph 4:1.

reality. Kierkegaard reminds us, as Karl Barth puts it, "God is in heaven, and thou art on earth."[126] One of the main struggles with doing apologetics, or any theological discipline, is turning God into an object of study. When I am in my day-to-day role—teaching students, reading theology, researching topics—I am all too quick to turn my vocation into a job. I have to publish something, so let me find a scandalous topic that piques my interests and will ruffle some feathers! I get into the groove of teaching the same classes, reading the same books, and answering the same questions. God then becomes *routine* in my life, an object on my daily planner like exercising or mowing the grass. I never want to fall into such a horrendous pit. What sadder reality exists than treating the king of the universe, the living God, as if he were a fairy tale? I have the privilege of knowing the one true God, the ineffable one.

Anselm has a rousing word for us all: "For I do not seek to understand so that I may believe; but I believe so that I may understand."[127] This should be all of our mottos. We investigate; we systematize; we study; we translate; we rationally think through arguments to better equip ourselves in our apologetic task; but we do it all in the name of *faith* in our God. Kierkegaard helps us to remember the limitations of our knowledge, of our inability to know God through our own, unaided efforts. Kierkegaard's categories of objectivity and subjectivity are needed in our discourse as a constant reminder of God's otherness and our creatureliness. The goal of apologetics is not just a rational basis of knowledge, but we seek to find new and novel ways to evangelize the lost. We want to take people's questions and doubts seriously, ready with an answer. We have to remember that Christianity is not just a set of tenets but a radical encounter with the resurrected Christ. Jesus rose from the dead in history, and every single individual encounters Christ in his or her conversion experience. We believe we still encounter Christ when we worship together. It saddens me that we often reduce Christianity to doctrinal statements or proofs of God's existence—not because I think these are bad per se but because they remove the vital, existential component of our faith. God is in heaven, thou art on Earth; but God came down, and "we have seen his glory, glory as of the only Son from the Father, full of grace and truth."[128]

126. Barth, *Epistle to the Romans*, 10.

127. Anselm, *Proslogion*, 1.

128. John 1:14

But when living becomes an earnest matter, then the question becomes: How shall one walk in order to walk the right road on the road of life? The traveler does not ask as one usually asks, "Where is the road?" but asks how one walks along the road and about how one ought to walk. Yet just to ask properly requires some consideration, because impatience does not mind being deceived and in fact merely asks where the road is, in the spiritual sense, as if that decided everything in the same sense as when the traveler found the highway. Worldly wisdom is very willing to deceive by again and again answering the question "Where is the road?" while the difficulty is omitted, that spiritually understood the road is: *how* it is walked.[129]

129. *UD*, 291 / *SKS* 8, 385–86.

2

That Doesn't Mean What You Think It Means

Fear and Trembling, Faith, and Absurdity

As an undergraduate student, I took a class on the Pentateuch. When it came time to pick a topic for my research paper, I decided to challenge myself. I chose Gen 22 as my text, the famous passage of Abraham offering up Isaac as a sacrifice to God. The reason was twofold. First, the passage was challenging, packed with layers of significance. Second, it gave me an excuse to finally read, in entirety, one of Søren Kierkegaard's most famous books: *Fear and Trembling*. As a wide-eyed twenty-one-year-old, I naively took up the arduous task of Kierkegaard's poetic reflection on Abraham's journey to Mount Moriah. Although I thoroughly misunderstood the book, it was my starting point in reading Kierkegaard beyond excerpts from philosophy textbooks.

The issue with *Fear and Trembling* being one's first foray into Kierkegaard is that it is a notoriously easy book to misread, so much so that even academics misconstrue Kierkegaard's purpose. C. Stephen Evans goes as far to say that *Fear and Trembling* "may also be [Kierkegaard's] most mystifying and misunderstood work."[1] Ronald Green agrees: "Few books have been as badly misunderstood as [*Fear and Trembling*]. Themes that Kierkegaard meant to serve only as a stimulus to reflection

1. Evans, "Faith as the *Telos*," 9.

have become the principal focus of modern commentary."[2] The irony is that my situation was not unique, for *Fear and Trembling* is often an undergraduate student's introduction to Kierkegaard's thought. Robert Perkins comments, "Since [*Fear and Trembling*] is the most studied of Kierkegaard's works in the undergraduate curriculum, each year many professors and students work their way through its difficult dialectic."[3] We have a complicated, easily misinterpreted book. I know what would be a good idea: let's tell everyone it is the best place to start reading Kierkegaard!

What is the nature of the misreading? Much of it is from Kierkegaard's vocabulary. Kierkegaard uses terms like "absurd," "ethical," "universal," and "faith"—all terms used in a myriad of disciplines from apologetics to philosophy to ethics to theology to sociology to psychology. Quite often, we attach our understanding of the term without inquiring Kierkegaard's usage. Now, Kierkegaard is partially to blame for the misunderstanding. He assumes that we all understand his context, and he rarely spends time defining terms—but in another sense, why would he? He is responding to specific issues in his native Denmark, continuing a philosophical conversation that was a part of the zeitgeist.

Let me give an example from *Fear and Trembling* that may be easily misread: "The ethical as such is the universal, and as the universal it applies to everyone, which from another angle means that it applies at all times."[4] If we read "ethical" as "referring to the discipline of ethics," then such a statement declares that an ethical action is always applicable in all situations. This does not seem controversial, yet *Fear and Trembling* also asks a grave question: "Is there a teleological suspension on the ethical?" Johannes de Silentio, the pseudonymous author of the work, implies that to maintain Abraham's status as the knight of faith, we have to suspend the ethical: "Thus, there is a paradox, that the single individual as the single individual stands in absolute relation to the absolute, or Abraham is lost."[5] Suspending the ethical—what is right and wrong—is irrational. If "right" and "wrong" are arbitrary, then how can we have confidence that anything is truly ethical? Martin Buber reads *Fear and Trembling* thusly: "The validity of moral duty can at times be suspended in accordance with something higher, of the highest. . . . What is more, that which

2. Green, "Enough Is Enough!," 191.

3. Perkins, "Introduction," 3.

4. *FT*, 54 / *SKS* 4, 148.

5. *FT*, 120 / *SKS* 4, 207.

is otherwise purely evil is for the duration of this situation purely good because it has become pleasing to God."[6] If God is holy, then how can evil please him? How can anyone give an apologetic defense to this sort of irrational, schizophrenic deity?

But what if the above understanding of "ethical," "universal," and "paradox" are *not* what Kierkegaard has in mind in *Fear and Trembling*? The above common reading derives from misunderstanding Kierkegaard's historical context and his theory of the stages of existence, particularly in relation to the pseudonymous author of *Fear and Trembling*, Johannes de Silentio. "Ethical" does not refer to right and wrong, but rather it refers to the *ethical sphere of existence* in Kierkegaard's thinking. Additionally, de Silentio assumes a Hegelian understanding of "ethical," and if we do not clearly comprehend this perspective then we will miss the point Kierkegaard makes. *Fear and Trembling* is *not* about ethics in the sense of doing right and wrong. *Fear and Trembling* is a reflection on the nature of faith as an existence category: we work out our faith with fear and trembling.[7] Faith is no easy task. As Dietrich Bonhoeffer puts it 100 years after Kierkegaard: "[Grace] is *costly* because it cost God the life of his Son: 'ye were bought at a price,' and what has cost God much cannot be cheap for us."[8] Kierkegaard lived in a cultural Christianity—what he calls Christendom—where faith "can be had at such a bargain price that it becomes a question whether there is finally anyone who will make a bid."[9] Christianity had become *objective*, a list of tasks to complete, a reflection of being a good person in society, a stamp on the passport to heaven. *Fear and Trembling* is a challenge to such unfortunate reality, showing the dynamics and difficulties of faith as opposed to an easy believism. Kierkegaard's most famous work[10] still challenges us today, giving us a fresh word to our contemporary context.

To understand *Fear and Trembling*, we must demystify the factors that inform the text. We start with an investigation of Kierkegaard's stages of existence. All people are in one of three spheres: aesthetic, ethical, or religious. We will examine these stages, along with their signs and effects

6. Buber, *Eclipse of God*, 115.

7. Phil 2:12.

8. Bonhoeffer, *Cost of Discipleship*, 45.

9. *FT*, 5 / *SKS* 4, 101.

10. In Kierkegaard's personal journal, he says, "Ah, some day after I am dead, *Fear and Trembling* alone will be enough to immortalize my name as an author. Then it will be read and translated into foreign languages." *KJN* 6, 237 / *SKS* 22, 235, NB12:147.

in the individual, for these stages directly relate to *Fear and Trembling* (and the bulk of Kierkegaard's writing at that). The second part of this chapter is a reading of *Fear in Trembling* in light of Kierkegaard's theory of stages. Kierkegaard's pseudonym in *Fear and Trembling* is Johannes de Silentio, and Johannes admits that he is not a man of faith. He consistently cites his befuddlement at Abraham's actions: "I cannot think myself into Abraham."[11] Silentio is an *outsider* to Christian faith, highly influenced by the Hegelian understanding of Spirit (*Geist*) operating in the world, yet Abraham's actions confound a Hegelian view of reality. Kierkegaard has a biting rebuke of the Hegelian view of ethics popular in his hometown of Copenhagen. I share Ryan Kemp's assessment of de Silentio's purpose in *Fear and Trembling*: "[He shows] the reader what faithfulness (and by implication faith) is *not*."[12] Lastly, I draw out some important teachings in *Fear and Trembling* that apply to apologetics. Kierkegaard's critique of Hegelianism is pertinent to contemporary times, and I believe *Fear and Trembling* is helpful for Christians living in a world with an improper understanding of God and how he works.

1. STAGES ON LIFE'S WAY

Kierkegaard believes that if we examine individuals in existence—meaning observing people as they go about their daily lives—we see some consistent patterns. We can broadly categorize all people into one of three stages of existence—the aesthetic, the ethical, or the religious—and we can predict how people will act and respond to life-events based upon the stage in which they exist. Gregor Malantschuk sees Kierkegaard's stages as "the first time in the history of man that a view of man has been formulated in which all the aspects and all the possibilities of human life have been consistently worked together in a developmental sequence."[13] The stages build upon one another, with the religious as the highest stage of existence, the stage of authentic humanity in proper relationship with God.[14] Kierkegaard is concerned that his fellow Danes have been lulled into a false sense of security, believing that they are true Christians when in fact they exist in a sub-faith stage. The fault lies in

11. *FT*, 33 / *SKS* 4, 128.
12. Kemp, "Johannes de Silentio," 145 (my emphasis).
13. Malantschuk, *Kierkegaard's Way to the Truth*, 19–20.
14. We will examine the dynamics of authentic humanity in chapter 3.

Christendom, the idea that Denmark is a Christian nation where all of its citizens are Christians.[15] Christendom also produces a faulty assumption: natural growth corresponds to spiritual growth. Children live in a world of make-believe, selfishly wanting their own way. After they sow all their wild oats and physically grow up, they take on responsibilities: marriage, work, and civilian life. Once they establish a family and settle down in a career, then they become religiously reflective. Progress is tied to objective check-boxes, and a good Christian ends up being someone who gets married, has children, throws a few coins in the coffer, and is an overall good person.

Yet faith is significantly more than checking boxes: it is a subjective leap of inward appropriation. Because the life of faith begins with a *decision*, faith is *not* a guarantee of natural progression. The life of faith is a new stage of existence, and a new stage of existence will result in a new way of living. At times, Kierkegaard uses the word "sphere" rather than stage, and this gives us a clue as to how these stages operate. They are not rungs on a ladder, but rather they are worlds in which we live. How we live tells which stage we are in, the world to which we belong. Just because I grow up physically does not mean I progress out of childlike thinking and living, as the apostle Paul reminds the Corinthians.[16] We can all think of individuals who are stunted in their personal development, who never seem to "grow up"—some even take pride in not growing up. In the same way, just because someone goes to church, receives baptism and the Lord's supper, and attends Sunday School does not mean she lives in the religious sphere of existence. The vast majority of the world lives in aesthetic or ethical categories, and Kierkegaard illuminates the shallowness and ultimate unlivability of the two lesser stages of existence. Knowing the characteristics of and borders between the stages aids us in unraveling the confusing web of *Fear and Trembling*. Malantschuk goes as far to say that "theory of the stages . . . is the basis of Søren Kierkegaard's whole authorship"; having a clear understanding is invaluable to walking through Kierkegaard's thought.[17]

15. *PV*, 23 / *SKS* 16, 11.

16. 1 Cor 13:11.

17. Malantschuk, *Kierkegaard's Way to the Truth*, 22.

1.1 The Aesthetic Stage

Kierkegaard, through pseudonym Frater Taciturnus, defines the aesthetic stage as "the sphere of immediacy."[18] Many of Kierkegaard's characters from his writings are firmly entrenched in the aesthetic sphere of life.[19] Kierkegaard often *demonstrates* an aesthetic lifestyle in his various works rather than an explicit philosophical treatise. He constructs characters and situations, and through his artistic expression, we *see* the deficiencies of such a life-sphere. As Evans explains, "Kierkegaard does not just tell us about the aesthetic life, but gives us aesthetic characters, people with whom we may identify or be attracted to, or, alternatively, feel compassion or even repugnance for."[20] Some of Kierkegaard's aesthetic characters we pity, like the Young Man in *Stages on Life's Way*, who refuses to fall in love because he does not understand it: "If I cannot understand the force to whose power I am surrendering, then I will not surrender to its power."[21] Kierkegaard's other characters repulse us, like Johannes the Seducer in both *Either/Or* and *Stages on Life's Way*. This character, who we will examine more in chapter 4, seduces women for the fun of it, abandoning them as soon as he gets what he wants. In Kierkegaard's personal journals, he describes Johannes the Seducer as a picture of "perdition."[22] These quick examples show that in order to understand the aesthetic sphere of existence, we ought to investigate one of Kierkegaard's aesthetic characters.

The most popular aesthete in Kierkegaard's writing is probably A, the unnamed author of *Either/Or, Part I*. He is full of artistic, morose sayings, and some of Kierkegaard's most pithy quips are usually from the mouth of the aesthetic A. For example, one of my favorite sayings is A explaining how empty he feels: "I am timorous as a *sheva*, as weak and muted as a *dagash lene*; I feel like a letter printed backward in the line, and yet as uncontrollable as a pasha with three horse tails."[23] While A is Kierkegaard's most popular aesthete, I want to examine the two characters from *Repetition* as examples of the aesthetic sphere of existence:

18. *SL*, 476 / *SKS* 6, 439.

19. We will explain Kierkegaard's purpose of pseudonyms in chapter 4. The following works are from the aesthetic stage: *Either/Or Part I*, *Repetition*, and *Stages on Life's Way*, part 1.

20. Evans, *Kierkegaard*, 70.

21. *SL*, 40 / *SKS* 6, 43.

22. *KJN* 2, 224 / *SKS* 18, 243, JJ:326.

23. *EO1*, 22 / *SKS* 2, 30. Biblical Hebrew fans will appreciate and grasp the image!

Constantin Constantius and the unnamed Young Man.[24] My reason for this is twofold. First, Kierkegaard published *Repetition* and *Fear and Trembling* on the same day, and there are subtle connections between the works. Second, many authors have analyzed A in *Either/Or*,[25] and I do not desire to retread old ground; but rather, I want to illuminate some of Kierkegaard's less popular characters from his other works. While we will use some examples from Kierkegaard's other aesthetic characters to describe the aesthetic sphere, we will mostly examine the oft-overlooked work *Repetition*.

Repetition is psychological report from Constantin Constantius, interspersed with letters from the Young Man. As a psychologist, Constantius wants to construct an experiment to test repetition. He explains his rationale:

> Say what you will, this question will play a very important role in modern philosophy, for *repetition* is a crucial expression for what "recollection" was to the Greeks. Just as they taught that all knowing is recollecting, modern philosophy will teach that all life is repetition. . . . What is recollected has been, is repeated backward, whereas genuine repetition is recollected forward. Repetition, therefore, if it is possible, makes a person happy, whereas recollection makes him unhappy.[26]

If you are already confused, you are in good company. Stephen Crites comments that "the author [Constantius] is a butterfly who leads [his audience] on a merry chase."[27] If that comment is too artistic for you, Robert Perkins is a little clearer: "Kierkegaard's *Repetition* is indeed a book that is hard to understand."[28]

Why is Constantius concerned with the esoteric concept of repetition? In fact, what even is repetition? Constantius puts repetition in opposition to recollection. The concept of recollection traces all the way back to Socrates (or rather, Plato's representation of Socrates), particularly in *Phaedo*. As I mentioned in the previous chapter, recollection is the idea that all of our learning is a mere recollecting of knowledge that we forgot.

24. Not to be confused with the Young Man from *Stages on Life's Way*, who may in fact be the same character.

25. For example, Evans has an excellent and robust analysis of A and the aesthetic life. See Evans, *Kierkegaard*, 68–89.

26. *R*, 131 / *SKS* 4, 9.

27. Crites, "Blissful Security of the Moment," 225.

28. Perkins, "Introduction," 195.

Socrates believed in the preexistence of the human soul, meaning our souls exist with perfect knowledge before our physical birth. At birth, our souls are thrown into our bodies, and this process causes us to forget all of the knowledge we once had. We did not *lose* the knowledge, for it still exists within us, latent in our minds.[29] As Kierkegaard himself summarizes in *Philosophical Fragments*, "Thus the ignorant person merely needs to be reminded"; we need to recollect what we forgot.[30] Constantius finds recollection unsuitable, for it makes all of existence *backward facing*. If we live our lives in recollection, then all we are doing is *remembering* something from our past. What about the here and now? Constantius wants to live in the present: "For hope is a beckoning fruit that does not satisfy; recollection is petty travel money that does not satisfy; but repetition is the daily bread that satisfies with blessing."[31]

In Constantius's quest for repetition, we see one of the main characteristics of the aesthetic stage of existence: *immediate desire*. When I say "immediate," I mean it in the most literal sense: without a medium; right here, right now. The aesthete does not want to recollect the past or hope in the future, for he desires the sensation of the present. Constantius shows an example of present desire through the actions of the Young Man he encounters and befriends. The Young Man became engaged, smitten by his beloved, yet something tragic begins to happen: the Young Man cannot recollect the love he once felt for his fiancée. Upon further reflection, the Young Man realizes that his love is not for his beloved but for the *ideal* of romantic love. Constantius comments that "[the Young Man] did not still love her, because he only longed for her. . . . She was the occasion that awakened the poetic in him and made him a poet."[32] The Young Man wants to love, but as soon as he has to *choose* to love, despair besets him. He desires all the warm tingles of romance, yet as soon as the sensations cease, he is at a loss. As Genia Schönbaumsfeld comments, "Since the aesthete is not interested in giving permanence to any of his experiences, as this would curtail his freedom and limit his potential to explore new possibilities, he is able to . . . use whatever life happens to provide as raw material that can be transformed into art."[33] The aesthete's problem is that

29. Plato, *Phaedo*, 72–73. For an in-depth explanation of Plato's concept, see Silverman, "Plato's Middle Period Metaphysics."

30. *PF*, 9 / *SKS* 4, 218.

31. *R*, 132 / *SKS* 4, 10.

32. *R*, 137–38 / *SKS* 4, 15.

33. Schönbaumsfeld, "Aesthetic as Mirror of Faith," 664.

such waffling is ultimately unsatisfying. We cannot have our cake and eat it, too. We have to choose: either have the cake or eat the cake.

The decision—to either eat or not eat the cake—terrifies an aesthete. The either/or of choice, reasons the aesthete, turns life into recollection. If I choose to eat the cake, it may be delicious. It may be the best cake in the entire world. That reality can then shackle me to always comparing subsequent cakes to that one amazing experience. Decisions in the past dictate the here and now, and the individual may never recapture said experience. It is kind of like the person who peaks in high school: his entire life is longing to recollect the past glory days. Aesthetes want to *live* in the sensation of the present, so they avoid any choices that may cause recollection. Merold Westphal has a great summary on the predicament of this sphere of existence: "For the aesthetic stage on life's way, the I is absolute."[34] If the I is absolute, then I must always be in control. Commitment to marriage turns the individual into a "we," a loss of autonomy. Settling down into a career is another bondage, for a job squashes spontaneity. The aesthetic sphere of existence is self-centered, and the echoing effects of living in a selfish world is that one's whims and fancies drive the bus.

Constantius obsesses over repetition because he wants to *feel* in the present. He wants to have all of the sensations he wants right when he wants them.[35] To test if repetition is possible, Constantius takes a trip to Berlin, recollecting a previous trip he had. On his first journey, Constantius stayed at a lovely apartment with a fine bachelor landlord. He went to an excellent performance at the Königstäder Theater. While at the theater, he had a great seat in the balcony by himself, spying a lovely young woman in the crowd. When he saw her, it opened a stream of emotions and memories of a beautiful woman in Denmark he encountered while out for a walk. All of these positive desires flowed through Constantius on his first trip to Berlin, yet on his experimental return voyage, everything is wrong. The landlord is married. The theater is filled to the brim, and worst of all, the lovely woman is nowhere to be seen. Constantius fears repetition is impossible, and he states, "I was plunged down almost into the abyss of despair."[36]

Why is he so upset that events do not play out like his previous excursion? Since he desires desire, he has to constantly seek desire in news ways. Attempting to do the same-old thing does not satisfy. Crites

34. Westphal, "Johannes and Johannes," 17.

35. Evans, *Kierkegaard*, 71.

36. *R*, 173 / *SKS* 4, 47.

explains that Constantius wants to live in "the eternal present," where Constantius's existence satisfies his poetic longing.[37] Constantius seeks what Charles Taylor calls *fullness*, a "way in which this life looks good, whole, proper, really being lived as it should."[38] Constantius has tasted and seen something *full*, something beautiful, and wants to do everything in his power to experience it again. For Constantius, and all aesthetes, the good life is desire, yet the insidiousness of desire is that it never satisfies and eventually dissipates. Kierkegaard discusses *Repetition* in the introduction of *The Concept of Anxiety*. His commentary is illuminative: "Repetition is a religious category, too transcendent for [Constantius]."[39] True repetition taps into the truly transcendent: God, the author of life, who makes all things new. Since God exists outside our understanding of time, he is eternally present, able to give us abundant life. God can only be found by faith, a *choice* to follow him. Either one has faith, or he does not. Constantius can never have a true repetition because he does not want to choose anything. His desire for desire is his god, yet this god is "[exchanging] the glory of the immortal God for images resembling mortal man and birds and animals and creeping things."[40] As T. F. Morris puts it, Constantius "is trying to avoid the world of actuality."[41] He desires a fullness that he can only achieve by giving up his selfish desire. Constantius is not free but a slave to the fancies of ever-increasing thrill seeking. A, the young aesthete in *Either/Or* has an entire essay about the inescapable despair of slowing down, titled "Rotation of Crops." He states that "boredom is the root of all evil," so he must constantly rotate crops—that is, find new and interesting ways to assuage boredom—in order to live a fulfilled life.[42] Any commitment will lead to boredom, so the aesthetic life is a never-ending quest for some form of existential fulfillment.

The irony of the aesthetic life is that it is ultimately unlivable. If the goal of life is to always desire, then the aesthete consumes himself with the latest and greatest; yet such a lifestyle is a *choice*. At one point in his life, Constantius chose to live the aesthetic life, and he is now recollecting that moment he *felt* something, attempting to regain some semblance of

37. Crites, "Blissful Security of the Moment," 224.

38. Taylor, *Secular Age*, 600.

39. *CA*, 18 / *SKS* 4, 326. Jeffery Hanson's work highlighted this connection for me. See Hanson, *Kierkegaard and Life of Faith*, 4.

40. Rom 1:23.

41. Morris, "Constantin Constantius's Search," 313.

42. *EO1*, 286 / *SKS* 2, 276.

completeness from his past. Kierkegaard explains that irony is a key signature of aesthetic existence, a border territory between the aesthetic and ethical stage.[43] John Lippitt explains how irony functions in the aesthetic sphere: "[The ironist] has realized that the aesthete endlessly toys with and reflects upon various existential possibilities, but perpetually postpones vital decisions concerning his own existence."[44] Both Constantius and the Young Man display such irony. The Young Man, unable to recollect his love for his fiancée, flees to Stockholm without addressing his problem. While there, he writes letters to Constantius about his struggling through the broken engagement. The Young Man takes solace in the sufferings of Job, and the Young Man has an intriguing statement: "Was Job proved to be in the right? Yes, eternally, by being proved to be in the wrong *before God*. So there is a repetition after all."[45] The Young Man realizes that true repetition—experiencing the eternal which will not leave us unsatiated—is connection to God, not his own self-centered desires. Yet how does the Young Man's story end? His former fiancée marries another, and he declares "I am myself again. . . . Is there not, then a repetition? . . . It is over, my skiff is afloat. In a minute I shall be there where my soul longs to be, there where ideas spume with elemental fury. . . . I belong to the idea. . . . When the idea calls, I abandon everything."[46] The Young Man's "repetition" is becoming master of his own self again. Disentangled from his fiancée, he can now search out poetic pursuits, rotating crops anew.

Constantius, too, is ironic. After reading the letters from the Young Man, Constantius knows the solution: "If [the Young Man] had had a deeper religious background, he would not have become a poet."[47] Constantius knows the solution to repetition—to be able to withstand the torments of life with unwavering purpose—is the leap to the religious sphere. With such knowledge of the objectively correct answer, we would assume Constantius takes his own advice, yet his irony is on full display: "I am unable to make a religious movement; it is contrary to my nature."[48]

We can say more about the aesthetic stage, but the above suffices for our understanding. Malantschuk has a great summary of the predicament of aesthetic existence: "At the top of the aesthetic scale is the one

43. *CUP1*, 501–3 / *SKS* 7, 455–57.

44. Lippitt, *Humour and Irony*, 63.

45. *R*, 212 / *SKS* 4, 79.

46. *R*, 220–21 / *SKS* 4, 87–88.

47. *R*, 229 / *SKS* 4, 95.

48. *R*, 187 / *SKS* 4, 57.

who has seen through the emptiness and despair of pure aestheticism but will not let it go and intoxicates himself with his own despair."[49] Aesthetes desire desire, so much so that they fill their lives with trivial activities to elicit emotional responses. They live in the world of daydreams and possibilities, too afraid to commit to something out of fear of either boredom or living a present life of past recollection. Whether it is music, art, or romance, the aesthete puts *himself* as the center of his reality. Any sort of commitment is bad because commitment is a fetter to something or someone else. The aesthetic life is ironic, for no one can sustain this level of existence. We pity Constantius and the Young Man because a life consumed with pleasure is fundamentally vapid. Such a sphere of existence is actual bondage, not freedom.

1.2 The Ethical Stage

While the aesthete consumes himself with the immediate moment of fleeting passion, the ethicist concerns himself with commitment. Kierkegaard's Frater Taciturnus states that the ethical is "the sphere of requirement."[50] The most famous ethical figure in the Kierkegaardian corpus is Judge William, and as a character, he shows up in two of Kierkegaard's works: *Either/Or* and *Stages on Life's Way*. Although Judge William is usually viewed through the lens of *Either/Or*, I want to look at him through *Stages* for two reasons. First, I find it odd that *Stages on Life's Way* does not get much attention, in either popular or academic circles. Walter Lowrie, the first translator of *Stages* into English, states his annoyance with part of the book: "I will say for my own part that I heartily wish S. K. had never written this Diary—nor written the hundreds of pages on the same theme which he confided to his Journal. I am tired of reading it all, and find it still more tiresome to translate it."[51] Like *Repetition*, I want people to engage this fascinating work. Although the Judge discusses marriage in both *Either/Or* and *Stages*, Kierkegaard's pseudonym Johannes Climacus comments that in *Stages*, "the Judge is preoccupied with marriage from an entirely different angle than in *Either/Or*."[52] The "different angle" is the second reason for examining *Stages*, for in *Stages*

49. Malantschuk, *Kierkegaard's Way to the Truth*, 35.

50. *SL*, 476 / *SKS* 6, 439.

51. Lowrie, "Introduction," 13.

52. *CUP1*, 287 / *SKS* 7, 261–62.

Kierkegaard more clearly differentiates the ethical from the religious sphere.[53] The addition of the religious sphere of existence in the last two-thirds of *Stages* highlights the ultimate dissatisfaction derived from the ethical sphere.[54] While we will peer into *Either/Or*, we primarily investigate *Stages on Life's Way*.

Judge William is a married man, and he states that "marriage is and remains the most important voyage of discovery a human being undertakes."[55] Why is this so? The aesthete, argues the Judge, never *decides* to do anything. He stays in the abstract world of fantasy rather than the concrete world of reality. As the Judge says to A in *Either/Or*, "You yourself are a non-entity, an enigmatical figure on whose brow stands Either/Or."[56] As fast as he can, the aesthete runs away from marriage. Marriage is a trap for the aesthete, for it cleaves a man to his wife. On the contrary, Judge William sees marriage as a beautiful expression of one's duty, "as the highest *τέλος* [goal] of individual life."[57] The aesthete lives in a state of constant turmoil, seeking novel experiences to keep the desire train rolling, but in choosing himself, the ethical man grows up to become a man of resolution. As Mark Taylor puts it, "The ethical person assumes responsibility for becoming himself."[58] Responsibility, commitment, putting down roots—all of these concepts exemplify the ethical sphere. The Judge says that "resolution is a person's ideality."[59] The ideal—what it means to be truly human, the goal to which we strive—is our resolution, our choice to exist as a part of our culture. So, argues William, take the plunge and put the ring on her finger!

Yet, who sets the definitive resolution? Will *any* resolution suffice, like someone choosing to be an axe murderer? At least the aesthete would just *think* about such macabre act rather than choosing to do it! For Judge William, resolution for resolution's sake is not the goal, as we see when

53. Some scholars argue that in *Either/Or*, Judge William is in the religious sphere, or some sort of ethico-religious sphere. See Watkin, "Judge William," 113–24. I disagree with such assessment, for *Either/Or* ends with a sermon from the Pastor who criticizes both A and Judge William, even though Judge William does not think the sermon applies to him.

54. For a discussion on *Stages* and its relation to the religious, see Lippitt, *Humour and Irony*, 75.

55. *SL*, 89 / *SKS* 6, 87.

56. *EO2*, 159 / *SKS* 3, 157.

57. *SL*, 101 / *SKS* 6, 97.

58. Taylor, *Journeys to Selfhood*, 241.

59. *SL*, 109 / *SKS* 6, 104.

William discusses romance and falling in love. Romantic love is not bad, but a juvenile pining for the beloved delays responsibility. The choice to love—that is, to get married—takes romantic sentiment and channels it in the appropriate direction. Judge William explains that "resolution knows how to *find the road to the society* of human beings and to *pave the safe way*."[60] Here, we see what sets the agenda: society, which tells us what resolutions we should make. The Judge sprinkles God into the equation, for in any true resolution, God "is present and completes the purchase."[61] God acts as a seal of approval on our formal papers. He, of course, is the ground of all ethics, but the way we experience God *is through the surrounding culture*. Herein lies the root of the ethical, and as Westphal correctly explains, "for the ethical the We is absolute."[62] The culture sets the agenda, and the culture is right in its assessment. The ethical individual must choose to participate in the group.

Kierkegaard claims that *humor* is the border territory between the ethical and the religious spheres. He explains in *Concluding Unscientific Postscript*,

> [The ethicist] grasps this misrelation and places the comic in between in order to be able more inwardly to hold fast the ethical within himself. Now the comedy starts, because people's opinion of a person like that will always be: for him nothing is important. . . . The humorist continually . . . joins the conception of God *together with something else* and brings out the contradiction—but he does not relate himself to God in religious passion.[63]

The ethicist is humorous because he takes the resolution that should belong to God and applies it to something finite. Think of the film *Monty Python's Life of Brian*.[64] Brian was born in the cave next to Jesus, and in the movie, the crowds follow Brian, thinking he is the Messiah. In one scene, Brian runs away from the crowd, losing a shoe in the process. The crowd takes the lost shoe as a divine sign, and they spread the good news of only wearing one shoe. The idea is hysterical that Brian's shoe sparks a religious movement.

60. *SL*, 162 / *SKS* 6, 152 (my emphasis).

61. *SL*, 110 / *SKS* 6, 105.

62. Westphal, "Johannes and Johannes," 17.

63. *CUP1*, 505 / *SKS* 7, 458 (my emphasis).

64. Jones, *Monty Python's Life of Brian*.

We laugh at the movie, but at the same time, the scenario is eternally tragic. People deceive themselves into thinking they have the answer, but they are simply following the requirements of the crowd. Judge William signifies such a sad situation in *Stages*. The Judge states that "marriage is the fullness of time," a phrase that instantly pricks up the ears of the devout Christian.[65] The apostle Paul defines the true "fullness of time" in Galatians: "God sent forth his Son, born of woman, born under the law, to redeem those who were under the law, so that we might receive adoption as sons."[66] The gospel, those wonderful words of life, William *equates to his marriage*. William's deception does not stop here, for when talking about the love of his wife, he states, "I believe that if I were ill, *sick unto death*, and this tender gaze rested upon me . . . I believe that it would summon me back to life if God in heaven did not himself use his power."[67] The phrase "sick unto death" has a special meaning in Kierkegaard's writing. In *The Sickness unto Death*, Kierkegaard equates the sickness with *sin*, a malady that pervades all people. What does William say? If he were "sick unto death"—that is, sinful—his wife could save him. Amy Hall explains, "As [Judge William] has construed the situation, a husband is to have reliant faith in the state of marriage (not, we note, faith in God)."[68] As George Connell astutely avers, "It seems, indeed, that marriage is the Judge's religion, just as his comment about marriage being the highest *telos* [purpose] would suggest."[69]

Another humorous perspective of the Judge is his negative view of people who skip the culture and go directly to God. A direct relation to God is too abstract for the Judge, for there is no concrete mediary between the individual and God. If resolution comes from society, then society is arbiter of *everything*, including religion. Bypassing the culture to go straight to God makes no sense to the Judge. As he explains, "[The individual] must not feel himself above the universal, but lower; he must [at all costs] want to remain within it."[70] The term "universal" can have multiple meanings in common usage, but Kierkegaard uses it specifically for the cultural consensus. Malantschuk explains, "The community—or the universal—has temporal goals. Here the individual stands lower

65. *SL*, 117 / *SKS* 6, 111.

66. Gal 4:4–5.

67. *SL*, 130 / *SKS* 6, 122–23.

68. Hall, *Kierkegaard and Treachery of Love*, 148.

69. Connell, "Importance of Being Earnest," 139.

70. *SL*, 181 / *SKS* 6, 168 (my emphasis).

than the universal and must surrender himself completely to the laws of the community."[71] According to William, it is nonsensical to subvert the crowd and directly go to God. The universal is God's way of instituting order. How can someone *not* submit to the universal? The universal means *universal.*

The ethical sphere is about choosing to submit to the culture. Be a good little boy, obey, and become a man! Have a wife, house, picket fence, and 2.5 children! Everyone else is doing it, and all of these nice, godly people cannot be wrong! Don't forget God! We need to go to church to be wholesome people of gumption and outstanding character! The ethical stage is mistaken, taking the characteristics of the infinite God-relationship and predicating them to something finite: marriage, work, hobbies, etc. Also, how do we know that the culture is correct in its portrayal of the good life?

1.3 The Religious Stage

The final sphere of existence is the religious stage, "the sphere of fulfillment," as Taciturnus puts it.[72] Kierkegaard has a few religious pseudonyms—primarily Anti-Climacus in *The Sickness unto Death* and *Practice in Christianity*—but Kierkegaard typically signs his name to his explicitly Christian discourses. These discourses are for upbuilding and awakening, focusing on the direct content rather than the indirect communication of pseudonyms. Because of the more direct nature of Kierkegaard's religious writings, we will not follow a particular character through a story but simply explain the stage.

Kierkegaard divides the religious sphere into two groups: Religiousness A and Religiousness B. Religiousness A is what Kierkegaard calls "the dialectic of inward deepening."[73] This step comes about as the ethical person realizes issues with her community. How does she know the culture is correct? What about biblical stories where God speaks directly to individuals? Taylor describes the process: "Kierkegaard's ethicist gradually discovers the depth of oppositions, the disparity of differences, and the exclusivity of the contraries within the self."[74] Furthermore, how

71. Malantschuk, *Kierkegaard's Way to the Truth*, 41.

72. *SL*, 476 / *SKS* 6, 439.

73. *CUP1*, 556 / *SKS* 7, 505.

74. Taylor, *Journeys to Selfhood*, 251.

can we measure up to society's values? None of us can obey all of the laws and values of a culture—as social media teaches us with gloating over flip-flopping, hypocrisy, and schadenfreude. The cracks in the ethical foundation lead down the path of pathos, an inward deepening that starts to corrode one's ethical existence. Despair fills the individual, and this "despair is veritably a self-consuming, but an *impotent self-consuming* that cannot do what it wants to do."[75] There is only one way out of despair: faith in God. With Religiousness A, subjectivity starts to emerge. The individual decides to internalize her *personal* relation to her surroundings, rather than filtering reality through her community. Subjectivity is more than having strong emotions. Aesthetes live for emotions but are not truly subjective. Subjectivity is more than choices—ethicists love to choose but are not truly subjective. Subjectivity is an honest assessment of our personal existence, realizing the holes in our way of life. Religiousness A starts the process of subjectivity.

Kierkegaard states that "Religiousness *A* must first be present in the individual before there can be any consideration of becoming aware of dialectical *B*."[76] The person in Religiousness A now stands at a crossroads: what is the root of the issue? Why does he feel how he does? Why is he incapable of keeping up with the culture? The answer, Kierkegaard declares, is *sin*. In *Postscript*, Kierkegaard explains that "sin is crucial for a whole existence-sphere, the religious sphere in the strictest sense."[77] Sin is not the depressed sentiment of the aesthete or transgression of societal norms of the ethicist. If sin were merely breaking cultural mores, then an individual sins against the culture, receiving absolution from public opinion.[78] Kierkegaard renounces such a view of sin: "The idea that what makes sin so terrible is that it is before God."[79] Sin is a *religious* category, something that science or logic cannot directly observe.[80] Religiousness B, authentic Christian faith, realizes that we have sinned against the God who is high and lifted up. We cannot come into God's presence on our own, whether through our own passions (aesthetic) or through being a moral person (ethical). Religiousness B is "paradoxical religiousness," for

75. *SUD*, 18 / *SKS* 11, 134 (my emphasis).

76. *CUP1*, 556 / *SKS* 7, 506.

77. *CUP1*, 268–69 / *SKS* 7, 244.

78. Does this sound familiar in our current context?

79. *SUD*, 80 / *SKS* 11, 194.

80. See Kierkegaard's discussion about psychological study vs. theological study of sin in *CA*, 9–24 / *SKS* 4, 317–31.

we must leap to faith in Christ, the God-man.[81] As Westphal puts it, "For the religious person God is the absolute."[82]

What, then, does Kierkegaard teach with his theory of stages? He wants to make sense of the many worlds in which we live. Aesthetes live in a world of selfish desire, making themselves the absolute standard of their existence. Aesthetes who become more reflective are ironic, for they can never live out their desires to the fullest. They must eventually make some sort of concrete decision. Ethicists "grow up" and submit to the culture. They become subservient to the goals of their community, making "common sense" or "the cultural good" the absolute standard of their existence. Ethicists who become more reflective are humorous, for they relate to ethical life as if it were God. Eventually, they realize the absurdity of this notion and the impossibility of living up to society's standards. Religiousness A is when the aesthete or the ethicist realizes that their existence-spheres are ultimately hollow.[83] They cannot live how they think they should, filled with despair and doubt. Only upon realizing their sinfulness, that they have sinned against the one true God, can they make the leap to faith. Religiousness B is the highest sphere of existence, the sphere of authentic Christian faith.

2. READING *FEAR AND TREMBLING*

Our discussion of the spheres prepares us for reading *Fear and Trembling*. Kierkegaard writes *Fear and Trembling* under the pseudonym Johannes de Silentio, a person in the ethical sphere of existence. Silentio's "dialectical lyric" opens with a quote from philosopher Johann Hamann: "What Tarquinius Superbus said in the garden by means of the poppies, the son understood but the messenger did not."[84] We spy something about the work in both the name of the pseudonym and the opening quotation. Being in the ethical sphere of existence, Silentio is on the *outside* looking at faith, attempting to understand its dynamics but failing to do so. Evans comments, "This motto [at the beginning of the book] hints that Johannes's message about faith is written in such a way that it is likely to

81. *CUP1*, 556 / *SKS* 7, 505.

82. Westphal, "Johannes and Johannes: Kierkegaard and Difference," 17.

83. I want to note that one can jump from aesthetic to religious and completely bypass the ethical. Kierkegaard himself considered this his personal story.

84. *FT*, 3 / *SKS* 4, 100.

be misunderstood by anyone who, lacking faith, is not 'in the family.' . . . Johannes accurately understands what faith is *not*, but as he himself insists, does not understand what faith *is*."[85] Johannes is *silent*: he does not make the leap to faith. He stands silent at the presentation of authentic faith, and he does not move forward: "By no means do I have faith. By nature I am a shrewd fellow, yet shrewd people always have great difficulty in making the movement of faith."[86] *Fear and Trembling* is the reflection of an admitted non-Christian analyzing Christian faith. As Ronald Green puts it, with the simple quote at the beginning of the book, "Kierkegaard signals that not everything that follows is as it seems."[87]

Fear and Trembling is Silentio's analysis of the harrowing passage of Gen 22 where God asks Abraham to offer his son Isaac as a sacrifice. Truly, such a task induces fear and trembling! We see the tension in God's request to Abraham: "Take your son, *your only son Isaac, whom you love*, and go to the land of Moriah, and offer him there as a burnt offering on one of the mountains of which I shall tell you."[88] Isaac, the child of promise, through whom God would make a great nation, the child Abraham and Sarah had so longed for, the miracle born in their old age—Abraham is to offer *him*. Silentio tries to walk in Abraham's shoes, to get into Abraham's mindset as he prepared for the hard road ahead. Surely, Isaac asked Abraham numerous questions on the path to Moriah! Surely, Abraham's household asked him what he was going to do! Surely, Abraham had to respond! The narrative tells us that Isaac had questions: "Behold, the fire and the wood, but where is the lamb for a burnt offering?" Abraham responds as the man of faith: "God will provide for himself the lamb for a burnt offering, my son."[89] What a response! God does not tell Abraham that he will spare Isaac, but Abraham has faith that God will move in a mighty way. Abraham passed the test, willingly trusting God for deliverance, and, as the author of Hebrew comments, "He considered that God was able even to raise [Isaac] from the dead, from which, figuratively speaking, he did receive him back."[90]

85. Evans, "Faith as the *Telos*," 11.

86. *FT*, 32 / *SKS* 4, 128.

87. Green, "'Developing' *Fear and Trembling*," 257.

88. Gen 22:2 (my emphasis).

89. Gen 22:7–8.

90. Heb 11:19.

2.1 Let's Talk about Your Suspension

Abraham's situation—the horror of the task and the beauty of faith—is something Silentio cannot grasp: "[Abraham] had faith by virtue of the absurd, for all human calculation ceased long ago."[91] Since Silentio is an outsider to the faith, it makes sense that the actions of true believers baffle him. We cannot fault Silentio for balking at the narrative. God wants Abraham to kill his child, the same child he claims as the means to bless the entire world. Silentio gives a metaphorical "I don't get it." Anything—whether it be a god or a culture or a tradition—requiring a parent to execute a child seems reprehensible to us modern readers. But Silentio does seem bothered by child sacrifice *qua* child sacrifice. Silentio approves of certain examples from history where fathers had to sacrifice their children. Agamemnon had to sacrifice his daughter Iphigenia to protect his nation. Jephthah gave over his daughter for Israel. A judge may have to execute his son if his son breaks the law. Abraham's actions are qualitatively different from these stories.[92] The above examples are tragic sacrifices *for the good of the community*, yet Abraham's sacrifice is *for his personal relationship to God*. Abraham appears selfish to Silentio, for Abraham puts himself before his culture. As Lippitt comments, "The absolute paradox is more offensive than 'ordinary nonsense,' not because it is somehow *more* nonsensical: it is so because, while appearing to be nonsense, it demands *existential allegiance*."[93] By answering God's call, Abraham is hitching his train to God rather than his culture.

Why does Silentio have an aversion to a direct relation to God? The answer, like a lot of Kierkegaard's thought, lies in the Hegelian understanding of Spirit (*Geist*) within history. Silentio links the "ethical" to the Hegelian understanding of *Sittlichkeit*, often translated as "ethical life," "social life," or "ethical system" in English.[94] Hegel, in his fun and easy-to-read style, explains the concept in detail in *Philosophy of Right*. Hegel states, "The ethical system [*Sittlichkeit*] is thus the conception of freedom developed into a present world, and also into the nature of self-consciousness."[95] As a reminder, Hegel's focus in philosophy is that

91. *FT*, 36 / *SKS* 4, 131.

92. *FT*, 57–58 / *SKS* 4, 151–52.

93. Lippitt, *Humour and Irony*, 58.

94. Westphal, "Johannes and Johannes," 19. *FT*, 55 / *SKS* 4, 149. See the Hongs' translation footnote 7 (*FT*, 346–47).

95. Hegel, *Philosophy of Right*, 155. For the original German, see Hegel, *Grundlinien*

absolute Spirit interacts through the process of human reflection in the world. We see Hegel's ethical life *in our experience of culture*,

> when the individual in his private will and conscience drops his self-assertion and antagonism to the ethical. His character, moulded by ethical principles, takes as its motive the unmoved universal which is open on all its sides to actual rationality. He recognizes that his worth and the stability of his private ends are grounded upon the universal, and derive their reality from it.[96]

Although I am confident, dear reader, that you completely understand what Hegel is saying with his clear vocabulary, for my own personal edification, I am going to break down the above. As individuals, we only become subjects when we reflect on our surroundings. Spirit is present in this process of mediation, our reasoning through the world to come to the truth. We as individuals, though, have a part to play. On the other hand, our reasoning and worldview come from our surroundings. Hegel notes that self-consciousness bears out in the real world by individuals, but self-consciousness also "finds in the ethical system its absolute basis and motive."[97] We are social creatures, part of a larger whole. We are a both/and: individuals and members of society. Philip Kain explains that "*Sittlichkeit* is found in culture . . . where it is socially constructed within and through our customs, traditions, practices, and public institutions."[98] Spirit works through the process of the both/and of individual/culture. In the most basic terms, if we want to know what Spirit requires of us, we look to the values and customs of our culture.

Hegel's conception of ethics has *drastic* implications for morality. The definition of "ethical" becomes "customary modes of behaviour," as J. N. Findlay puts it.[99] Silentio buys into Hegel's teaching and rightfully becomes concerned with Abraham's narrative. The issue for Silentio is not that Abraham was going to kill Isaac. As stated above, Silentio cites how Agamemnon is ethical in his sacrifice of his daughter, for his sacrifice *was mediated through the culture*. A judge who executes his murderous son bases his justice upon the customs and laws of the people. The examples Silentio cites remain within their cultural understanding of right and

---

Der Philosophie Des Rechts, 133.

96. Hegel, *Philosophy of Right*, 162.

97. Hegel, *Philosophy of Right*, 155.

98. Kain, *Hegel and Right*, 86.

99. Findlay, *Hegel*, 318.

wrong. What do we have with Abraham? Abraham hears a direct word from God, and God *directly* deals with Abraham. There is no religious council, formalized church, or court of law. Westphal explains the issue Kierkegaard raises: for Hegel, "Man's relation to God is so thoroughly mediated via the social order that *faith becomes indistinguishable from socialization*."[100]

Yet what do we encounter in Gen 22? Silentio realizes a *big* problem with Hegelian philosophy and the story of Abraham as a titan of faith in the Bible: "Either there is a paradox, that the single individual as the single individual stands in absolute relation to the absolute, or Abraham is lost."[101] *Either* Abraham is justified in his sacrifice to Isaac, *or* he is not. The good Sunday School answer is that Abraham is right because God asked him to do it, yet if we buy into Hegelian philosophy, then Abraham's actions *cannot* be right. He overrides the laws and customs of his time, grounding morality in a God who *speaks* rather than an immanent Spirit who mediates. Silentio reasons that to save Abraham, there must be a teleological suspension of the ethical, meaning God may trump the ethical, *Sittlichkeit*, our culture's understanding of right and wrong. Silentio explains, "By [Abraham's] act he transgressed the ethical altogether and had a higher τέλος [purpose] outside it, in relation to which he suspended it."[102] Abraham violates the ethical, meaning *he goes against his culture*. Transgressing the ethical is *not necessarily sinning*, for sin is only a category for the religious sphere of existence.[103]

Silentio brings up another issue: how can an individual—who finds his definition in the culture—even achieve a teleological suspension? Silentio's answer is that "he exists as the single individual in contrast to the universal."[104] If we want to save Abraham, Silentio reasons, then we must reevaluate our understanding of both ethics and selfhood. Our existence cannot be solely derived from the ethical/universal, but rather it must come from a higher source. Otherwise, we would not be able to go *beyond* the ethical. Jeffery Hanson has an excellent analysis of the situation:

100. Westphal, "Abraham and Hegel," 74 (my emphasis).

101. *FT*, 120 / *SKS* 4, 207.

102. *FT*, 59 / *SKS* 4, 152.

103. Ontologically, people sin in every stage of existence. What Kierkegaard means is that the individual does not recognize any action as sin until he is in the religious sphere. In other words, lost people do not know they are lost. Only after they are found do they realize what lostness is.

104. *FT*, 61–62 / *SKS* 4, 155.

> Similarly, if faith puts the single individual higher than the universal, this implies that there is more to the good itself than the order of moral life can disclose, which again means not only that the laws and customs of the people are not the final authority over the individual but that *Sittlichkeit* simply does not exhaust all there is of good. . . . Once again, *the target is not just Hegel but any natural notion of the good life.* The teleological suspension is shorthand for an alteration in the relationship of good to conscience that is *mandated by a serious reckoning with revelation.*[105]

Examining Abraham's offering of Isaac leaves Hegelian philosophy in dire straits. If we believe in a God who *reveals* himself to us, then we cannot endorse Hegel's view of ethics. Hegelianism is a type of moral relativism, changing whenever a new mediation occurs. Kierkegaard consistently critiques Hegel on this point, claiming that "Hegelian philosophy has no ethics" and makes God "pantheistically abolished."[106] In short, if we adopt Hegel's understanding of existence, then we cannot accept the God as revealed in the Bible without seriously reinterpreting the Christian message.[107]

So what is *Fear and Trembling* about? It is the dismantling of the Hegelian notion of Spirit being equivalent to the Christian God. It shows how accepting Hegel's presuppositions leads to Abraham, the knight of faith, as a villain rather than a hero. Faith must be something other than *Sittlichkeit*, something beyond the ethical sphere of existing as a good member of the state. Silentio remarks, "The paradox of faith, then, is this: that the single individual is higher than the universal, that the single individual—to recall a distinction in dogmatics rather rare these days—determines his relation to the universal by his relation to the absolute, *not his relation to the absolute by his relation to the universal.*"[108] The person in the religious stage of existence, the person of authentic Christian faith, defines herself first and foremost in God (the absolute). The God-relationship determines the relationship to the culture (the universal)—*not the other way around.* The teleological suspension of the ethical is not saying God will ask us to sin. Sin is within the religious sphere, between

105. Hanson, *Kierkegaard and Life of Faith*, 139 (my emphasis).

106. *BA*, 129; *SUD*, 117 / *SKS* 11, 229.

107. Westphal has a great summary of how Hegel interprets the Christian message through his understanding of Spirit. See Westphal, "Johannes and Johannes," 25–29.

108. *FT*, 70 / *SKS* 4, 162 (my emphasis).

the individual and God.[109] God is holy, and he will not ask us to go against his ways. The teleological suspension of the ethical means that God may require us *to go against our culture*. Authentic faith grounds itself in God, not a group or a nation.

2.2 That's Absurd!

Whenever someone uses the A-word in philosophical discourse—"absurd"—he means business.[110] In *Fear and Trembling*, Silentio claims faith is absurd. Is this not proof again that Kierkegaard is anti-rational? He wants an absurd faith! Absurdity, philosophically speaking, is "any belief that is obviously untenable."[111] Various Christian apologists and philosophers claim Kierkegaard endorses fideism. James Dew and Paul Gould offer a succinct definition of "fideism": "One does not base belief in God on rational argument or scientific evidence. Rather, one simply has faith, and this is what is pleasing to God."[112] The reasoning, so it goes, is that because Kierkegaard declares faith "absurd," then any objectively true formulations of Christianity run counter to authentic faith. Francis Schaeffer comments on the "danger" of reading Kierkegaard:

> As a result of [Kierkegaard posing the leap of faith], from that time on, if rationalistic man wants to deal with the really important things of human life . . . he must discard rational thought about them and make a gigantic, nonrational leap of faith. The rationalistic framework had failed to produce an answer on the basis of reason, and so all hope of a uniform field of knowledge had to be abandoned.[113]

Kierkegaard's emphasis on absurdity leads to a world without rationality or reason, claims Schaeffer. Louis Pojman offers a similar take on Kierkegaard: "Kierkegaard's thesis is: A Christian should have nothing to do with historical research into the materials which involve the articles of Christian faith. There are two basic reasons for this: 1. The results of such objective inquiry do not matter for faith in the least. 2. The process

109. I will discuss sin and spirituality more in chapter 3.

110. I must give credit to my philosophy professor Robert Stewart for teaching me about the A-word!

111. Blackburn, *Oxford Dictionary of Philosophy*, 3.

112. Dew and Gould, *Philosophy*, 64–65.

113. Schaeffer, *God Who Is There*, 1:16.

of inquiry involves a temptation, an infidelity to the Gospel."[114] Is there not a danger in speaking of faith as absurd, throwing rationality and truth that corresponds to reality out the window? In fact, does not a leap to the absurd render all apologetics moot?

Dew and Gould have a criticism of fideism, *which they link to Kierkegaard*: "It should be noted that having an interest in God does not require us to jettison reason, science, or historical considerations the way fideism suggests we must."[115] Kierkegaard, once again, is not using "absurd" the way analytic philosophers use it. We must remember that Silentio is *an outsider observing Christian faith*. His philosophical musings have led him to a choice: to either leap to faith, standing as an individual before the absolute, or sink back into the universal. To an outsider steeped in Hegelian philosophy, the idea that the eternal would put on flesh and enter history as a decisive act is absurd. Spirit simply does not work that way. It is like attempting to square a triangle: nonsense. *Yet Kierkegaard is not Silentio*. Kierkegaard abhors Hegelianism, seeing it as the malady of his day. He demonstrates that Christianity—the religion everyone in his nation claims to believe—is absurd to Hegelianism. If we truly believe in the revelation of God, then we cannot endorse the entirety of Hegel's project. As Kierkegaard states in *Postscript*, "What, then, is the absurd? The absurd is that the eternal truth has come into existence in time, that God has come into existence, has been born, has grown up, etc."[116]

God is not absurd. Faith is not absurd. It is absurd to think that God would love me, that the Prince of Peace would die for me, that God would take his enemy and make him a son and heir. As Kierkegaard says in his personal journals, "What shamelessness—it is, then after all, you [God] against whom I have sinned, and then to demand that you should console me for it. And yet, infinite Love, I know that this does not displease you, because in one sense it is a sign of progress."[117] To the one requiring proof—the one who buys into the modernist dictum that I am the arbiter of truth—it is absurd to believe God must reveal himself to me. The Enlightenment thinker does not need God, tradition, or history—only reason. Christianity teaches that all of my righteousness, *including my reasoning*, is like filthy rags before God.[118] Kierkegaard clarifies his use

114. Pojman, *Logic of Subjectivity*, 41.

115. Dew and Gould, *Philosophy*, 66.

116. *CUP1*, 210 / *SKS* 7, 193.

117. *KJN* 10, 170 / *SKS* 26, 170, NB32:72.

118. Isa 64:6.

of "absurd" in his personal journals: "The absurd is a category, the negative criterion, of the divine or of the relationship to the divine. *When the believer has faith, the absurd is not the absurd—faith transforms it.*"[119] To those in either the ethical or aesthetic sphere, Christianity will *appear* to be nonsense. It is most definitely *not* nonsense; Kierkegaard never intimates that it is contradictory or illogical, but rather faith is something to be *lived.* J. Heywood Thomas notes there is a "surprisingly long-living myth that Kierkegaard is an irrationalist."[120] I agree. *Kierkegaard is not a fideist.* He stresses the necessity of faith and our inability to achieve salvation on our own—like all orthodox Christians. His use of "absurd" relates to the perspective of the non-Christian attempting to understand the life of faith unaided by the illumination of the Holy Spirit.

Let us use an example from the Bible to illustrate Kierkegaardian absurdity. On the night Jesus is handed over to be crucified, his followers scattered. They thought the movement was over, for the Messiah would be killed. Everyone "knew" that the Jewish Messiah was supposed to be a political ruler who would lop off the heads of the Romans! Peter was ready: he drew his sword, and in a very Peter-like fashion, only sliced off Malchus's ear rather than successfully liberating Jesus. Jesus chastised Peter: "Put your sword away! Shall I not drink the cup the Father has given me?"[121] In fact, Jesus constantly referenced that he would be crucified, but the apostles did not believe him. It was "absurd" to think that the Messiah would be put to death—*from the cultural perspective of the apostles.* After Christ's burial, Mary Magdalene finds the glorious empty tomb. After reporting what she saw, Jesus appeared to the disciples, and they "were overjoyed when they saw the Lord."[122] Yet someone was missing: Thomas. He refused to believe: why would anyone resurrect in the middle of history? That's nonsense! Thomas defiantly stated, "Unless I see the nail marks in his hands and put my finger where the nails were, and put my hand into his side, I will not believe." The disciples drug Thomas to their next gathering, and Jesus appears. He lovingly says to Thomas, "'Put your finger here; see my hands. Reach out your hand and put it into my side. Stop doubting and believe.' Thomas said to him, 'My Lord and my God!'"[123] Upon seeing Jesus—experiencing the resurrected Christ—the

119. *JP* 1, 10 / *Pap.* X6 B 79 (my emphasis).

120. Thomas, "Revelation, Knowledge, and Proof," 147.

121. John 18:11.

122. John 20:20.

123. John 20:25, 27–28.

"absurd" notion that he resurrected vanished. Christ, in his patience and kindness, revealed himself to Thomas. *This* is what Kierkegaard means by absurd: the gospel runs contrary to our normal expectations—whether one is Hegelian or not! As Paul reminds us, "we preach Christ crucified, a stumbling block to Jews and folly to Gentiles."[124] As Sylvia Walsh correctly comments, "The absurd is a category of interpretation employed by human understanding, not a qualification of the absolute paradox itself as the content of faith. Second, the absurd more specifically is a category employed only by nonbelievers, not by believers."[125] For Kierkegaard, faith is not absurd in the logical sense of being untenable, but rather to the outsider, steeped in logic and proofs and *Sittlichkeit*, it *seems* absurd that anyone would accept such a belief. As Kierkegaard explains, "Thus God is a supreme conception that cannot be explained by anything else but is explainable *only by immersing oneself in the concept itself*."[126] God's ways may not make sense to us, but that does not mean he is nonsensical.

2.3 Getting a Little Personal: Kierkegaard's Own Isaac

Fear and Trembling is not solely an attack against the prevalence of Hegelianism in Copenhagen. Like many of Kierkegaard's works, *Fear and Trembling* is Kierkegaard working out his own personal faith with fear and trembling. In Problema II, Silentio discusses how God may directly speak to the individual to do a particular task, which leads to "a paradoxical expression [of love], such as, for example, that love to God may bring the knight of faith to give his love to his neighbor—an expression opposite to that which, ethically speaking, is duty."[127] God may suspend the ethical for a particular individual for a particular purpose, but the suspension is always to serve God and others. God does not suspend the ethical for us to do whatever we want or to chase a selfish desire. As Hanson comments, "The ethical . . . is at most relativized, never invalidated."[128] Silentio remarks, "The absolute duty can lead one to do

124. 1 Cor 1:23.

125. Walsh, "Echoes of Absurdity," 40.

126. *CUP1*, 220 / *SKS* 7, 201.

127. *FT*, 70 / *SKS* 4, 162.

128. Hanson, *Kierkegaard and Life of Faith*, 158.

what ethics would forbid, but it can never lead the knight of faith to stop loving."[129] God transposes the ethical requirement to a different situation.

What, then, did Kierkegaard believe to be his Isaac—his something to give up for the sake of the religious? It was actually a *someone*, his fiancée Regine Olsen. Kierkegaard's journals tell us of his initial meeting, engagement, and later sundering with Regine. Søren met Regine at a mutual friend's house and was smitten with her immediately. After some pursuing, Søren approached both Regine and her father to ask for her hand in marriage. They both accepted, and Søren and Regine were engaged. Kierkegaard states, "But within [myself], the next day I saw that I had made a mistake. Penitent that I was, my vita ante acta, my melancholia, that was enough. I suffered indescribably during that period. She seemed to notice nothing."[130]

Why did Kierkegaard regret the engagement? It was not displeasure with Regine: he loved her deeply.[131] Kierkegaard totters back and forth between various explanations for ending the engagement. The first possible reason is that Kierkegaard suspected Regine was not yet in the religious sphere of existence: "She has no clue about the specifically religious."[132] He wanted a wife on the same page as him in regard to religious life. I find Kierkegaard's reason a little odd since we know that in addition to attending normal Sunday services in the Lutheran church, Regine and her family frequented Moravian prayer meetings.[133] While attending prayer meetings does not automatically make someone a Christian, Regine's participation in more pietistic, personal devotion seems to betray Kierkegaard's assessment. We see a second possible reason in Kierkegaard's character Quidam in *Stages on Life's Way*, where he chooses the religious over his betrothed.[134] Kierkegaard believed that his task as a religious author would take all of his focus and strength, and it would be unfair to subject Regine to his lifestyle.[135] The final reason he gives is his melancholy:

129. *FT*, 74 / *SKS* 4, 165.

130. *KJN* 3, 432 / *SKS* 19, 434, Not15:4.

131. In fact, on his deathbed he was still talking about her, saddened by the broken engagement. See Kirmmse, *Encounters with Kierkegaard*, 121–22.

132. *KJN* 5, 220 / *SKS* 21, 212, NB9:24.

133. Moravians were a religious group who emphasized personal piety and religious experience. See Garff, *Søren Kierkegaard*, 176.

134. *SL*, 222 / *SKS* 6, 207.

135. We get hints of this reasoning in the pseudonym Nicolaus Notabene in

> But if I were to explain myself, I would have to initiate her into terrible things, my relationship to Father, his melancholy, the eternal night brooding deep inside me, my going astray, my desires and excesses, which in the eyes of God are nevertheless perhaps not so glaring, since it was, after all, anxiety that led me to go astray, and where was I to find a roof when I knew or suspected that the only man I had ever admired for his strength and power wavered?[136]

Regardless of the particular reason, Kierkegaard called off the engagement, something that was wrong in the eyes of his culture but righteous in the eyes of God (at least according to Kierkegaard). Regine did not go quietly. As Alastair Hannay puts it, "She fought a woman's fight to keep him at all costs."[137] Kierkegaard constructed a plan to break the relationship and hopefully push Regine toward the religious sphere: "I went there [to see her] and made her see reason. She asked me: Will you never marry? I answered: Well, yes, in ten years, when I have begun to simmer down and need a lusty young miss to rejuvenate me. A necessary cruelty."[138] Kierkegaard feigned a lack of love for Regine to drive her into a despair that only God could alleviate. Kierkegaard reflects on the whole ordeal in what I think is one of the most tragic entries in his personal journals:

> Had I faith I would have stayed with Regine. Praise and thanks be to God, I have now understood it. I have been on the point of losing my mind these days. [Humanly] speaking I have done the right thing for her; perhaps I should never have become engaged, but from that moment on I treated her chivalrously. In an aesthetic and chivalrous sense, I loved her far more than she

---

Prefaces, whose wife does not let him write a book. Notabene states, "A married man who is an author is not much better than a married man who goes to the club every evening, yes, even worse, because the one who goes to his club must still admit that it is an infraction, but to be an author is a distinguished unfaithfulness that cannot evoke regret even though the consequences are worse" (*P*, 9 / *SKS* 4, 473). More from Notabene in chapter 4!

136. *KJN* 2, 165–66 / *SKS* 18, 179, JJ:115. Søren's relationship with his father really shattered his confidence. Michael Kierkegaard was a paragon of pietistic, Christian virtue. Kierkegaard looked up to him, yet on Michael's deathbed, he confessed to Søren that as a youth, he cursed God for his hard life. Michael also admitted that Kierkegaard's mother, Ane, was actually Michael's second wife. While remarrying is not shocking, the situation around it was. Ane was Michael's first wife's personal maid, and Ane became pregnant mere months after Michael's first wife passed away. The "perfect" Christian father had, in fact, been a flawed man.

137. Hannay, *Kierkegaard*, 157.

138. *KJN* 3, 434 / *SKS* 19, 436, Not15:4.

> loved me, for otherwise she would neither have acted proudly toward me nor alarmed me later with her scream. . . . She has not become any theater princess, so she should, if possible, become my wife. Good Lord, that was all I wished for! And yet I had to deny myself that [wish].[139]

Whether or not Kierkegaard acted chivalrously with Regine is beside the point—and as a sidebar, I think Kierkegaard's ploy was a *horrible* way to try and turn Regine toward religious faith. Kierkegaard believed God was asking him to do the unthinkable: give up his love for the kingdom of God. Kierkegaard admits that if he would have held strong in his faith, then he would have stayed with Regine, yet his anxiety got the best of him. Abraham held firm; he had faith God would handle the seemingly impossible—that God would preserve Isaac no matter what. Kierkegaard did not stand firm. The teleological suspension of the ethical is no easy task, and Silentio cites Jesus' difficult saying in Luke 14:26: "If anyone comes to me and does not hate his own father and mother and wife and children and brothers and sisters, yes, and even his own life, he cannot be my disciple." The suspension may lead us to places we do not personally want to venture, but if we are obedient to God, we must follow him. One thing is for sure, Kierkegaard's broken engagement led to *Fear and Trembling*, a book we are still discussing, a book still challenging us to authentic Christian faith. The suspension may lead to a temporary heartache, but the kingdom of God is a sweeter gift than momentary discomfort.

3. CONCLUSIONS

We could fill an entire book with an analysis of *Fear and Trembling*, but our short exploration offers much food for thought. Kierkegaard's dynamic reflection on Abraham's offering of Isaac fascinates our imaginations, causing us to ponder the nature of faith. One important facet of *Fear and Trembling* for us today is the Hegelian concept of the culture being the representation of Spirit in the world. Although not many people walk around saying they believe in Hegelian philosophy, Western culture drinks deeply of the Hegelian concept of cultural progression moving in the correct direction. How often do we hear someone say to Christians, "You don't want to be on the wrong side of history" regarding some modern cultural value? Why, pray tell, is the culture correct? If we buy

139. *KJN* 2, 164–65 / *SKS* 18, 177–78, JJ:115.

into Hegel, then it is obviously correct, and whatever the culture values is the de facto ethical position. Yet, we have examples from history where the culture progressed in a *horrific* direction. Just because certain values change in the eyes of the culture does not mean they change for the better. Kierkegaard gives a good word on the problems of a Hegelian view of culture and the relativism it creates.

"Amen, brother!" you may say to me. "The culture has gone to hell in a handbasket!" It is easy to point the finger at the licentiousness of the West, but does the Hegelian concept of ethical life leak into the church? I have lived most of my life in the United States of America. I love my culture, warts and all, but there are some troubling, contra-gospel values I see infiltrate the church with little to no resistance from the faithful. One example is the concept of Sabbath. We live in a constant society, a culture that never sleeps. With twenty-four-hour news and customer service, we expect knowledge and services whenever we want them. The "always on" culture creeps its way into the church; we are always so *busy*. Although I was never explicitly taught so as a youth, the church's implied teaching was that if I was not spending every free second of my life passing out gospel tracts then I was damning people to hell. There was no discussion of Sabbath, that God created us to work *and rest*. In fact, any sort of resting was seen as laziness: you rest when all the work is done! Losing ourselves in work is an American cultural value. Melissa Davis quips that "the famous 'I think, therefore I am' of René Descartes has given away to, 'I do, therefore I am.'"[140] How many pastors burn out because they run themselves ragged? How much strife happens in our homes because we do not spend time resting with our families? How often does the local church treat its pastor as an on-call worker, not giving him the chance to unwind? How much do we pack the week with church activities so that there is no down time to recharge? The biblical concept of Sabbath is *countercultural*, and we must not let the American value of being defined by work influence our teaching and praxis in the church. Davis explains the plight: "Busyness is an insidious cultural liturgy that teaches us to bow down to the idol of self. It teaches us that security, salvation, and significance are defined by what we do. Sabbath offers a robust, formative rhythm that breaks the idol of busyness in renewal."[141] Sabbath is so important that it is both in the creation narrative and one of the Ten Commandments. Our culture should not overwrite the teaching of God.

140. Davis, "Sabbath as Counter-Formational Practice," 573.

141. Davis, "Sabbath as Counter-Formational Practice," 580.

A second lesson from *Fear and Trembling* is a tough one: faith is hard. We often teach an easy believism, the "cheap grace" that Bonhoeffer explains as "forgiveness without requiring repentance, baptism without church discipline, Communion without confession, absolution without personal confession."[142] When we look to Abraham and what God asked of him—*that* was difficult. Isaac was the child of promise, the fulfillment of Abraham's destiny, yet God asked for Isaac as a sacrifice. What a difficult teaching, but Abraham is not the only one who went through trials. Hebrews 11—the great chapter of faith—goes through the Old Testament saints' struggles. The New Testament bears witness to the persecution of the faithful. Church history shows us the brave men and women who faced adversity. Kierkegaard reminds us that we take up the same task, a task we live out with fear and trembling. While we go through seasons of great peace, joy, and growth, standing for Christ is no easy task. The harsh reality should not shock us—our savior was beaten to death on a cross—yet we often want to avoid a difficult faith at all costs. Part of the avoidance is our normal frailty: adversity *hurts*, and who wants to hurt? Part of it may be Hegelianism of American culture. American culture is all about doing what makes me happy. I am not *happy* to suffer. I do not purposefully seek it out as some sort of holy bona fides, but I also do not run from it. I have a *joy* in following my savior. I want to be a man of costly grace. Faith may cost us something we love dearly, but the joy of being in God's kingdom trumps any temporary hardship or sadness.

Lastly, *Fear and Trembling* demonstrates the personal nature of faith. God speaks to you and me personally; He has a task for you and me personally. We often want to hide in the crowd, acting as if God does not call us as individuals: "I was baptized at age eight with everyone else in my Sunday school class, so I am a Christian!" The life of faith is *subjective*, meaning a personal, internalization of the truth. Some critique Kierkegaard's emphasis on individual faith. The first salient criticism is how do we differentiate between what we think is from God and what is actually from God? I have heard stories of people saying, "God directly told me to do *x*," where *x* is some flagrant sin. The check to my experience should be God's word: if the supposed word from God goes against the plain teaching of the word, then we go with the written word. To critique Kierkegaard, I believe his lying to Regine about why he was breaking off the engagement was wrong. We ought to speak the truth

142. Bonhoeffer, *Cost of Discipleship*, 44.

in love, and he should have honestly explained his concerns to Regine. A second criticism of Kierkegaard is that he overly-individualizes faith to the detriment of the community. I understand such criticism, but I believe Kierkegaard's over-emphasis on individual faith is to oppose his context of Christendom in Denmark.[143] *Everyone* claimed to be a Christian because they were Danish. We need to have a balanced view: we are saved as *individuals* to be a part of the *community* of faith. As the apostle Paul reminds the Corinthians,

> For just as the body is one and has many members, and all the members of the body, though many, are one body, so it is with Christ. For in one Spirit we were all baptized into one body—Jews or Greeks, slaves or free—and all were made to drink of one Spirit. For the body does not consist of one member but of many. . . . But as it is, God arranged the members in the body, each one of them, as he chose. If all were a single member, where would the body be? As it is, there are many parts, yet one body.[144]

We all have roles to play as individual parts to the betterment of the entire body of Christ. Our culture is consumer focused: What can you do for me? We turn Sunday morning into a public event that gives me something rather than worshiping the one true God in faith. Authentic faith is self-sacrifice: What can I do for *you*? As members of the body, we have a function, but we must not forget the whole body. While in the community of faith, we need to be personally active, seeking to serve the church in the manner God has called us.

The application of *Fear and Trembling* for apologetics is myriad. Kierkegaard's dismantling of Hegelianism reminds the apologist to check his or her presuppositions: do I endorse said virtue because it is from God or my culture? We all need a reminder that culture is like a pair of glasses we forget we are wearing. God is the absolute who can remove our lenses, declaring that no earthly kingdom is completely right in its assessment of values. Examining *Fear and Trembling* in its context also dispels the oft-circulated myths about Kierkegaard and fideism. Kierkegaard does stress faith and absurdity but not as a means to relativism. If authentic faith is "proving oneself to be right," *then faith is merely Hegelianism in a new wrapping*. Faith has the absolute as its ultimate *subject*, not my objective formulations.

143. I will discuss Christendom in Denmark thoroughly in chapter 5.

144. 1 Cor 12:12–14, 18–19.

Fear and Trembling is a classic, and people will continue to read it. Understanding Kierkegaard's stages of existence sheds light on his profound work. The aesthetic, ethical, and religious spheres help us to see our neighbors and understand where they are in life. Kierkegaard's polemic against the Hegelian concept of *Sittlichkeit*—the culture's actions as the manifestation of Spirit—brings us a constant reminder of how easy it is to fall into the trap of uncritically following the culture. Faith is taking up a *cross*, not an easy task for the faint of heart, but as Peter reminds us, "After you have suffered a little while, the God of all grace, who has called you to his eternal glory in Christ, will himself restore, confirm, strengthen, and establish you. To him be the dominion forever and ever."[145] May we all work out our faith in fear and trembling, knowing that the God who commands sacrifice is the one who resurrects!

> No, away, pernicious sureness. Save me, O God, from ever becoming completely sure; keep me unsure until the end so that then, if I receive eternal blessedness, I might be completely sure that I have it by grace! It is empty shadowboxing to give assurances that one believes that it is by grace—and then to be completely sure. The true, the essential expression of its being by grace is the very fear and trembling of unsureness. *There* lies faith—as far, just as far, from despair and from sureness.[146]

145. 1 Pet 5:10–11.

146. *CD*, 211 / *SKS* 10, 219.

3

The Wound and Blessing of Existence

Selfhood, Sin, Necessity, and Human Freedom

My favorite film is 2006's *Children of Men*, directed by Alfonso Cuarón.[1] The setting is the United Kingdom in the not-too-distant future, but rather than thriving, the world is staring at an existential crisis: humanity has lost the ability to reproduce. The youngest person on the planet is only eighteen years old, and scientists have no idea why humanity is infertile. The world is barreling toward extinction with no possible solution. Societies are collapsing, so the United Kingdom closes its borders to all foreigners, hunting them down for deportation. The story centers on Theo, a former political activist that gave up "the good fight" years before the start of the film, when his two-year-old son died during a flu pandemic. Separating from his wife, Theo wastes his subsequent years at a mundane office job. One day, he receives an unannounced caller: Julian, his wife, contacts him for help. Kee, a young African immigrant in London, is pregnant—the first pregnancy in over eighteen years—and Julian knows the only person she can trust is Theo. Theo has a twofold task. First, he must protect Kee against the various groups who want to use her pregnancy for political gain. Second, he has to transport Kee safely through a dystopic police-state to the Human Project, a non-partisan group of world-class scientists, who will hopefully solve humanity's dilemma.

Seeing as this is my favorite movie, when I started dating my now wife, I introduced her to the film. I was so excited to have her experience

1. Cuarón, *Children of Men*.

the story, but she hated it. Flummoxed, I asked, "Why?!" Her response: "It was so depressing. People were dying. There was no hope in the world. It was so bleak." While I will not spoil the movie—it is really that good . . . you should stop reading this book and go watch the film immediately—I came to different conclusions than she, but I understand why my wife was appalled. The movie effectively depicts the brokenness of the world. It demonstrates how easily people turn on each other, how the worst of humanity rears its ugly head in a crisis. Theo's heartache of losing his child in a childless world reminds us how fragile life is.

I think one of the reasons I love the movie so much is that it taps into something within all of us. We have all been marred by tragedy in our lives, and we are all desperately looking for a solution to our pain, a bit of hope that in the end, all will be fine. One of the few things that unites all humans is that we will face pain or suffering or disappointment at some point. When we ponder our surroundings, it seems like some people get extra portions of suffering. I recall three friends who have had to bury their children. What is more, these three friends are all involved in ministry. They went to seminary. They gave their lives to serving God through the church—a God they proclaim to be omnipotent, who had the ability to heal their children yet chose not to. Their families are now lacking members. Every missed birthday or milestone is a deep wound with reverberating effects. Something feels wrong deep in our bones that a loving God would not heal a child.

C. S. Lewis makes a poignant remark in *The Problem of Pain*: "In a sense, [Christianity] creates, rather than solves, the problem of pain, for pain would be no problem unless, side by side with our daily experience of this painful world, we had received what we think a good assurance that ultimate reality is righteous and loving."[2] Professing a God who is omnipotent and omnibenevolent in the midst of a suffering world gives rise to a great challenge for Christians. As atheistic philosopher William Rowe effectively argues,

> In the light of our experience and knowledge of the variety and scale of human and animal suffering in our world, the idea that none of those instances of suffering could have been prevented by an omnipotent being without the loss of a greater good seems an extraordinary, absurd idea, quite beyond our belief. It seems that although we cannot *prove* that premise 1 [that there are instances of intense suffering that an omnipotent, omniscient

2. Lewis, *Problem of Pain*, 14.

> being could have prevented] is true, it is, nevertheless, altogether *reasonable* to believe that 1 is true, that it is a *rational* belief.[3]

As the popular apologetic phrase goes, the evidence demands a verdict.

Rowe's challenge is difficult for the Christian, and the usual response is the "free will argument." Alvin Plantinga summarizes the argument well:

> To create creatures capable of *moral good*, therefore, [God] must create creatures capable of moral evil; and He can't give these creatures the freedom to perform moral evil and at the same time prevent them from doing so. As it turned out, sadly enough, some of the free creatures God created went wrong in the exercise of their freedom; this is the source of moral evil.[4]

The "moral good" mentioned is usually equated with love. It is good to love. Scripture tells us that "God is love."[5] Each person of the Trinity willing loves the other, making love essential to who God is. As Augustine explains it,

> For whether [the Holy Spirit] is the unity of both, or the holiness, or the love, or therefore the unity because the love, and therefore the love because the holiness, it is manifest that He is not one of the two, through whom the two are joined, through whom the Begotten is loved by the Begetter, and loves Him that begat Him. . . . If equal, equal in all things, on account of the absolute simplicity which is in that substance. And therefore they are not more than three: One who loves Him who is from Himself, and One who loves Him from whom He is, and Love itself.[6]

The doctrine of the Trinity shows us that God did not have to create the world in order to exercise love—God *is* love. Love entails a choice: God *chose* to act on his love by creating humanity in his image. If God creates us to love, then humans can indeed choose *not* to love, to misbehave, to seek their own way instead of God's. Although the appearance of evil throughout the world is terrible, God is not the cause. Humanity, in its rebellion, brought sin into the world. Adam and Eve, despite a clear command from God, willingly disobeyed. As Gen 3 tells us, "So when the woman saw that the tree was good for food, and that it was a delight to the eyes, and that the tree was to be desired to make one wise, she took of

3. Rowe, *Philosophy of Religion*, 101.
4. Plantinga, *God, Freedom, and Evil*, 30.
5. 1 John 4:8.
6. Augustine, *On the Trinity*, 6.5.7.

its fruit and ate, and she also gave some to her husband who was with her, and he ate."[7] God did not force Adam and Eve to eat the fruit. He decreed the prohibition and explained the consequences.

God cursed humanity because of Adam and Eve. Sin and death spread to Adam and his offspring. Paul clarifies in Rom 5: "Therefore, just as sin came into the world through one man, and death through sin, and so death spread to all men because all sinned."[8] The consequence of Adam is usually dubbed as original sin, and as John Calvin elucidates, "After the heavenly image in man was effaced, [Adam] not only was himself punished . . . but he involved his posterity also, and plunged them in the same wretchedness."[9] Humans are now broken, "by nature children of wrath."[10] Because of our sinful status, "all we like sheep have gone astray; we have turned—every one—to his own way."[11] We make bad decisions. We hurt people. We add to the evil in the world. In philosophical discourse, we call this moral evil.

The effects of the fall do not stop with humanity and its moral agency. God describes a bitter consequence stemming from Adam's disobedience: "Because you have listened to the voice of your wife and have eaten of the tree of which I commanded you, 'You shall not eat of it,' *cursed is the ground because of you*; in pain you shall eat of it all the days of your life."[12] The earth itself is corrupted, "groaning together in the pains of childbirth."[13] We call this natural evil. As Charles Taliaferro succinctly states, "Natural evils include ills that are inflicted on persons by 'nature,' as when suffering results from birth defects, disease, floods, volcanoes, and the like."[14] To summarize, everything is messed up in the world, both morally and naturally, *because of humans freely choosing sin*, not because of God's direct action.

Yet, does not the free-will argument simply kick the can down the road? Adam and Eve had a choice; they messed up; *but now we do not have a choice*. God, in his omniscience knew Adam and Eve would fall, so in a functional sense, it appears we are all destined to perform evil. If

7. Gen 3:6.
8. Rom 5:12.
9. Calvin, *Institutes of Christian Religion* 2.1.5.
10. Eph 2:3.
11. Isa 53:6.
12. Gen 3:17 (my emphasis).
13. Rom 8:22.
14. Taliaferro, *Contemporary Philosophy of Religion*, 301.

the individual is unable to do otherwise because of the sin of Adam, then God is the author of evil in some way, right? The Bible clearly teaches that post-fall humans cannot do good on their own. The view that humans, unaided by God, can will righteousness—called Pelagianism—has been thoroughly rejected by all forms of orthodox Christianity. We do not view a cat killing a mouse as evil—that is just what cats do.[15] Why, then, are humans damned to hell by a God who does not allow them to be good in-and-of-themselves? What is more, why does God even create humans to reciprocate love at all? Considering the known consequences of the fall, why would God allow the world to become so evil? The questions that arise from Christianity's firm convictions about the nature of God and our experience of evil cause our heads to spin. I truly see how thinkers like Rowe come to the conclusions they do. Borrowing Rowe's categories in his *Philosophy of Religion*, I consider myself a "friendly theist," a person who "believes that someone may well be rationally justified" in atheism based off the prevalence of evil.[16]

How do Christians respond to the problem? I am under no delusion that I will sufficiently answer all the minutia entailed in the problem of evil in a single chapter. What I offer are insights from Kierkegaard's thought that aid us in such an arduous task. Often Kierkegaard is left out of the discussion regarding the problem of evil and the interplay of necessity and freedom. I find this ironic, since Kierkegaard wrote an entire monograph on the issue of hereditary sin titled *The Concept of Anxiety*. Furthermore, the doctrine of sin permeates all of Kierkegaard's writing, and I have argued elsewhere that it is a lynchpin to his entire system of thought.[17] In this chapter, we will examine Kierkegaard's writings as they relate to evil, freedom, and necessity. First, Kierkegaard argues that sin is inevitable without being necessary while also denying any form of Pelagianism. Second, Kierkegaard clearly demonstrates that the cause of sin and evil lie solely at the feet of humans, not God. Third, Kierkegaard's depiction of existence shows the overwhelming blessedness of living, a clear reason for *why* God creates us with freedom at all.

15. Herbert McCabe argues along these lines when thinking about natural evil, essentially making natural evil not a thing in itself but a matter of perspective. He writes, "In fact there can never be a defect inflicted on one thing except by another thing that is, in doing so, perfecting itself. . . . The things that inflict evil on me, therefore, are not themselves evil; on the contrary, it is by being good in their way that they make me bad in my way" (McCabe, "God, Evil, and Divine Responsibility," 618–19).

16. Rowe, *Philosophy of Religion*, 109.

17. See Steinmetz, *Severed Self*.

To achieve our goals, I start by examining Kierkegaard's anthropology, particularly in *The Concept of Anxiety* and *The Sickness unto Death*. Kierkegaard envisions humans as dynamic agents in the world. God creates humans as *beings*, meaning they seek to develop into authentic selfhood. Second, I explain the role of anxiety in the life of individuals. Anxiety happens when we have a choice. How we respond in anxiety has drastic consequences. Third, I investigate Adam and the fall. Kierkegaard has an intriguing explanation of Adam, innocence, and the results of his misdeeds. Fourth, I look to the effects of sin in the everyday lives of individuals and the implications of the possibility and necessity of sin. Sin is not simply something we do, but it is the world we inhabit. Lastly, I offer a positive apologetic. Kierkegaard shows us *why* it is good to be a human with choices. God created us *to be*, and this means we can bless others in this world.

1. WHO EVEN ARE YOU?

Genesis 2:7 recounts the creation of the first man: "Then the Lord God formed the man of dust from the ground and breathed into his nostrils the breath of life, and the man became a living creature." We see a physical component (the dust) and a spiritual component (breath of life). The vast majority of Christians see the composition of humanity as having at *least* two constituent parts: body (physical) and soul/spirit (spiritual)—called a dichotomy. Others claim three parts of the human composition—body, soul, and spirit—arguing that the soul is the "animating principle" in life, while the spirit "comes from or is like unto God"—called a trichotomy.[18] For Kierkegaard, the relationship between the eternal and the temporal components of humankind is dynamic, and how humans live in this world directly ties to the relationship between their body/temporal/finite aspect and their soul/eternal/infinite aspect. This relationship develops *in existence*, meaning that humans are on a journey. As Arne Grøn puts it, "To exist is to be *in becoming*, in the middle of life, on one's way. . . . Existence is not just motion but *like* motion in that we are ourselves *in* becoming."[19]

Who even are we? What makes humans different from angels or avocados? Angels, avocados, and I are all "alive" in the sense that we exist,

18. Garrett, *Systematic Theology*, 1:446. The main scriptural text for trichotomy position is 1 Thess 5:23, where soul and spirit seem to be two separate entities. Dichotomy argues that soul/spirit are synonyms for our spiritual makeup.

19. Grøn, "Concept of Existence," 75.

but there seems to be something different about my human existence. Angels are pure spirit; avocados are physical; and I am some mixture of both.[20] How can two opposites—spiritual and physical—exist together in the entity we call a human?

In *The Concept of Anxiety*—written under pseudonym Vigilius Haufniensis[21]—Kierkegaard states that "man is a synthesis of the psychical and the physical; however, a synthesis is unthinkable if the two are not united in a third. This third is spirit."[22] Humans have a spiritual (psychical) component and a physical component. How can they exist together? Opposites should repel, yet you and I are walking around with bodies and souls that operate together. Something must *synthesize*—that is, bring together in a form of unity—body and soul so that they function within the individual. Kierkegaard calls this third something "spirit." Well, you may think, that is not *that* complicated. That sounds similar to the trichotomy of body/soul/spirit explained above. Yet Kierkegaard takes a different angle on trichotomy. Diving deeper, Kierkegaard explains the concept of "spirit" in *The Sickness unto Death*. Hold onto your horses:

> A human being is spirit. But what is spirit? Spirit is the self. But what is the self? The self is a relation that relates to itself, or it is that in the relation which is the relation's relating to itself. The self is not the relation but is *that* the relation relates to itself. A human being is a synthesis of the infinite and the finite, of the temporal and the eternal, of freedom and necessity, in short, a synthesis. A synthesis is a relation between two terms. Considered in this way, a human being is not yet a self.[23]

That is how Kierkegaard decides to *start* his book—not the catchiest intro. Although, as Alastair Hannay notes, Kierkegaard is poking fun at Hegel's writing style, Kierkegaard's obtuse passage *does* say something important.[24] Allow me to translate. First, humans are not automatically "selves." The simple existence of a human with a body and soul does not denote true selfhood. Second, "spirit" is the third separate something that *relates*

20. A mixture of both spirit and matter, not angels and avocados. In the Bible, angels do take on physical manifestations at times, but their composition is spiritual in nature. For more on this, see Erickson, *Christian Theology*, 408–10.

21. I promise, we will eventually get to a discussion on Kierkegaard and his pseudonyms in chapter 4!

22. *CA*, 43 / *SKS* 4, 349.

23. *SUDk*, 13 / *SKS* 11, 129.

24. Hannay, "Spirit and Idea of Self," 23.

multiple things together. Lastly, although his definition borrows numerous terms from Hegel, Kierkegaard thoroughly refutes Hegel's concept of *mediation*. "Spirit" for Kierkegaard does not *mediate* body and soul into a new substance. Spirit retains the uniqueness of body and soul. Kierkegaard is always careful to use the term "synthesis" and not "mediation."[25]

If all humans are not automatically "selves," then who even are we? Kierkegaard calls our baseline of existence—our simple body/soul unity—a *negative unity*. By "negative" Kierkegaard does not mean "evil" or "sinful." He simply means that the individual does not have a positive, concrete form. Recall the example used in chapter 1. There is a difference between driving a car and thinking about what it means to drive a car. I do not have to contemplate my existence to drive to get Chipotle for dinner. Acting without reflecting is the life of the negative unity, for I have not posited any deeper existence. I remain in the physical as a negative unity; all humans start as negative unities. Kierkegaard explains the state of the negative unity: "The world is preoccupied with frivolity, mindlessness and prattle, and therefore, as a rule, becomes quite solemn and deferentially doffs its hat at the mention of anything deeper."[26]

A *positive unity* is when I move beyond mere existence to thinking about my existence and *relating to the power who established it*.[27] If we are a synthesis of spiritual and physical, then living only a physical existence (driving a car to eat Chipotle to survive) means I am not living up to who I really am. I must engage my spiritual side in order to *live* rather than just exist. I have to *actualize* my spiritual side. My spirituality does not happen "naturally" because it is supernatural. That does not mean that the spiritual person is *unnatural*; it simply means that spirituality is not something that occurs without effort. Kierkegaard states that a *positive unity* is when spirit is "in equilibrium," "relating itself to itself and in *willing* to be itself . . . rests transparently in the power that established it."[28] Spirit, the third something that allows body and soul to exist together, has a dual function. First, it relates body and soul together in equilibrium.

25. Hegel uses the term "synthesis" in his writings, but it is almost always used in relation to *mediation*. Kierkegaard despises the concept of mediation. When Kierkegaard uses "synthesis," it is an example of using the same term but having a different dictionary. See Dupré, "Of Time and Eternity," 112.

26. *SUDh*, 143 / *SKS* 11, 224.

27. Here is also a key difference from the philosophy of Hegel. With Hegel, reflection is *Geist*/Spirit working in the world. For Kierkegaard, simple reflection is not enough. God exists apart from the world, and we should relate to him.

28. *SUD*, 14 / *SKS* 11, 130 (my emphasis).

Second, it relates the human back to its source: God. Being a true self is the life of the positive unity, of spirit. We are all negative unities by our mere existence, and not all people become positive unities.

We see a key aspect of becoming a self: *willing*. The emphasis on willing is where many of the atheistic, existential philosophers of the twentieth-century take only part of Kierkegaard's view of the self. Kierkegaard is not saying that *only* willing is required to become a self. It is not the throwing off the "they" of Martin Heidegger or the revolt against the "absurd" of Albert Camus. As Louis Dupré states, "spiritual selfhood requires more than active self-realization."[29] The only way to become a true self for Kierkegaard is willing *faith*, choosing to submit to God. As John Glenn explains, "Kierkegaard ultimately stresses here the *volitional* rather than the cognitive element of the self-relation. Again the issue is, Does the self will or not will to be itself?"[30] Willing to follow God forms a *positive* unity because I have *posited* something.

2. I'M FEELING REALLY ANXIOUS

With a cursory understanding of Kierkegaard's anthropology, we can now look at the relationship of our personal existence to sin and freedom. Kierkegaard takes us all the way back to Adam in the Garden of Eden in *The Concept of Anxiety*. Adam was originally in a qualitative state of innocence. Kierkegaard explains, "Innocence is ignorance. In innocence, man is not qualified as spirit but is psychically qualified in immediate unity with his natural condition."[31] In innocence, Adam is a *negative unity*.[32] To stress again, *negative does not mean sinful*—it means it has no positive form. In his innocence in the garden, Adam is merely existing, not yet living as a true self. A *negative* unity strives to be a *positive* unity: we long to have both physical and spiritual lives. Yet, how is Adam to strive in the garden? Kierkegaard comments, "In this state [of innocence] there is peace and repose, but there is simultaneously something else that is not contention and strife, for there is indeed nothing against which to strive. What, then, is it? Nothing. But what effect does nothing have? It

29. Dupré, "Of Time and Eternity," 122.

30. Glenn, "Definition of the Self," 11.

31. *CA*, 41 / *SKS* 4, 347.

32. Kierkegaard uses the term *immediate* unity in *CA*. The two terms are synonymous.

begets anxiety."[33] Adam, by his composition of being both physical and spiritual, needs *to be*, but he can only *be* by willing to follow God.

In innocence, Kierkegaard explains that Adam is "only qualified as dreaming spirit[;] the eternal appears in the future."[34] Adam is "dreaming" in the sense that he has not awakened to his full potential as a human being, and Adam longs to exercise his spiritual dimension at some point in the future. One may protest Kierkegaard's understanding of Adam and innocence. Was not Adam perfect in the Garden? Why was he lacking something, created in a dreamlike state? To answer the charge, we need to think about *why* God created humans in the first place. Now I know this question can fill an entire book, but the creation narrative tells us a simple response: "The LORD God took the man and put him in the garden of Eden to work it and keep it."[35] God gives Adam a *task*, and the task is both physical and spiritual in nature.[36] God also commands Adam and Eve to be fruitful and multiply. Work, family, culture—God mandates all of these missions *before* the fall. Adam, in solitary innocence, is dreaming, but God plants a particular tree in the garden to wake up Adam.

The tree of knowledge of good and evil in the garden comes with a prohibition: "You shall not eat [of it], for in the day that you eat of it you shall surely die."[37] When we sit back and ponder the conversation, Adam must have been confused. Death has not yet occurred, and, as Kierkegaard comments, "Adam does not know what it means to die."[38] Adam knows, though, that he has a choice, a *possibility*: to follow God and his ways, or to disobey and eat the fruit. When we have possibility, says Kierkegaard, we have anxiety:

> Adam must have had a knowledge of freedom, because the desire was to use it. The explanation is therefore subsequent. The prohibition induces in him anxiety, for the prohibition awakens in him freedom's possibility. What passed by innocence as the nothing of anxiety has now entered into Adam, and here again it is a nothing—the anxious possibility of *being able*.[39]

33. *CA*, 41 / *SKS* 4, 347.

34. *CA*, 91 / *SKS* 4, 394.

35. Gen 2:15.

36. "Work" and "keep" are used throughout the Pentateuch in relation to the work of priests. See Waltke and Fredricks, *Genesis*, 87.

37. Gen 2:17.

38. *CA*, 45 / *SKS* 4, 350.

39. *CA*, 44 / *SKS* 4, 350.

Kierkegaard is clear in his writings that anxiety is not sin: "The anxiety that is posited in innocence is in the first place no guilt, and in the second place it is no troublesome burden."[40] Adam was anxious because he had a choice to make, and the anxiety he experienced was a type of blessing.

The word "anxiety" does not usually elicit positive emotions, and we often use "anxiety" flippantly in society. I can be anxious about the direction of the newest *Star Wars* property, or I can be anxious that I will lose my job. I can have anxious butterflies in my stomach when I ride a roller coaster, or I can be so anxious that I cannot get out of bed and need to take medication to help me function. We can become so anxious that we are frozen in fear, yet anxiety can also be a gift. If I see a lion, I get anxious. The anxiety alerts me to potential danger. Kierkegaard sees anxiety as the natural consequence of having choices. When Adam encounters the tree in the garden, he must *do* something. Anxiety eats at him until he chooses.[41] The choice to follow God allows us to live a spiritual life.

The ambiguity of "anxiety" in English muddies the waters of Kierkegaard's discourse. What does Kierkegaard actually mean by "anxiety?" In Danish, the book's title is *Begrebet Angest*, and *Angest* does not have a direct English equivalent. The first English translation of *Begrebet Angest* was titled *The Concept of Dread*, but all modern English translations title it *The Concept of Anxiety*. Because there is no direct equivalent in English, it is easy to misinterpret what Kierkegaard means by "anxiety." Anxiety is not a mere emotion we feel. As Arne Grøn explains, "Anxiety points towards the future. . . . It is not this or that specifically but the unspecific or undetermined future."[42] It is a present unease at the possibility of the future. The irony of anxiety is that it comes *from* freedom, but we can never be free from it.[43] In Kierkegaard's thinking, we cannot live an anxiety-free life because anxiety always derives from possibility, and possibility appears whenever we are faced with a choice. The unease we feel

40. *CA*, 42 / *SKS* 4, 348.

41. The dynamic of anxiety as a positive force is similar to pain as a positive force. None of us likes pain, but it serves a positive purpose. Without the pain I experience when I touch something hot, I would severely injure myself. C. S. Lewis has a great remark about the positive side of pain: "God whispers to us in our pleasures, speaks in our conscience, but shouts in our pain: it is His megaphone to rouse a deaf world" (Lewis, *Problem of Pain*, 91).

42. Grøn, *Concept of Anxiety*, 5.

43. Kierkegaard calls it "entangled freedom, where freedom is not free in itself but entangled, not by necessity, but in itself" (*CA*, 49 / *SKS* 4, 354).

comes from the *ambiguous* nature of what we ought to do. Kierkegaard calls the object of anxiety "nothing."[44] We should think of this statement as "no thing": there is not one specific thing that we can do to vanquish anxiety. As Grøn clarifies, "Ambiguity stems from the fact that a human being in anxiety is put before himself as a *self who can relate in one way but also another*."[45] Choice leads to ambiguity because we do not know with *certainty* where the outcome will lead.

Let us use Adam as an example. God prohibits eating of the tree of knowledge, yet the serpent deceives Eve—and in turn Adam—with a simple rejoinder: "You will not surely die. For God knows that when you eat of it your eyes will be opened, and you will be like God, knowing good and evil."[46] Adam has a choice, but he does not know the outcome in an existential sense because he has not experienced said outcome. He cannot comprehend "death." He knows some things: God clearly explains the consequences. Yet the serpent interjects new information, a new *possibility* that eating the fruit may be a good idea. What Adam cannot do is *not make a choice*. He has to either eat of the tree or not eat of the tree. In the moment of possibility, the choice is *ambiguous* to Adam—it is not a physical "thing." Kierkegaard illustrates that the effects of anxiety are akin to standing on the edge of a cliff:

> Anxiety may be compared with dizziness. He whose eye happens to look down into the yawning abyss becomes dizzy. But what is the reason for this? It is just as much his own eye as in the abyss, for suppose he had not looked down. Hence anxiety is the dizziness of freedom, which emerges when spirit wants to posit the synthesis and freedom looks down into its own possibility.[47]

I look down and realize I am on the precipice. Do I back away? Do I steady myself on a tree? Do I keep walking and end it all? The choices may overpower me, paralyzing me to my core. Yet, I have to do something about the chasm before me. Kierkegaard says this ambiguous dynamic is "*a sympathetic antipathy* and *antipathetic sympathy*."[48] Kierkegaard elaborates in his personal journals: "Anxiety is in fact a desire for what one fears, a sympathetic antipathy; anxiety is an alien power that seizes

44. *CA*, 41 / *SKS* 4, 347.

45. Grøn, *Concept of Anxiety*, 15 (my emphasis).

46. Gen 3:4–5.

47. *CA*, 61 / *SKS* 4, 365.

48. *CA*, 42 / *SKS* 4, 348.

the individual, and yet one cannot tear oneself free of it and one does not want to, for one fears, but what one fears is what one desires."[49] We fear the outcome because it is uncertain, but we also desire the outcome because *we seek to develop into selves.* A desire for what we fear, and a fear of what we desire—anxiety operates whenever we have possibilities.

Anxiety occurs in a moment of choice, and Kierkegaard notes that "the moment is not properly an atom of time but an atom of eternity."[50] These possibilities that elicit anxiety are not simple choices without real-life consequences. Kierkegaard is not talking about options like what to eat for supper or what to wear to a party. In the journey of personhood, those types of choices do not really matter. Whether I eat steak or fish for dinner does not affect my life in the sense of being a positive unity. One may protest this point. Eating unhealthful vs. healthful food can drastically affect one's life. This is true in one sense. Eating junk food may lead to an early grave, but in another sense, it still does not matter because what happens *after* death is not predicated on what I ate. This is what I mean by "real-life consequences," because "real-life" in the Kierkegaardian sense deals with the body/soul/spirit synthesis, the positive unity of relating to self and relating to God. Anxiety, in Kierkegaard's thinking, pertains to issues of our existence, not the accoutrements that fill modern people with analysis paralysis. Since we are a synthesis of physical and spiritual, then our choices, the moments of decision, have both physical and spiritual consequences. *Anxiety is neutral: it is a tool that pushes us to choose to either follow God or our own way.*

3. ADAM AND THE FALL

Let us return to Adam. Adam existed in a *state of innocence*. In the Garden, God planted the tree of knowledge of good and evil. At this point, Adam has possibility, and possibility breeds anxiety. In Kierkegaard's example of anxiety as dizziness, he notes that the chasm fills us with a type of vertigo. We are spun around, and we attempt to find ways to steady ourselves. In that illustration, Kierkegaard explains the consequences of how we respond to the abyss: "Hence anxiety is the dizziness of freedom, which emerges when the spirit wants to posit the synthesis and freedom looks down into its own possibility, *laying hold of finiteness to support itself.*

49. *KJN* 2, 286 / *SKS* 18, 311, JJ:511.

50. *CA*, 88 / *SKS* 4, 391.

Freedom succumbs in this dizziness . . . and freedom, when it again rises, *sees that it is guilty*."[51] Anxiety and possibility are not sin. Sin occurs when we "lay hold of finiteness" in our response to the issue at hand. In anxiety, Adam has a choice to eat—in direct opposition to God—or to not eat—in direct concord with God. Adam's choosing the fruit is choosing *himself* rather than God: he lays hold to a finite, personal solution. Adam has now exited the state of innocence and entered a new *qualitative state of existence*. Kierkegaard comments that "the first sin constitutes the nature of the quality: the first sin is the sin. . . . The new quality appears with the first, with the leap."[52] We see "leap" again, and we must remember that the leap has to do with a volitional act of the entire person. Adam willingly chose to sin—body, soul, and spirit. In the moment of possibility, he willed to be himself rather than obeying the voice of God, and his action had severe consequences: "One must say that by the first sin, sinfulness came into Adam."[53]

Kierkegaard's ensuing discussion on Adam, innocence, sin, and the fall has to do with *qualitative* distinctions. A qualitative difference is a difference of *kind* or *genus* or *essence*, or as Leo Stan explains, "a quintessential trait of an object or person."[54] A dog is qualitatively different from a cat. A quantitative difference is a difference of *quantity* or *attributes*: Beagles and Pomeranians are *qualitatively* the same—because they are dogs—but *quantitatively* different—size, color, behavior, etc. Kierkegaard argues that innocence, sinfulness, and faith are *qualitative categories of existence*, and humans, as they develop through life, enter different categories as they progress in the stages on life's way. A qualitative or quantitative difference is easy to recognize when looking at the natural world, but in human development, we may overlook these shifts. Let me use a mundane example to illustrate the concept: becoming a father. When my daughter was born, I entered a new sphere of existence, that of "being a father." No matter what happens during the rest of my life, I will still be in the category of "being a father." Even if the unthinkable happens and I lose my child, I will still "be a father" because I have had a child. My example highlights another aspect of qualitative changes in Kierkegaard's thought: *they are asymmetrical in nature*. I chose to become a father, yet once I made the choice and my daughter was born, there is nothing I

51. *CA*, 61 / *SKS* 4, 365–66 (my emphasis).

52. *CA*, 30 / *SKS* 4, 336.

53. *CA*, 33 / *SKS* 4, 339.

54. Stan, "Qualitative Difference," 15:179.

can do to change my status. I can choose to dye my hair blue, but this is merely a quantitative change: I am still me whether my hair is blue or blond or pink.

In *The Sickness unto Death*, Kierkegaard's pseudonym Anti-Climacus states, "Despair is the misrelation in the relation of a synthesis that relates itself to itself."[55] When we choose our own way rather than God's, we effectively sever our relational connection to God. Let us remember that "spirit" in Kierkegaard's thinking relates body and soul together, *but it also relates the human back to God.* When Adam chose himself in anxiety, he *misrelated* to both his individual self and to God. He no longer functions the way God intends, and the consequences reverberate in everything that he does. Anxiety comes from an *external* possibility, a choice to do or do not. On the other hand, despair is *internal*, and as James Marsh notes, "because I inflict it on myself, despair comes from within."[56] Adam mortally wounds himself through his disobedience. No one *makes* Adam eat of the tree. The serpent deceives, but the choice to act lies with Adam. He cannot blame anyone but himself.

In theology, the result of Adam's sin is labeled original/hereditary sin. Theologians have numerous interpretations of the connection of Adam to his progeny. Space does not allow us to entertain all theories of original sin, but I will explain two of the most popular theories that relate to Kierkegaard's Protestant context.[57] The first is called *federal headship*, where Adam acts "as our 'federal' or 'representative' head."[58] Since Adam sinned as our representative, all of his offspring receive his sinfulness and guilt. His actions are credited to us. The second theory is *natural headship*, where all humans are "*really* one [with Adam] rather than just viewed as one in a legal sense."[59] We are one with Adam: his sin passes to us in a real/natural/genetic way. The Danish Lutheran Evangelical Church of Kierkegaard's day followed *The Augsburg Confession*, which states, "All men begotten after the common course of nature are born with sin."[60] Kierkegaard shockingly goes against his tradition with an explicit denial of both federal and natural headship: "Consequently,

55. *SUD*, 15 / *SKS* 11, 131.

56. Marsh, "Kierkegaard's Double Dialectic," 68.

57. For an excellent summary of the major positions regarding original sin, see McCall, *Against God and Nature*, chapter 4.

58. McCall, *Against God and Nature*, 162.

59. McCall, *Against God and Nature*, 166.

60. *Augsburg Confession* 1.2

every attempt to explain Adam's significance for the race as *caput generis humani naturale, seminale, foederale*, to recall the expression of dogmatics, confuses everything."[61]

How do the two traditional Protestant perspectives "confuse everything?" In these formulations, Adam is in a state of innocent perfection. When he sins, sin comes into the world. Adam's first sin is the *original* sin. Our current relationship to sin is actually a relationship to Adam, "not through [our] primitive relation to sin."[62] The classic view understands sin as punctiliar actions we perform, not a qualitative state we inhabit. Kierkegaard argues if we make Adam the "creator" of sin, and we in turn are related to him as creator, then Adam "would actually stand outside the race."[63] Adam was born in a qualitative state of innocence. He then sins, bringing sin into the world, entering a new qualitative state of sinfulness. The consequence is that his progeny are born in a qualitative state of sinfulness. If that is the case, then all of us are *qualitatively unlike Adam*, for we never existed in a qualitative state of innocence. How, then, is Adam truly human? As Kierkegaard explains,

> Does the concept of hereditary sin differ from the concept of the first sin in such a way that the particular individual participates in inherited sin only through his relation to Adam and not through his primitive relation to sin? *In that case Adam is placed fantastically outside of history.* Adam's sin is then more than something past. . . . Hereditary sin is something present; it is sinfulness, and Adam is the only one in whom it was not found, since it came into being through him. Hence one would not try to explain Adam's sin but instead would explain hereditary sin in terms of its consequences.[64]

Adam sinned even though—from the conventional, Protestant understanding—he did not have hereditary sin. *If sin is an existence state one enters, then Adam is just like you and me.* Sin in general and hereditary sin in particular are not "created" by Adam because they both are not a "thing." Kierkegaard stresses that sin "presupposes itself," for sin is only possible when we have possibility.[65] The fall, for Kierkegaard, is a qualitative leap into sin, an existential reality. The same body/soul/spirit dynamic

61. *CA*, 29 / *SKS* 4, 336.
62. *CA*, 26 / *SKS* 4, 333.
63. *CA*, 30 / *SKS* 4, 336.
64. *CA*, 26 / *SKS* 4, 333 (my emphasis).
65. *CA*, 32 / *SKS* 4, 338.

in Adam operates in all humans because both Adam and his offspring are beings-in-process. As Kierkegaard articulates, "Just as Adam lost innocence by guilt, so every man loses it in the same way. If it were not by guilt that he lost it, then it was not innocence that he lost; and if he was not innocent before becoming guilty, he never became guilty."[66] Furthermore, Kierkegaard states, "Now sin is precisely that transcendence, that *discrimen rerum* [crisis] in which sin enters into the single individual as the single individual. Sin never enters into the world differently and has never entered differently."[67] Kierkegaard views Adam's fall as a *historical example of a reality we all experience*: we willingly become sinners, fall from grace, and bring sin into the world.

4. THE RESULTS ARE IN

What are the results of sin in the individual? Kierkegaard defines sin in *The Sickness unto Death*: "Sin is: before God in despair not to will to be oneself, or before God in despair to will to be oneself."[68] We can see that Kierkegaard's definition of sin is quite broad, and he has a purpose in such a construction. If I were to ask the average Christian to define sin, I would probably receive a blank stare. It is easy to list sins, and we have asinine slogans for it: "I don't smoke, drink, dance, or chew, and I don't go with girls who do!" But what *is* sin? What happens when we sin? Kierkegaard states his "definition embraces every imaginable and every actual form of sin."[69] By having a broad definition, we focus on sin as a qualitative state rather than creating an objective list of sins. The temptation in listing sins is to deceive ourselves; to think we can balance the scales and declare ourselves righteous; to objectify sin in the Kierkegaardian sense. But sin is no mere action: it is the reality of the person as a negative unity.

Kierkegaard starts his definition with the spiritual reality of sin as "before God," and "what makes sin so terrible is that it is before God."[70] We remember that King David, after caught in his sin with Bathsheba, cries out, "Against you [God], you only, have I sinned and done what is

66. *CA*, 35 / *SKS* 4, 342.
67. *CA*, 50 / *SKS* 4, 355.
68. *SUD*, 81 / *SKS* 11, 195.
69. *SUD*, 82 / *SKS* 11, 196.
70. *SUD*, 80 / *SKS* 11, 194.

evil in your sight."[71] Or we can think of Samuel's dealing with Israel. The Israelites wanted a king to rule over them rather than God. God says to Samuel, "Obey the voice of the people in all that they say to you, for they have not rejected you, but they have rejected me from being king over them."[72] Sin is against God, and such a verdict is terrifying for sinners. Kierkegaard emphasizes the individual aspect of sin: we stand as *individuals* before God to give an account of our actions. The popular Christianity of Kierkegaard's day had a group-mentality. "I am citizen of Denmark; therefore I am a Christian. Sure, I may sin, but I am not as bad as other people. I can hide in the crowd, pointing my finger at the really bad sinners!" Kierkegaard summarizes the sentiment: "And now in our enlightened age . . . it is still not inappropriate to think of God as . . . an ordinary district judge. . . . Therefore, let us just stick together and make sure that the clergy preach this way. . . . It is nonsense, an antiquated notion, that the many can do wrong. What many do is God's will."[73] Kierkegaard reminds us that we sin as individuals *before God*. Since sin is a personal choice, it affects the totality of the person. As Kristen Deede explains, "The crucial idea for [Kierkegaard] is that sin is neither a matter of ignorance nor of wrongdoing, but of *willful misrelation* to oneself and to God."[74]

Sin is before God, severing our relationship to him, leading to judgment and condemnation. Sin does not only affect my relation to God, for I am both spiritual and *physical*. The next portion of Kierkegaard's definition is that sin is "in despair not to will to be oneself." What does it mean to not to will to be oneself? When an individual begins to understand despair—that is, she starts to see that there is something wrong, something amiss in her life[75]—she looks for a solution to the problem. She realizes that there is a spiritual reality that she must consider. Yet the task seems too great, too difficult, too hard—she instead despairs over her despair. She becomes ashamed that she cannot move forward, cannot enter through the narrow gate. As Kierkegaard says, "Like a father who disinherits a son, the self does not want to acknowledge itself after having been so weak."[76] Kierkegaard calls such action "despair in weakness," for the individual does not take the leap to faith.

71. Ps 51:4.

72. 1 Sam 8:7.

73. *SUD*, 123 / *SKS* 11, 234–35.

74. Deede, "Infinite Qualitative Difference," 34 (my emphasis).

75. As explained in chapter 2, this self-reflection is the stage of Religiousness A.

76. *SUD*, 62 / *SKS* 11, 177.

The last part of the definition is "to will to be oneself." Unlike despair in weakness, Kierkegaard calls this "despair in defiance." The weak individual is too afraid to become a self—the task is too difficult. The defiant individual wants to be a self, but he does not want his self to be grounded in God. Kierkegaard states, "The self in despair wants to be master of itself or to create itself, to make his self into the self he wants to be, to determine what he will have or not have in his concrete self."[77] We see such despair in the New Testament with the rich young ruler. He followed the law his whole life, and he came before Jesus to ask what he must do next. Christ commanded him to sell all that he had and give the proceeds to the poor. Luke tells us, "But when [the rich young ruler] heard these things, he became very sad, for he was extremely rich."[78] The young man wanted to build his identity on his riches—his own idea of his self—rather than on Jesus Christ, God incarnate.

The prevalence of despair in defiance is obvious in western culture. We must forge our own way. We determine who we are. No culture, society, or religion can say what we should be. We take Christianity and reinterpret it to fit our own ideas of self and purpose. When our vision of self clashes with the Bible, we simply ignore the requirements of Christianity. This is not some conservative vs. liberal talking point: all Christians of every stripe struggle with despair in defiance. Like father Adam so long ago, we all think we know our true selves. The irony is that we tell the omniscient God that we know better than he. The qualitative sphere of sin is dynamic. Because humans are a synthesis, we seek to become ourselves. The problem is that the qualitative leap into sin severs our relationship to God. Although we have no ability to remedy the malady, we press on with our fool's errand, trying to create ourselves, impotent in our efforts.

5. THE REST OF US

Now our theological "Spidey sense" is tingling. Kierkegaard's understanding of the self, Adam, sin, and the fall leaves us with a glaring question. If all people are born qualitatively innocent, then does this not open the door to Pelagianism? Pelagianism is a heretical viewpoint that cropped up early in church history. Shirley Guthrie offers a straightforward definition:

77. *SUD*, 68 / *SKS* 11, 182.

78. Luke 18:23.

> The position [of Pelagianism] argues that God has given us laws and commandments to tell us how we must live, [*sic*] and the freedom to obey and disobey them. If we choose to obey, God will be gracious to us and will help and save us; if we refuse to obey, we will get the rejection and punishment we deserve. In other words, we save (or damn) ourselves by the "good works" we do (or refuse to do).[79]

Based on Kierkegaard's statements, he *could* be read as Pelagian, yet Kierkegaard consistently denies any form of Pelagianism in *The Concept of Anxiety*: "It hardly needs to be said that this view is not guilty of Pelagianism."[80] How does Kierkegaard answer the serious charge of Pelagianism? Kierkegaard addresses the Pelagian issue in two ways. First, he reminds us that Adam and all people are not merely individuals but a part of the human race. In fact, Kierkegaard states that "at every moment, the individual is both himself and the race."[81] We are individuals, but we belong to a broader community. Our actions affect others, even when we deceive ourselves into thinking that our sins pertain only to ourselves. Kierkegaard writes, "[Pelagianism] permits every individual to play his little history in his own private theater unconcerned about the race."[82] If Adam is a part of the race, and we are a part of the race, then his sin will affect us in some way. Let me use an illustration. Let us say that I stay up late watching television even though I know I have to be up early for work. I think to myself, "No big deal. I'll just be a little tired tomorrow morning." Indeed, the next morning I am exhausted, and that makes me irritable. As I swing by the café on the way to work, a car cuts me off. I then lay on my horn and make a nasty face to the person who cut me off. This person is now upset because I shamed and accosted him. He now goes about his day in a foul mood. He gets home and snaps at his wife, and now she is upset. I think you get the picture: because humans are a race—meaning we are more than just individuals—our actions are interconnected. Pelagianism thinks that our actions do not have such drastic effects on others.

Kierkegaard's second response to the charge of Pelagianism is what he calls the transmission of *sinfulness*. We are all different than Adam in one major *quantitative* way: we live post-fall. Adam lived in a world

79. Guthrie, *Christian Doctrine*, 126.

80. *CA*, 34 / *SKS* 4, 341.

81. *CA*, 28 / *SKS* 4, 335.

82. *CA*, 34 / *SKS* 4, 341.

without sin for a time. We have only ever lived in a world with sin. Kierkegaard calls this the *quantitative issue* of sin. Quantitatively, sinfulness *does* pass through generations: "It has been said several times that the view presented in this work does not deny the propagation of sinfulness through generations."[83] For Kierkegaard, we do not inherit Adam's guilt (sin), but we do inherit his corruption (sinfulness). Let us return to my previous example of yelling at the man who cut me off in traffic. Now let us consider that dynamic at the macro level. All people are born with sinfulness because sin affects both the sinner and the sinner's surroundings. As we sin, we are quantitatively begetting more evil into the world. We are surrounded by sin on all fronts. My actions put people in bad situations, and in return, other people's actions put me in a bad situation. The reciprocity multiplies and multiplies, like the reverberations from a stone chucked into a placid lake. Yet, even that analogy is not accurate, because in reality, the lake is not placid. It is turbulent, tossing to and fro. We cannot escape sinfulness because God created us to be together. There is nowhere to run. Sinfulness affects you and me in everything we do, but sinfulness does not *cause* me to sin. Sure, the waves hit me, but I still chucked the rock. *For Kierkegaard, sin is not essential, but it is inevitable because God created us to be, to grow, to actualize, to create.* Once our being becomes corrupted, the cat is out of the bag. Sinfulness drastically influences me, but there is no *causal* relationship between Adam and me.[84]

Kierkegaard wants to emphasize the existential dimension of our sin. If we turn Adam into an objective story that explains our sin, we miss the fact that we are *just like Adam*: "Precisely in the same way is it true of every subsequent man's first sin, that through it sin comes into the world."[85] Even though quantitative factors tempt us, we choose to sin. We cannot blame Adam in the same way Adam could not blame God—which is exactly what Adam tried to do. Adam blamed God for giving him Eve.

83. *CA*, 47 / *SKS* 4, 352.

84. While Kierkegaard's view is not the common perspective in Reformed Protestantism, it is not an unorthodox view. His view sounds similar to the reformer Ulrich Zwingli: "I have said that the original contamination of man is a disease, not a sin, because sin implies guilt, and guilt comes from a transgression or trespass on the part of one who designedly perpetrates a deed" (Zwingli, "Declaration of Huldreich Zwingli," 5). Adam Harwood argues along similar lines when thinking about sin and infants: "infants inherit from Adam a sinful nature but not guilt. The sinful nature that infants inherit will eventually result in their becoming guilty by knowingly committing acts of sin" (Harwood, *Spiritual Condition of Infants*, 153).

85. *CA*, 31 / *SKS* 4, 337.

Eve blamed God for the presence of the serpent. And what do we do? We blame God for putting us in a situation, declaring him the cause of our sin. Kierkegaard is clear: I am the one who sinned. Lee Barret has an astute observation on Kierkegaard's view of Adam: "[Kierkegaard] uses the story of Adam as the *archetype* of human motivation rather than as a deterministic explanation of the race's sinfulness."[86] Adam is an archetype, but Adam is not merely an archetype. Pelagius saw Adam as *only* an example. If God did not create us to *be*, then Pelagius is correct: there cannot be a connection between Adam and me. But because God created us to exist in reciprocating relationships—with body and soul relating via spirit—our actions are not in a vacuum. The sad reality is that our story is Adam's story.

6. THE GOOD GIFT OF BEING HUMAN

Faith, like sin, is a *qualitative category of existence*. Like the leap into sin, people must leap to faith in God. Only then will one be a *positive unity*, a true self. In *The Concept of Anxiety*, Kierkegaard bluntly states that "the real 'self' is posited only by the qualitative leap."[87] In *Practice in Christianity*, Kierkegaard explains the call of faith:

> Will you be offended or will you believe. If you will believe, then you push through the possibility of offense and accept Christianity on any terms. So it goes; then forget the understanding; then you say: Whether it is a help or a torment, I want only one thing, I want to belong to Christ, I want to be a Christian.[88]

When one leaps to faith in Christ, she is finally who she was created to be. She lives the life of the positive third, of spirit, for by the forgiveness of God, she now relates properly to both God and herself. The category of "sinner" is existence as a negative unity with its corresponding fruits: despair and a never ceasing drive to create oneself, perpetuating the curse of Adam. The category of faith is existence as a positive unity with its corresponding fruits: faith and being who God created one to be, blessing the world.

I know what you may be thinking. Kierkegaard is kicking the can down the road like all other Christians, posing some form of free-will

86. Barrett, "Kierkegaard's 'Anxiety,'" 55 (my emphasis).

87. *CA*, 79 / *SKS* 4, 382.

88. *PC*, 115 / *SKS* 12, 122.

defense to the problem of evil. Still, why does God create us to reciprocate, to develop, to have possibility? We turn to Kierkegaard's signed discourses for an answer. In part 2 of *Upbuilding Discourses in Various Spirits*, Kierkegaard has three short discourses on the beauty of being human. All three have Matt 6:24–34 as their text, which is Christ's discussion of the lilies of the field and the birds of the air. Kierkegaard notes that this biblical passage "addresses itself to those who are worried"—those who are *anxious* with the possibilities of life.[89] Possibility can overwhelm us, but Kierkegaard argues that *it is a good thing to be a human being.*

The first of Kierkegaard's discourses is titled "To Be Content with Being a Human Being." Kierkegaard points to the lilies and the birds as prime examples of contentment, for they are happy in what they are: "[The lilies] actually do not do anything but adorn themselves or, more correctly, [are] adorned."[90] As humans, we become so worried about our livelihood, and we fall into the trap of comparisons, "[forgetting] . . . what it is to be a human being."[91] A lily is just what it is: beautiful. Kierkegaard tells a parable of a worried lily to illustrate how we forget about being ourselves. A bird comes to see a lily, and the bird tells the lily of all the beautiful flowers it has seen on its journeys, sowing doubt in the mind of the lily—is it pretty enough? After being consumed with comparison, the lily confides in the bird, and the bird has a solution: it will carry the lily to where the other flowers live so that the lily may grow like them. Kierkegaard ends the parable with a curt statement: "Alas, on the way the lily withered. If the worried lily had been contented with being a lily, it would not have become worried."[92] The life of comparison leads to despair, for we are looking to a finite something to fulfill the longings of our heart. Lilies and birds do not have the problem of comparison, for as Peter Kline puts it, "They simply are what they are without any possibility of being otherwise. They entrust themselves entirely to the precarity of their existence, without hesitation. They are entirely content to be creatures, happy in their finitude."[93]

The discussion causes us to reflect: Why are we so worried about various things? If we live in a world without a God who desires for us to reciprocate, then we are truly alone. The God of deism creates but does

89. *UD*, 160 / *SKS* 8, 260.

90. *UD*, 163 / *SKS* 8, 263.

91. *UD*, 165 / *SKS* 8, 265.

92. *UD*, 169 / *SKS* 8, 268.

93. Kline, "Imaging Nothing," 702.

not wish for us to beseech it in prayer. It gave us the tools to succeed; we need to get on with it and live our lives. An atheistic world obviously has nothing transcendent upon which to rely. In a non-reciprocative world, humans must rely on themselves, and only themselves, to make it through life. This may sound liberating at first blush, but it is ultimately a crushing weight. If we are truly alone, then I must consume myself with all the possible outcomes of the various conundrums that cross my path. If every decision comes down to me, then I cannot make a mistake. What if I choose the wrong career? The wrong car? The wrong spouse? What if I don't exercise enough? What if I exercise too much? If I need help, I may reach out to others, but they, too, might let me down. There is no assurance that all will be fine in the end. Kierkegaard eloquently states, "To be dependent on one's treasure—that is dependence and hard and heavy slavery; to be dependent on God, completely dependent—that is independence."[94] If God creates us to reciprocate, *it means that we have an ultimate friend who is looking out for us, helping us*. We are never alone.

The second discourse is titled "How Glorious It Is to Be a Human Being," where Kierkegaard examines the gloriousness of being made in God's image. This glory is not as obvious as the beauty of the lily, but rather, "to be spirit, that is the human being's invisible glory."[95] Since humans have both physical and spiritual components synthesized via spirit, "[humans are] the place where the eternal and the temporal continually touch each other, where the eternal is refracted in the temporal."[96] When we consider God's relationship to his creation, we see an active agent who cares deeply about the universe. Colossians 1:15–17 states that Jesus

> is the image of the invisible God, the firstborn of all creation. For by him all things were created, in heaven and on earth, visible and invisible, whether thrones or dominions or rulers or authorities—all things were created through him and for him. And he is before all things, and in him all things hold together.

Although Genesis tells us that God rested on the seventh day of creation, God did not remain at rest. He is providentially working in the world.

I mentioned earlier how God created Adam and Eve to work and keep the garden. Kierkegaard sees a positive to work: "To work is a human being's perfection. By working, human beings resemble God, who

94. *UD*, 181 / *SKS* 8, 279.

95. *UD*, 193 / *SKS* 8, 290.

96. *UD*, 195 / *SKS* 8, 292.

indeed also works."[97] The gloriousness of being human means that, like God, we can be active agents in the world. A world without possibility means a world without work. To some, this may sound fantastic. As a professor, I love my summer breaks. I kick my feet up and do nothing . . . for about two weeks, until I start going insane from doing nothing. Since I have spirit, I will have a drive to do something. This does not mean that my worth is based on what I produce; it simply means that God creates humans *to be*. This "doing" is not just a job or a profession, but it is tied to doing *good* in the world. Sylvia Walsh demonstrates that our task involves worship: "Just as God has clothed the lily with its beauty, so also the human has been created in God's image. Since it is worship that best expresses that resemblance, human beings are obligated to worship and have faith in God."[98] What a privilege to be able to create, to dynamically interact with the world in such a beautiful way. As the psalmist cries out, "I will praise thee; for I am fearfully and wonderfully made: marvellous are thy works; and that my soul knoweth right well."[99]

The final discourse is titled "What Blessed Happiness is Promised in Being a Human Being," where Kierkegaard focuses on Matt 6:24: "No one can serve two masters, for either he will hate the one and love the other, or he will be devoted to the one and despise the other. You cannot serve God and money." The birds and the lilies do not "serve" God, for serving implies a choice. Humans, on the other hand, can serve, and this is a "glorious thing: *that the human being is granted a choice*."[100] God is the one who allows us to choose, and as Kierkegaard states in *Christian Discourses*, "Every human being at some time, at the beginning, stands at the crossroads—this is his perfection and not his merit."[101] To actively will the good is us being like God, for God always wills the good.

Furthermore, choice exhibits where one's heart is. I am forced to pay taxes: I do not love doing it at all. I choose to tithe, and it is a blessing to do so. There is something to possibility, being able to refuse, that makes the right choice all the sweeter. Choice denotes will, desire. God chose to make the world and humans in his image *because he wanted to be with us*. God was not forced to create the world. The fact that he did shows how very valuable we are to him. The same stands true for when we choose

97. *UD*, 198–99 / *SKS* 8, 295.

98. Walsh, "If the Lily Could Speak," 126.

99. Ps 139:14, KJV.

100. *UD*, 205–6 / *SKS* 8, 301.

101. *CD*, 20 / *SKS* 10, 31.

the good: we show how valuable God is to us. Possibility means we can do wrong, and oftentimes, it is difficult to make the right decision. Kierkegaard comments,

> Therefore the human being must choose. The struggle is terrible, the struggle in a person's inner being between God and the world. To have the choice is the glorious perilousness of the condition, but what, then, is the eternal happiness that is promised if the choice is rightly made or, what amounts to the same thing, what should a person choose? He should choose God's kingdom and his righteousness.[102]

God's kingdom is the eternal happiness. We choose to be with God; God chose to be with us by sending Christ—Immanuel. As Stephen Dunning comments, "Since [Kierkegaard] has already identified the kingdom of God with the promised blessed happiness, this is tantamount to saying that blessed happiness is identical with true righteousness rather than its reward."[103] The struggle is real, but the gloriousness of being a part of the kingdom of God is worth every toil along the way. I am reminded of a powerful passage from *The Return of the King*. After Sam and Frodo toss the ring into Mount Doom, they wake up days later from the trauma and see their friends. They celebrate that they achieved their goal, that Sauron is finally vanquished:

> And all the host laughed and wept, and in the midst of their merriment and tears the clear voice of the minstrel rose like silver and gold, and all men were hushed. And he sang unto them, now in the Elven-tongue, now in the speech of the West, until their hearts, wounded with sweet words, overflowed, and their joy was like swords, and they passed in thought out to regions where pain and delight flow together and tears are the very wine of blessedness.[104]

For Kierkegaard, it is good to be human in a reciprocal relationship with God. We are never truly alone, having a firm foundation, not bound by the whims of random chance. God created us to develop. Work is a good gift given by God, a relationship we have to the cosmos that allows for untold possibilities of art, beauty, grace, and forgiveness. If God does not reciprocate, then there is no need for us to be active in any sense.

102. *UD*, 208 / *SKS* 8, 303.

103. Dunning, "Transformed by the Gospel," 124.

104. Tolkien, *Return of the King*, 232.

We are created with freedom so that we can *will*, demonstrating our affection for the good. Without choice, we are cogs in the machine, not beings-in-process.

7. CONCLUSIONS

How does Kierkegaard's understanding of anthropology, hereditary sin, and freedom assist us when dealing with the problem of evil? I have tried to tease out some insights to help us think through the difficult conundrum. First, Kierkegaard's emphasis on qualitative categories helps us to think about the pervasiveness of sin and evil. This is not to say that those who are qualitatively in the state of sin are wicked, malevolent actors trying to destroy the fabric of reality. The atheist and Christian alike can do morally good deeds in this world. Yet, the nature of qualitative categories is that no amount of good can "fix" the root issue of evil. We need someone who is not evil, powerful enough to reestablish our righteousness, granting us pardon and new life. When we look at the evil in this world, it is a tragic byproduct of people attempting to posit themselves apart from God.

Second, Kierkegaard persuasively argues that sin is the fault of the individual, not God. No one makes me sin other than me. At the same time, Kierkegaard highlights the interconnectedness of all humans. I am *pressured* to sin in my life. I grew up seeing it everywhere. Even with loving Christian parents, I could not escape the brokenness of the world. Yet, the brokenness does not *cause* me to sin. All people will unfortunately *choose* sin without being *forced* to sin.

Lastly, Kierkegaard's focus on being-in-process shows us *why* it is good to have freedom. Choice means I can love, but it also means I can create. I can grow in my knowledge. The downside of choice means that if I qualitatively leap into sin, then my potential for growth is cancerous. I foment more death in the world. But if I am forgiven, made righteous by the work of Christ, I can now grow in goodness. I can add beauty to the world. I can develop into who God wants me to be. It is interesting that Gen 1 starts in a garden. What does a good gardener do? She makes sure that the plants are watered and the weeds are removed. She also sculpts and prunes, allowing the plants to reach their full potential. She arranges the flowers in a way that is beautiful, pointing us to the One who made a beautiful world.

I am not trying to overlook evil in the world. I also understand that Kierkegaard's perspective may not quell the anxious thoughts of those going through intense suffering. We do not know why some experience such horrors while others seem to get off scot-free. What we can know is that God created us to *be* with him. When we walked away, Immanuel came, as the classic Christmas carol proclaims, "to make his blessings flow as far as the curse is found."

I end with the beginning, *Children of Men*. I am about to spoil the ending. You have been warned. Kee gives birth to a healthy baby girl, whom she names "Dylan" in honor of Theo's child he lost so many years before. In the process of protecting Kee, Theo is mortally wounded. As Theo rows the boat to the meeting point to get Kee to the Human Project, he smiles and tells her it is going to be OK. Why? He is about to die. He lost his child so many years ago. He lost his wife and his future and his friends and everything. But now he has hope: the world is saved through the birth of a child. His "tears are the very wine of blessedness."

> [Self-annihilation] is the highest and the most difficult thing of which a human being is capable—yet what am I saying—he is incapable even of this; at most he is capable of being willing to understand that this smoldering brand only consumes until the fire of God's love ignites the blaze in what the smoldering brand could not consume.—Thus man is a helpless creature, because all other understanding that makes him understand that he can help himself is but a misunderstanding, even though in the eyes of the world his is regarded as courageous—by having the courage to remain in a misunderstanding, that is, by not having the courage to understand the truth. But in heaven, my listener, there lives the God who is capable of all things.[105]

105. *EUD*, 309–10 / *SKS* 5, 302.

4

Multiple Personalities

Indirect Communication and Apologetics

I WAS RECENTLY AT the pediatrician with my daughter for her two-and-a-half-year check-up. The pediatrician asked me a dreaded question that all parents of toddlers must answer: "Have you started potty training yet?" My wife and I *attempted* potty training a few months previously because my daughter showed the typical signs that she was ready, but alas, we failed. I could see that my daughter understood the process. I pumped her full of liquid, set a timer, and when I knew she had to use the bathroom, I put her on the toilet. Defiantly, she stared right back at me. I was not shocked; she gets her stubbornness from me, so I was prepared to wait her out. After ten minutes, I placed her on the toilet once again, and I received the same defiant gaze. Three hours later, defeated, I realized my daughter simply did not want to use the potty. She knew that she could, but she would not. My wife and I caved, and we put her back in a diaper, where she immediately proceeded to use it. I relayed our frustration to the pediatrician, lamenting that the sins of the father clearly passed to the daughter, when he offered us some advice: stop trying to force her to use the potty. Instead, we should praise her any time she is interested in the potty, encouraging her to be a "big girl." He told me that strong-willed toddlers respond better to positive reinforcement rather than rigid timetables and forced potty sessions. Essentially, he told us that we have to make her think it was her idea. Easier said than done!

As adults, we really have not outgrown our inner toddler—we just get better at hiding it. We especially do not like being treated like a child who needs a parent. I love the show *Survivor*, and one of the *quickest* ways to get voted off the island is to tell people what to do. When people confront us, we naturally become defensive. Who are you to tell me how to live? Why are you trying to control me? Even when we need help or correction, we hate being proven wrong. Sometimes we would rather hold onto the delusion of being right than to admit we are mistaken. None of us wants to be potty trained—we want to forge our own path.

Søren Kierkegaard understood the interpersonal dynamics of telling people a truth that they may not want to hear. In the posthumously published *The Point of View for my Work as an Author*, he lays out his method and purpose of writing. He directly states, "I am and was a religious author, that my whole authorship pertains to Christianity, to the issue: becoming a Christian, with *direct* and *indirect* polemical aim at that enormous illusion, Christendom, or the illusion that in such a country all are Christians of sorts."[1] Nineteenth-century Denmark was a "Christian" nation. The state church was the Danish Evangelical Lutheran Church, and by law, all children were baptized into the church shortly after birth.[2] Church attendance and tithing were part and parcel of being a good citizen. Although the average Dane participated in these "objective" markers of faith, Paul Tyson notes that "Kierkegaard thought that respectable Christian religion and theology in his milieu was almost entirely functionally atheistic."[3] Kierkegaard has a curt word for his situation: "Christendom has abolished Christianity without really knowing itself. As a result, if something must be done, one must attempt *to reintroduce Christianity into Christendom*."[4]

If people are under the illusion of Christendom and Kierkegaard has a drive "in service of the truth," then how does he go about awakening the masses from their stupor?[5] One may think the best bet is to *prove* to someone that he is deceived. Although he goes to church and was baptized and confirmed he really lives "just as sensately as any pagan ever

1. *PV*, 23 / *SKS* 16, 11 (my emphasis).

2. As the nineteenth century wore on, religious toleration was extended, particularly to Baptists who refused infant baptism. See Kirmmse, *Kierkegaard in Golden Age Denmark*, 43.

3. Tyson, *Kierkegaard's Theological Sociology*, 13.

4. *PC*, 36 / *SKS* 12, 49 (my emphasis).

5. *PV*, 24 / *SKS* 16, 12.

did."[6] Once our duped friend sees the error of his ways, he will accept the truth wholeheartedly! The problem is that humans do not make decisions based solely off logical reasoning. My daughter refuses to potty-train *because she does not want to potty train, not because it makes more sense to stay in diapers*. Kierkegaard likens the problem to filling a jar with water. If someone is receptive to a message, then a direct explanation works well. He explains, "In relation to pure receptivity, like the empty jar that is to be filled, *direct* communication is appropriate, but when illusion is involved, consequently something that must first be removed, direct communication is inappropriate."[7] Why is direct communication—that is, demonstrating directly the faults in one's assumptions—inappropriate? If someone is under an illusion that everything in his life is in order, then he has placed a lid on his jar. The matter is already settled, so why waste one's time entertaining such a thought? Pouring water on top of a closed jar achieves nothing. In fact, Kierkegaard believes such direct dealing with close-mindedness will "only [strengthen] a person in the illusion and also [infuriate] him."[8]

What is the solution? Kierkegaard declares that we must *indirectly* dismantle the illusion, which, in turn, will make the person realize he ought to unscrew the lid: "If you can do it, if you can very accurately find the place where the other person is and begin there, then you can perhaps have the good fortune of leading him to the place where you are."[9] How does Kierkegaard go about indirectly perturbing the illusion of Christendom? Kierkegaard uses *pseudonyms*, characters from different perspectives who reflect on their existence. We have encountered some of Kierkegaard's pseudonyms previously, but we will explore Kierkegaard's method of communication in this chapter and how it applies to apologetics. Formal apologetics is a direct discipline; it has proofs and demonstrations and polemics. This is all well and good *if the person on the other side of the argument is truly open to the truth*. Often, we say we are open to another perspective when we actually are not. Kierkegaard's concept of *indirect* communication is a blind spot in modern apologetics. If we are called to always have an answer, to proclaim our faith, then we need to have *every* tool in our tool belt. Kierkegaard gives us a smattering of tools to assist us in our quest.

6. *PV*, 48 / *SKS* 16, 30.
7. *PV*, 8 / *SKS* 13, 15.
8. *PV*, 43 / *SKS* 16, 25–26.
9. *PV*, 46 / *SKS* 16, 28.

In what follows, we investigate Kierkegaard's method of indirect communication. First, we examine Kierkegaard's method and rationale for his writing project. Kierkegaard's posthumous *The Point of View* gives a detailed description of his purpose and method of writing in his various works. Second, we discuss *how* to read indirect communication through Kierkegaard's various pseudonyms. Each pseudonym exists in one of Kierkegaard's three spheres of existence, and understanding the sphere unlocks the character. Lastly, we analyze two writings from Kierkegaard's pseudonyms as indirect apologetics of Christian faith: "The Seducer's Diary" in *Either/Or* by Johannes the Seducer and *Prefaces* by Nicolaus Notabene.

1. INDIRECT COMMUNICATION

As we know from previous chapters, Kierkegaard employs pseudonyms. In fact, Kierkegaard's most famous works are not "written" by him at all. Why does Kierkegaard purposefully confound his audience? *The Point of View* was originally envisioned to be released in 1849, along with the second edition of *Either/Or*, but Kierkegaard withheld the work until after his death. In *The Point of View*, Kierkegaard reflects on his entire authorship because the popularity of *Either/Or*, Kierkegaard's first published work in his writing project,[10] compelled him to offer "a direct commination, [a] report to history."[11] Kierkegaard admits that his authorship "has been misunderstood, interpreted as pride, arrogance, and God knows what," but his reason for his subterfuge was "direct and indirect polemical aim at that enormous illusion, Christendom."[12] As Benjamin Daise expresses, "Christendom needed a midwife."[13]

Kierkegaard explains that "an illusion can never be removed directly. . . . One who is under an illusion must be approached from behind." Directly attacking one who is under an illusion "only strengthens a person in the illusion and also infuriates him. Generally speaking, there is nothing that requires as gentle a treatment as the removal of an illusion."[14] The illusion Kierkegaard envisions is not a disagreement on ancillary issues

10. Kierkegaard had published a few articles and book reviews while he was a student, and his Magister's dissertation is titled *The Concept of Irony*. Kierkegaard did not consider these works as a part of his writing project (*PV*, 29 / *SKS* 16, 15).

11. *PV*, 21 / *SKS* 16, 7.

12. *PV*, 23 / *SKS* 16, 11.

13. Daise, *Kierkegaard's Socratic Art*, vii.

14. *PV*, 43 / *SKS* 16, 25–26.

like our favorite sports team or if Apple is better than Microsoft. Kierkegaard refers to issues of existential force in our lives, issues of worldview. Worldview concepts are foundational; our daily actions derive from core principles we hold—whether we articulate them or not.[15] If someone assaults our perspective, it may put us on edge, catching us off-guard; and we generally double down on our firmly held beliefs. As Anderson, Clark, and Naugle illuminate, "once a worldview is in place within an individual's heart, the individual tends (all other things being equal) to preserve the worldview."[16] We should expect a vice grip on worldview issues: if we build our identity on certain presuppositions, uprooting our sense of self and transplanting to another venue is a monumental task. If a direct assault elicits clutching to our beliefs more feverishly, then what can we do? Kierkegaard states, "I can compel him to become aware" that something may be amiss.[17] As Daise clarifies, Kierkegaard "[presents] figures, who, by articulating themselves, expound conflicts in the ways in which his culture thought about the most fundamental of matters, its understanding of what it is to be a person, its understanding of the self."[18]

How does Kierkegaard go about "approaching from behind?" Kierkegaard adumbrates the process:

> The religious author first of all must try to establish rapport with people. That is, he must begin with an esthetic piece. This is earnest money. The more brilliant the piece is, the better it is for him. Next, he must be sure of himself, or rather he must in fear and trembling relate himself to God. . . . Therefore he must have everything prepared in order, yet without any impatience, to bring forth the religious as swiftly as possible as soon as he has gained their attention.[19]

A biblical example of such tactic is 2 Sam 12. King David committed rape and adultery, impregnated Bathsheba, and had her husband Uriah killed to cover his tracks. The prophet Nathan confronts David, but Nathan does not begin by directly attacking David. Instead, Nathan uses a story about a rich man coming and taking a poor man's lamb. David is rightfully incensed by the injustice: "As the Lord liveth, the man that hath done this

15. Sire, *Naming the Elephant*, 19.
16. Anderson et al., *Introduction to Christian Worldview*, 42.
17. *PV*, 50 / *SKS* 16, 32.
18. Daise, *Kierkegaard's Socratic Art*, 14.
19. *PV*, 44 / *SKS* 16, 26.

thing shall surely die"; yet Nathan replies to David: "Thou art the man."[20] In *For Self-Examination*, Kierkegaard notes Nathan's transition: "See, the tale the prophet told was a story, but this '**Thou** art the man'—this was another story—this was the transition to the subjective."[21] By presenting the truth to David indirectly, the existential nature of his deeds packed a severe punch, sealing the gravity of the situation in David's life, leading to repentance.[22] Robert Roberts comments,

> As Nathan has calculated, David responds to the story with indignation, thus appreciating its moral import. But as I say, he doesn't yet get *Nathan's* point. He doesn't make the connection to *himself.* When David does make the application, it occasions a deep understanding of his crime. In a phrase which Kierkegaard describes some of his own moral and spiritual efforts at rhetorical induction of understanding, Nathan's story is "a thought that wounds from behind, for edification."[23]

We want to maintain the appearance that everything is fine, and we do not entertain the contrary. When we avoid introspection, we flee from subjectivity. There exists "a problematic relationship between the speaker and the hearer," as Ronald Marshall puts it. Marshall continues, "The difficulty we have in reading Kierkegaard's writings serves the noble end of helping his readers become Christians. Because the appropriation of the Christian way is so difficult, he believed his books had to be tough if they were going to help us become Christians."[24] Kierkegaard openly admits to being deceptive in his indirect method, but his intention is not malicious in the same way Nathan was not malicious in his treatment of David. Kierkegaard explicates, "What, then, does it mean 'to deceive'? It means that one does not begin *directly* with what one wishes to communicate but begins by taking the other's delusion at face value."[25]

20. 2 Sam 12:6, 7, KJV.

21. *FSE*, 38 / *SKS* 13, 65. The Hongs' translation does not put "Thou" (*Du*) in bold, but it is present in Danish. I included it in bold to match the original because the emphasis of David being the one is important to Kierkegaard's point.

22. In Ps 51:3–4, David gives a powerful confession of his guilt: "For I know my transgressions, and my sin is ever before me. Against you, you only, have I sinned and done what is evil in your sight, so that you may be justified in your words and blameless in your judgment."

23. Roberts, "Rhetoric and Understanding," 45.

24. Marshall, "Traversed Path," 130, 147.

25. *PV*, 54 / *SKS* 16, 36.

Indirect communication leads to introspection, to Religiousness A, "the dialect of inward deepening."[26] It prods the sleeper from slumber to ask deep-seated questions about *individual* existence. Kierkegaard's pseudonymous works are *beautifully* written. The level of poetics and philosophical insight truly cement Kierkegaard as one of the greatest in his craft, yet Kierkegaard had a mission in mind when he wrote. As Stephen Crites comments, "What takes place on the stage of our little theater [of the pseudonymous work] is always 'interesting,' but to the extent that we do in fact become interested in it we discover that *the essential action is being conducted offstage*."[27] The interesting theater of Johannes de Silentio, William Afham, Constantin Constantius, etc. should move us, the readers, "offstage" to contemplate our place in this world. When we ruminate that we may not be living in truth, we start to unscrew the lid on our proverbial jar.

To use indirect communication effectively, we must know our audience, and knowing our audience is more than adjusting our presentation to the appropriate educational level or avoiding technical jargon. *We must understand where our audience comes from*, which is more than knowing facts about their lives; we attempt to visualize from their perspective how they exist in the world. As much as possible, we need to ask ourselves, "Why does so and so make the choices she makes? Why does she live the way she lives? Why is she *not* a Christian at this moment?" Only upon identifying with our audience may we attempt to compel them to pay attention. As Kierkegaard quips, "No, to be a teacher is truly to be the learner."[28] Is this not what Jesus did? John tells us, "The Word became flesh and dwelt among us."[29] Christ spent time with the tax collectors, prostitutes, and sinners. He met them where they were at, speaking in parables—a form of indirect communication. Jesus did not come to tell fun stories; he came that we may have abundant life, forgiveness of sin. As Kierkegaard reminds us,

> If you are able to do so, portray the esthetic with all its bewitching charm, if possible captivate the other person, portray it with the kind of passionateness whereby it appeals particularly to him, hilariously to the hilarious, sadly to the sad, wittily to the

26. *CUP1*, 556 / *SKS* 7, 505.
27. Crites, "Pseudonymous Authorship as Art," 222 (my emphasis).
28. *PV*, 46 / *SKS* 16, 28.
29. John 1:14.

witty, etc.—but above all *do not forget one thing*, the number carried that you have, *that it is the religious that is to come forward.*[30]

2. READING IN STAGES

We turn to reading Kierkegaard's pseudonyms. Let us take *Either/Or* as an example. *Either/Or* is edited by Victor Eremita, which contains the writings of "A," Johannes the Seducer, Judge William, and the Pastor. If *Either/Or* is indirect communication on the part of Kierkegaard, how can we know what he is trying to portray? How does Kierkegaard "approach from behind"? How do we read *with* these pseudonyms?

Before answering the question, I must deal briefly with the academic controversy on reading Kierkegaard.[31] *The Point of View* appears clear: "I am and was a religious author. . . . There *is* such a duplexity [in signed and pseudonymous works] from beginning to end."[32] If we take Kierkegaard at face value, then we can look back and see his point of view; yet, Kierkegaard has an odd, signed statement at the end of *Postscript*: "Therefore, if it should occur to anyone to want to quote a particular passage from the books, it is my wish, my prayer, that he will do me the kindness of citing the respective pseudonymous author's name, not mine."[33] Are we betraying Kierkegaard's wishes? Does not the statement in *Postscript* sound contradictory to the point of view in *The Point of View*? Various Kierkegaard scholars do *not* see a unity in perspective across Kierkegaard's works. Roger Poole gives a succinct statement on Kierkegaard's apparent inconsistency: "Kierkegaard remains a mystery to this day. In what follows, I shall do the very opposite of suggesting that there is one right final reading. I shall suggest that the mystery is impenetrable to the end, and that is because Kierkegaard's writing has made all solutions impossible."[34] The mix of characters, artifice, and deception make Kierkegaard an unreliable narrator, especially when he directly tells us how to understand his authorship. In *The Point of View*, Kierkegaard explains that he was so concerned with indirect communication that it

30. *PV*, 46 / *SKS* 16, 28 (my emphasis).

31. For an excellent summary of the major perspectives on reading Kierkegaard, see Westfall, "Introduction," 1–25.

32. *PV*, 23, 29 / *SKS* 16, 11, 15.

33. *CUP1*, 627 / *SKS* 7, 571.

34. Poole, *Kierkegaard*, 1.

impacted his personal life. He purposefully portrayed himself in public as "nothing but a streetcorner loafer." Kierkegaard regales us with a story of being so consumed with writing *Either/Or* that he was almost unable to maintain his facade. In a panic, he rushed to the theater to be seen by the intelligentsia so that no one would expect he was working on a book.[35] Such antics cause us to question his reliability. Joakim Garff shares Poole's concerns:

> The reader is tempted to ask whether Kierkegaard is writing in good faith, or whether he is the rather impious (stage-)producer of a pious deception. How can the reader know whether Kierkegaard, with his revelation of having spent 'a certain part of every day' in prayer and meditation, is not merely repeating the self-staged act he enacted—only a few pages earlier—by appearing for 'five or ten minutes' at the theatre?[36]

David Law sees *The Point of View* as "a battleground for Kierkegaard's self-understanding" rather than "a definitive explanation that resolves all the issues and ties up the loose ends of the authorship."[37] In short, ought we trust an author who focuses on indirect communication (subjectivity) to directly tell us how to understand his works (objectivity)?

Such concerns from Poole, Garff, and Law—along with other scholars—are valid. What are we to make of Kierkegaard explaining a grand vision of authorship, particularly when many of the works are contrary to one another? Mark Tietjen has a criticism of a "postmodern" reading of Kierkegaard in general and Poole in particular: "Surely Poole is correct that one cannot ignore the start-to-finish religious interests or the priority of the Christianly religious. . . . There is no excuse for Kierkegaard scholars to attend unevenly to the unsigned literature."[38] Kierkegaard's works are religiously focused from the beginning, both his signed and pseudonymous writing. Every one of his works ties to theology in some way.[39] Niels Cappelørn gives an astute observation: "I therefore hold that this is a legitimate way, indeed the *only* legitimate way, of interpreting Kierkegaard, namely, to proceed from his own writings about the authorship and then attempt with

35. *PV*, 61 / *SKS* 16, 41–42.

36. Garff, "Eyes of Argus," 87.

37. Law, "Cacophony of Voices," 42.

38. Tietjen, *Kierkegaard, Communication, and Virtue*, 82.

39. I argue in *The Severed Self* that the doctrine of sin is a unifying theme throughout every one of Kierkegaard's works. There is not a single one of Kierkegaard's signed or pseudonymous works from *Either/Or* forward that fails to mention sin in some way.

him to live forwards and understand backwards through the various works in order to understand his production as a whole."[40] In *The Point of View*, Kierkegaard is looking backward at his life, making sense of his authorship with amazement:

> If, for example, I were to go ahead and say that I had had an overview of the whole dialectical structure from the very beginning of the whole work as an author . . . it would be a denial and an unfairness to God. . . . It is Governance that has brought me up, and the upbringing is reflected in the writing process. To that extent, then, what was developed earlier, that all the esthetic writing is a deception, proves to be in one sense not entirely true, since this expression concedes a little too much along the lines of consciousness. Yet it is not entirely untrue, because I have been conscious during the upbringing, and from the beginning.[41]

Kierkegaard admits he did not have a "road map" of every work when he started *Either/Or*. God led him through it, and some themes Kierkegaard did not at first realize came to the forefront in process. How can this be? I agree with Lee Barrett's assessment: "In *The Point of View* the Christian life, epitomized by Kierkegaard's activity as an author, is depicted as being both a human task and a divine gift."[42] Kierkegaard wrote the works, and he believed that God guided him in the process. I side with scholars like Cappelørn and Tietjen who see a uniform method to Kierkegaard's writing project. I take Kierkegaard's statements in *The Point of View* at face value. If Kierkegaard is actively deceiving us in *The Point of View*, then we should be able to suss out his deception as we analyze his works. In this way, we are testing Kierkegaard's method as we read.

How does Kierkegaard tell us to read his works? Kierkegaard categorizes his pseudonymous writing into three divisions: "The first division of books is esthetic writing; the last division of books is exclusively religious writing—between these lies *Concluding Unscientific Postscript* as the *turning point*."[43] Let us examine the first division, the aesthetic writing. Below are the pseudonymous works from *Either/Or* until *Postscript*:

40. Cappelørn, "Retrospective Understanding," 21.

41. *PV*, 76–77 / *SKS* 16, 56–57.

42. Barrett, "Kierkegaard's Authorship," 76.

43. *PV*, 31 / *SKS* 16, 17.

Title	Date	Pseudonym(s)
Either/Or	1843	Victor Eremita (Editor), "A," Johannes the Seducer, Judge William, the Pastor
Repetition	1843	Constantin Constantius (primary author), the Young Man (excerpts of letters)
Fear and Trembling	1843	Johannes de Silentio
The Concept of Anxiety	1844	Vigilius Haufniensis
Prefaces	1844	Nicolaus Notabene
Stages on Life's Way	1845	Hilarious Bookbinder (editor), William Afham, Judge William, Frater Taciturnus

The second division is the "turning point" to the religious, neither is it "esthetic writing, but, strictly speaking, neither is it religious." Interestingly, Kierkegaard signs his name as *editor* in these works, which he claims is "a hint."[44] These are as follows:

Title	Date	Pseudonym
Philosophical Fragments	1844	Johannes Climacus, Søren Kierkegaard (editor)
Concluding Unscientific Postscript to Philosophical Fragments	1846	Johannes Climacus, Søren Kierkegaard (editor)

The final division is the religious stage:

Title	Date	Pseudonym
Two Ethical-Religious Essays	1849	H. H.[45]
The Sickness unto Death	1849	Anti-Climacus, Søren Kierkegaard (editor)
Practice in Christianity	1850	Anti-Climacus, Søren Kierkegaard (editor)
The Book on Adler	Unpublished	Petrus Minor, Søren Kierkegaard (editor)

44. *PV*, 31 / *SKS* 16, 17–18.

45. *Two Ethical-Religious Essays* is actually excerpts from Kierkegaard's unreleased *BA*.

The movement of Kierkegaard's authorship is from 1) the aesthetic pseudonyms of indirect communication to 2) the "turning point" of indirect communication, with directly posing the question of Christianity, to 3) the explicitly religious pseudonyms post-*Postscript*.

How do we read indirect communication under a pseudonym for Kierkegaard's ultimately religious purposes? We ought not automatically accept a perspective of a particular character. Some of Kierkegaard's pseudonyms are downright villainous, as we will see below with Johannes the Seducer. If Kierkegaard writes these characters as a way of removing the illusion of Christendom, then we should see signs of the ultimate bankruptcy of such worldviews. As C. Stephen Evans comments, "Through the pseudonyms, Kierkegaard presents his readers with various views as to how a human life should be lived, various answers to the question 'How should a person exist?' The pseudonyms do not simply write about these various answers to this question; they embody those answers."[46] Kierkegaard's characters embody one of the three spheres of existence we discussed in detail in chapter 2: aesthetic, ethical, or religious. If we are to read Kierkegaard's indirect communication well, then we must consider the sphere of the pseudonym. Both the aesthetic and the ethical are sub-faith spheres of existence, part of the illusion of Christendom. Kierkegaard presents these characters with their "bewitching charm," yet they ultimately lead to an unlivable life.[47] The following is the breakdown of each of Kierkegaard's pseudonyms' sphere of existence:

Writing Stage	Work	Pseudonym	Sphere of Existence
Aesthetic	*Either/Or, Part I*	Victor Eremita, "A," Johannes the Seducer	Aesthetic
Aesthetic	*Either/Or, Part II*	Judge William, the Pastor	Ethical
Aesthetic	*Repetition*	Constantin Constantius, the Young Man	Aesthetic
Aesthetic	*Fear and Trembling*	Johannes de Silentio	Ethical
Turning Point to Religious	*Philosophical Fragments*	Johannes Climacus	Ethical

46. Evans, *Kierkegaard*, 37.

47. *PV*, 46 / *SKS* 16, 28.

Writing Stage	Work	Pseudonym	Sphere of Existence
Aesthetic	*The Concept of Anxiety*	Vigilius Haufniensis	Religious[48]
Aesthetic	*Prefaces*	Nicolaus Notabene	Ethical
Aesthetic	*Stages on Life's Way*	Hilarious Bookbinder, William Afham	Aesthetic
Aesthetic	*Stages on Life's Way*	Judge William, Frater Taciturnus	Ethical
Turning Point to Religious	*Concluding Unscientific Postscript*	Johannes Climacus	Ethical
Religious	*Two Ethical-Religious Essays*	H. H.	Religious
Religious	*The Sickness unto Death*	Anti-Climacus	Religious
Religious	*Practice in Christianity*	Anti-Climacus	Religious
Religious	*The Book on Adler*	Petrus Minor	Religious

We see some books hold to one sphere, while others have varying perspectives. Knowing the sphere helps us decipher the indirect communication. Cappelørn has a concise statement on the matter:

> What Kierkegaard calls the aesthetic stage or sphere can be understood better from the perspective of the aesthetic-religious stage than in isolation. Similarly, one can better understand the earlier ethical stage in terms of the later religious one towards which it points and to which it is related. *But both of these*

48. *CA* is pseudonymous, but it *directly* addresses an issue of Christian doctrine *before Kierkegaard pivots to the religious stage of his writing.* Interestingly, Kierkegaard originally planned to sign his name to the work, but at the last moment chose a pseudonym. While Kierkegaard does not elaborate the reason for the change, *CA* is markedly different from his other works in the aesthetic stage of his writing career. *CA* has more in common with *SUD*, an explicitly religious work, than with the pre-*Postscript* pseudonyms. In *Postscript*, Johannes Climacus comments on *CA*: "*The Concept of Anxiety* differs essentially from the other pseudonymous works in that its form is direct and even somewhat didactic. Perhaps the author thought that at this point a communication of knowledge might be necessary before a transition could be made to inward deepening" (*CUP1*, 269–71 / *SKS* 7, 245). I believe the pseudonymity of *CA* results from the nature of Kierkegaard's signed works during this time. Kierkegaard released numerous signed upbuilding discourses during his aesthetic stage of writing, yet all of them are sermonic in nature for the everyday Christian. *CA* is a philosophical and psychological deliberation on sin, a specialized work. Signing his name to *CA* may also have given away that he was the author of the aesthetic pseudonyms.

> *stages are best understood retrospectively, that is, from the rigorously Christian point of view which is the final or ultimate one in Kierkegaard's entire authorship*. The point is that Kierkegaard's stages of existence are finally understandable only in terms of the goal to which they lead and from which they are described, namely, the specifically Christian, the mark of which is the striving to imitate Christ.[49]

We now turn to examining two pseudonyms. The first is Johannes the Seducer in *Either/Or*, who exists in the aesthetic sphere. The second is Nicolaus Notabene from *Prefaces*, who exists in the ethical sphere.

3. THE SEDUCTION

"The Seducer's Diary" is the final part of *Either/Or, Part I*. The bulk of the diary is written by Johannes the Seducer, with a brief introduction from "A"—the primary author of *Either/Or, Part I*[50]—and a few letters from the object of Johannes's seduction. On April 4th, while in a shop, Johannes spies a young woman's reflection in a mirror. He does not know this woman, but he is taken by an insatiable drive to seduce. Notice I say, "is taken," using the passive voice. Johannes acts as if some other force causes him to chase after the girl. In this, we see that the Diary is not merely a story of conquest of a master pick-up artist. Johannes is seeking something else entirely. As he states in an excerpt from May 5th,

> Cursed chance! Never have I cursed you because you made your appearance; I curse you because you do not make your appearance at all. . . . Cursed chance! You, my only confidant, the only being I deem worthy to be my ally and my enemy. . . . I shall be your poet! I do not want to be a poet for others; make your appearance, and I shall be your poet. I shall eat my own poem, and that will be my food. . . . I have consecrated myself to your service; light, thinly clad, limber, unarmed, I renounce everything.[51]

49. Cappelørn, "Retrospective Understanding," 37 (my emphasis).

50. "A" technically does not identify himself in the work *EO1*. Victor Eremita, the editor of *EO1*, gives him this moniker as opposed to "B," the author of *EO2*; B does identify himself as Judge William. Victor Eremita also suspects that A is the author of the Diary and that "Johannes" is a pseudonym of A (*EO1*, 8–9 / *SKS* 2, 16–17). I see Johannes and A as separate, but ultimately, it is a moot point. Johannes the Seducer is a clear and defined character, so we will proceed as such. For more on this confounding discussion, see Kramer, "Johannes the Seducer," 160–62.

51. *EO1*, 326–27 / *SKS* 2, 316–17.

Johannes's acts are more than sexual urges. He declares, "I am an esthete, an eroticist, who has grasped the nature and the point of love."[52]

As he ambulates throughout Copenhagen, Johannes finally learns the object of his desire. Her name is Cordelia Wahl, and she is a seventeen-year-old orphan who lives with her aunt. Once he finds her name and address, we would expect that he would try to smooth-talk her immediately, but Johannes has other plans. He explains his understanding of love:

> How beautiful it is to be in love; how interesting it is to know that one is in love. This, you see, is the difference. I can become furious at the thought that she disappeared before me the second time, and yet in a certain sense I am glad of it. The image I have of her hovers indefinitely somewhere between her *actual* and her *ideal* form.[53]

The "ideal" is something abstract, something ephemeral as opposed to the real life he lives. Johannes idealizes his passion for Cordelia, and as Aaron Edwards notes, "It is not, after all, the experience of true love that the Seducer seeks, but an unquenchable and impossible pursuit of the image of unattainability itself."[54]

Johannes commences his battle to woo Cordelia, but he wants Cordelia *in a particular manner*. Daniel Berthold is correct in his assessment: "What Johannes really loves is his own artistic recreation of Cordelia."[55] What is this "artistic recreation?" Johannes decides to orchestrate a relationship between Cordelia and another man named Edward. Edward is head-over-heels in love with Cordelia, but he does not have the courage to engage her: "His bashfulness verges on the unbelievable. If it were a guise, then Edward would be a dangerous rival to me."[56] Johannes befriends Edward, takes him under his wing, and escorts him on his dates with Cordelia. As Edward and Cordelia court, Johannes sits with Cordelia's aunt, chatting her up and gaining rapport. During these supervised dates, Johannes plants seeds of desire in Cordelia, demonstrating that Edward is a bore while Johannes is an intriguing mystery. As soon as Edward musters the courage to propose marriage, Johannes swoops

52. *EO1*, 368 / *SKS* 2, 356.
53. *EO1*, 334 / *SKS* 2, 323 (my emphasis).
54. Edwards, "Thrill of the Chaste," 18.
55. Berthold, "Kierkegaard's Seductions," 1050–51.
56. *EO1*, 347 / *SKS* 2, 336.

in and asks the aunt for Cordelia's hand instead, which she promptly accepts. Although "Edward is beside himself with indignation," Johannes proceeds with his plans.[57]

As readers, we think, "Surely, Johannes has won his illicit 'reward,'" but his conquest is not complete. Johannes lists his next steps:

> What I have to do now is, on the one hand, to organize everything so that the engagement is broken in such a way that I thereby secure a more beautiful and significant relationship to Cordelia. . . . When I have brought her to the point where she has learned what it is to love and what it is to love me, then the engagement will break like a defective mold and she will belong to me.[58]

You read that right. Johannes's plan is to make Cordelia fall madly in love with him, break off the engagement, and push her to the point of desperation. What is more, he plans to make her think the broken engagement is all her idea! As if anticipating our disgust, Johannes writes, "Do I love Cordelia? Yes! Sincerely? Yes! Faithfully? Yes—in the esthetic sense, and surely this should mean something."[59] After successfully manipulating Cordelia into breaking off their engagement, the Seducer springs his final trap. He finds out that she will be in the countryside, staying at a small inn. He stages her room to mimic the locale where their courtship blossomed, where he started the manipulation of her desiring him. He leaves a note about their love, and after she reads it, he goes in for the kill. The Diary ends abruptly: "Why cannot such a night last longer? . . . But now it is finished, and I never want to see her again. When a girl has given away everything, she is weak, she has lost everything."[60]

3.2 Analysis

In this shocking and scandalous story, what is Kierkegaard attempting to indirectly communicate with us? Johannes the Seducer is firmly entrenched in the aesthetic stage of existence. Nathaniel Kramer dubs Johannes as "the aesthete *par excellence*," and Bradley Dewey claims "that the figure of Johannes provides central clues to what Kierkegaard meant

57. *EO1*, 376 / *SKS* 2, 364.
58. *EO1*, 376 / *SKS* 2, 365.
59. *EO1*, 385 / *SKS* 2, 373.
60. *EO1*, 445 / *SKS* 2, 432.

by the aesthetic stage."[61] We recall that the aesthetic sphere is the stage of immediacy, abstraction, and possibility, as opposed to the harsh reality of the ethical sphere. Aesthetes long for longing: they chase after sensations, not wanting to make concrete decisions. When we look at Johannes's actions, we see the aesthetic sphere taken to its logical conclusions, and the results are not pretty.

An interesting thing about Johannes is that Cordelia is not his first conquest.[62] Furthermore, he cannot satiate his desire during his seduction of Cordelia, for he is always seeking a new prize. In the midst of his project, he spies another beautiful girl, and he fantasizes about her. He goes on for five pages, lusting after a new woman while actively hatching his plot with Cordelia.[63] As Amber Bowen comments, "For Johannes, the desire for actuality, in this case a relationship that becomes a fixture in his life, is nauseatingly naive and even presumptuous. One must instead work up the sheer courage to embrace the flux, to expect nothing beyond what each moment can offer, and to find a new 'first.'"[64] The never-ending task of a new "first," a sensation to experience rather than an event to recollect, rules Johannes's life. Aesthetes desire possibility; any commitment is a bondage. Ironically, in his attempt at unfettered desire Johannes is imprisoned in a never-ending cycle of pleasure-seeking.

Johannes is a despicable character, and his actions are profoundly cruel. We do no envy Johannes's prowess with women. Céline Léon succinctly states the sentiment: "The seducers' pleasures consist not so much in their enjoyment qua subjects as in the control exercised over another human being. . . . Clearly what excites these men, more than sensuality, is the ability to subjugate women and to lead them out of their paths."[65] Johannes neither cares for nor loves Cordelia. He proffers a rationale to his existence: "If she promptly sees a deceiver in me, then she misunderstands me, for I am no deceiver in the ordinary sense; if she sees a faithful lover in me, then she also misunderstands me. It is a matter of having her soul be determined as little as possible by this episode."[66] He is not deceiving! He is helping her to advance toward ideal love and passion! If she would simply understand him, she would agree! As Dewey expounds, "In

61. Kramer, "Johannes the Seducer," 160; Dewey, "Seven Seducers," 160.

62. *EO1*, 346 / *SKS* 2, 335.

63. *EO1*, 354–59 / *SKS* 2, 343–48.

64. Bowen, "Real Love," 577–95.

65. Léon, "No Woman's Land," 231.

66. *EO1*, 372 / *SKS* 2, 360–61.

the 'Diary' Johannes displays his 'modern' consciousness, seeing himself on a world stage without God. . . . He surveys the stage emptied of God and steps into the divine role himself."[67] Johannes's subjugation of Cordelia is the ultimate art experiment and, from his view, not immoral. The Seducer quips, "A man can never be as cruel as a woman. . . . A Don Juan seduces them and abandons them, but he has enjoyment not in abandoning them but rather in seducing them; therefore, it is in no way an abstract cruelty."[68]

As you are reading this analysis, I bet you are thinking, "This guy is delusional." You are correct! Johannes paints his misdeeds as strokes on an abstract canvas, but his actions are happening in the real world. Cordelia is an actual person, not some fantasy. Although Johannes creates a plan in the abstract, his execution is in the concrete. Dewey comments, "The special demands of the aesthetic lifestyle . . . produce a deep split within the aesthete himself. . . . [Johannes's] manipulative, deceitful lifestyle demands what might be called an aesthetic *bifurcation of the self*."[69] Johannes believes he escapes morality—the ethical sphere—because he does not stay tethered to a choice. He splits his passion from his decisions and thus justifies his behavior. Such an explanation is utter nonsense to outside observers. David Stern has a keen observation on Johannes's worldview: "[The aesthete] fails to appreciate the way in which he is dependent on immediacy, a tie which is subtle and elastic, constituting not a material but a formal limit that cannot be severed."[70] We cannot live "abstract" lives. Our actions happen in existence. Johannes may rationalize that his *intentions* are different than the consequences, but such is merely marketing, ignoring the pain he willingly inflicts on Cordelia.

Kierkegaard comments in his personal journals that Johannes the Seducer is an example of "perdition, a 'marked' individual."[71] The Seducer believes he has won; he got the girl without having the girl. He avoids ethical requirements while indulging in the passion of the moment. From the aesthetic perspective, he is *not* immoral because he stayed in the abstract realm of immediacy. He chases after seduction, not trying to hurt anyone. Cordelia's hurt is her own fault because she does not understand the ideality of true love. We, as readers, see through the charade. The

67. Dewey, "Seven Seducers," 192.

68. *EO1*, 432 / *SKS* 2, 419.

69. Dewey, "Seven Seducers," 185 (my emphasis).

70. Stern, "Ties That Bind," 252.

71. *KJN* 2, 224 / *SKS* 18, 243, JJ:326.

aesthetic sphere is hollow, leading to a flight from reality wherein one may construct all sorts of justifications for his actions. Johannes the Seducer lives a life of despair, not pleasure. He may fool himself into thinking he is an enlightened, ephemeral poet, but the actual, existing world around him sees him for what he is. If he looks like a scoundrel and acts like a scoundrel, he *is* a scoundrel.

4. POOR NICOLAUS

Kierkegaard published *Prefaces: Light Reading for People in Various Estates According to Time and Opportunity* under the pseudonym Nicolaus Notabene. *Prefaces* is a specific type of literature popular in Copenhagen during Kierkegaard's epoch. As Lasse Kjældgaard explains, "The subtitle specifies the generic format of the text: 'Morskabslæsning,' literally *amusement reading*, was a kind of popular literature that thrived in the literary marketplace of the day, consisting of literary *divertissements* that required little effort to read and served to make time pass agreeably."[72] Such departure in genre from Kierkegaard's other pseudonyms informs us that the work is comical in nature, yet the work is more than mere amusement.

Nicolaus Notabene, a happily married man, decides he wants to write a book. After gathering the materials and choosing the topic, he beams with purpose, declaring that "it would be an irretrievable loss to humanity if my writing did not see the light of day."[73] Authorship is not a hobby like other hobbies: it requires the author to consistently think, rewrite, and edit, and unfortunately, Nicolaus's wife does not share his creative passion. Notabene regales us with a tense conversation between the two:

> "Your thought belongs to me," she said, "it must belong to me. Your attentiveness is my daily bread. Your approval, your smile, your jests are my life, my inspiration. Grant me that—oh, do not deny me what is justly due me—for my sake, for the sake of my joy, so that with joy I may be able to do what is my only joy: to think of you and to find all my satisfaction in being able, day in and day out, to continue wooing you as once you wooed me."[74]

72. Kjældgaard, "Age of Miscellaneous Announcements," 7.
73. *P*, 7 / *SKS* 4, 471.
74. *P*, 9 / *SKS* 4, 472–73.

Notabene attempts to reason with her, to reassure her that she is his muse, but he acquiesces because “even if I can debate with the devil himself, I cannot debate with my wife.”[75] Notabene’s wife halts the enterprise, for she argues that “to be an author when one is a married man . . . is downright unfaithfulness.”[76] Nicolaus loves and respects his wife, yet he has an inner need to become an author. A paragon of marital stability, they strike a compromise. Nicolaus will only write prefaces to books rather than the books themselves. According to Notabene, his wife has nothing to fear because a preface “must then have no subject to treat but must deal with nothing, and insofar as it seems to discuss something and deal with something, this must nevertheless be an illusion and a fictitious motion.”[77] *Prefaces*, therefore, is a compilation of Notabene’s prefaces to his unfinished books. This way he can remain faithful to his wife while also becoming an author: “The little or the trifles that I hereby publish I was able to write [with good conscience].”[78]

Prefaces contains nine prefaces and a postscript. While each of these prefaces are independent from one another, we can deduce a common theme: the cultural climate of the literary elite in Copenhagen. In Preface I, Notabene comments that to be an excellent author, one ought to “make sure that [the book] will be of benefit. To that end, [the author] asks a publisher or a philosophical fellow or his barber or a passerby what it is that the times demand.”[79] Yet, what the times demand does not guarantee success or understanding, as Notabene notes in Preface II. An author releases a book, then the literary who’s-who discuss amongst themselves if they have read the book. One responds, “No, not yet, but I have heard it is not great.” These erudite readers wait from a review by a literary critic to determine a book’s worth, but one replies, “I have not read [the review of the book] yet, but I heard from a friend out in the country, who has a damned good head and is a connoisseur, that the book falls short, even though there are some beautiful passages in it.”[80] Notabene remarks, “The author is a wretched bungler who knows nothing and understands

75. *P*, 7 / *SKS* 4, 471.
76. *P*, 10 / *SKS* 4, 474.
77. *P*, 5 / *SKS*, 4, 469.
78. *P*, 12 / *SKS* 4, 476.
79. *P*, 13 / *SKS* 4, 477.
80. *P*, 16 / *SKS* 4, 480.

nothing but with anxiety and horror waits for the rigorous judge, for the wise and insightful judgment of the most esteemed public."[81]

Preface V is a preface to a speech for the Total Abstinence Association. If one is a teetotaler on his own, what does that benefit him? Nicolaus remarks, "But what reward is it to lose oneself in the whole or to remain alone by oneself? No, praise be to our association, glorious is its reward. . . . If he joins our association, he acquires by this an infinite significance for the whole, something that is known by everyone who is a member."[82] Preface VI is an introduction to a new form of Christian devotional literature. Older devotional work is too archaic, a vestige of a bygone era. "The cultured are, of course, Christians," Notabene remarks, and "just as the essentially Christian was not concluded in the past, so also it is not concluded in the present moment either but has the future open and can still become what it wants to be."[83] Preface VII talks about the ease of writing a modern book: "One takes ten older works on the same subject and out of them puts together an eleventh on the same subject."[84] An eleventh book is a mediation of the previous ten, delivering on the promise of presenting the truth the previous ten left unfinished.

Preface VIII is an introduction to a new journal titled *Philosophical Deliberations*—whose mission statement is to eradicate all "remaining doubt." But Nicolaus has a fear:

> There is one thing that I do desire of my contemporaries: it is an explanation. Consequently I do not deny that Hegel has explained everything; I leave that to the powerful minds who will also explain what is missing. I keep my feet on the ground and say: I have not understood Hegel's explanation.[85]

Notabene has tried to make sense of philosophy, and he confesses, "My obtuseness must signify that I lack possibility."[86] What if he cannot understand philosophy, especially if it is the pathway to truth? Nicolaus's journal is an attempt to create "an original Danish system," which includes people like himself.[87] Notabene's postscript to *Prefaces* has a simple

81. *P*, 19 / *SKS* 4, 483.
82. *P*, 28 / *SKS* 4, 490.
83. *P*, 33 / *SKS* 4, 495.
84. *P*, 35 / *SKS* 4, 497.
85. *P*, 51, 56 / *SKS* 4, 512, 516–17.
86. *P*, 58 / *SKS* 4, 519.
87. *P*, 65 / *SKS* 4, 525.

rejoinder: "It hardly needs saying that this light reading cannot possibly . . . initiate conflict and quarreling."[88]

4.2 Analysis

What are we to make of Nicolaus Notabene and his *Prefaces* full of prefaces? What does Kierkegaard attempt to communicate indirectly? Notabene is in the ethical sphere of existence,[89] and we recall that the ethical sphere is concerned with shaking off the passion of youth and growing into one's ethical responsibilities. Ethical life is determined by one's culture, and its values trump those of individual desire. We start by examining Nicolaus Notabene's name. The name serves a dual function. As Nassim Jordán explains, *Notabene* "comes from the Latin *nota bene*, which is also a common expression in the Danish language used to make critical remarks, and it literally means 'note well.'"[90] Although the work is "light reading," Kierkegaard is "also capturing the paradox of approach" by asking us to "note well."[91] "Pay attention to my unserious remarks" appears to be a performative contradiction, and Kierkegaard hides his remarks under satire. Jordán explains the second aspect of Notabene's name: "The initials of the name, 'N.N.,' probably correspond to the Latin phrase *nomen nescio*, which can be translated as 'I do not know the name,' and is frequently used as a sort of anonym."[92] "N. N." denotes an unknown, someone who has no definition. Notabene is declaring to us: "Note well that I am a nobody!"

Why is N. N. a nobody? If Notabene is in the ethical sphere, then he finds his self identity in the ethical obligations of society. We must ask, "How does he know that his culture has found the correct solution?" Preface VII underlines the conundrum. If we need an eleventh book to understand the previous ten, then how do we know that the eleventh

88. *P*, 68 / *SKS* 4, 527.

89. Some may challenge my categorization of Notabene as in the ethical sphere. For example, Perkins states that "there is no suggestion that Nicolaus was anything but the aesthete he shows himself to be" (Perkins, "Reading Kierkegaard's *Prefaces*," 114). While Notabene does have some aspects of the aesthetic sphere, the facts that he is married, concerned with Hegelianism, and obsessed with cultural trends firmly place him in the ethical sphere.

90. Jordán, "Nicolaus Notabene," 196.

91. Kjældgaard, "Age of Miscellaneous Announcements," 9.

92. Jordán, "Nicolaus Notabene," 196.

book is correct? Would it not get lumped into the previous ten, and then we need a twelfth book to tell us what the previous eleven mean? As Mark Peterson notes well, "[Kierkegaard's] critique focuses on authors who writes books that are merely derivative, posture behind a curtain of technical vocabulary, and promise *philosophical insights that are never delivered*."[93] Kjældgaard agrees, "*Prefaces* does . . . resume a theme that is recurrent in Kierkegaard's authorship: the problem of *motion*."[94] If I always defer the truth to the next latest and greatest work, then I *exist* in a nebulous state. I cannot *know* anything subjectively. All I can do is gather the objective facts as presented, yet this leaves me empty, unable to *become* anything of substance. As Peterson explicates, "If the author is merely an observer . . . then the author may be a conveyer, but never a producer, of truth. Thus, the degree to which an author is a good philosophic author is the degree to which he becomes transparent or, even better, absent."[95] I am a nobody, and academic discourse simply becomes rearranging deck chairs on the Titanic, offering no solution for the existing individual. If everything is relative in forward progress, then nothing means anything, and anything means nothing. Mediation acts as a carrot on a stick, but we are on a treadmill, unable to arrive at any answers about our existence.

Furthermore, Nicolaus is obsessed with integrating into Copenhagen's society, as Preface V highlights with the Total Abstinence Association. For Nicolaus, what is important is not that someone practices abstinence in the privacy of her own home. That does not matter; N. N. needs a group, an association, a gathering of peers to tell him that his choices matter. He wants to become a nobody, not an individual. As he states at the end of Preface V, "It is fitting for every member of our association to be as intoxicated as a drunken man, but, note well, intoxicated with enthusiasm, which is all the more marvelous the less there is of that which produces intoxication."[96] For Notabene the problem is not intoxication *qua* intoxication. The issue is intoxication *as an individual*. Once the crowd determines which type of intoxication is amenable, then have at it!

Lastly, Notabene's desire to be absorbed by the culture is ultimately unachievable. In Preface VIII, Nicolaus expresses his fear of misunderstanding Hegelianism. He admits that "I do realize that [understanding

93. Peterson, "Ringing Doorbells," 87–88 (my emphasis).

94. Kjældgaard, "Age of Miscellaneous Announcements," 26.

95. Peterson, "Ringing Doorbells," 100.

96. *P*, 30 / *SKS* 4, 485.

philosophy] was no place for me, but that it must be glorious to be able to go there."[97] N. N. wants to be a part of the whole but cannot achieve such a lofty position by his own faculties—but he is a part of the whole, despite his stupidity. He exists as a living being and, by definition, a part of larger humanity. His appearance as a questioning individual contradicts the presupposition of said philosophy. As Stephen Crites says,

> But Nicolaus's demand to be initiated into philosophy is also an attack on philosophy itself, for he suggests that its incapacity is even greater than his. If his stupidity consists by definition in the fact that philosophy cannot understand him, the essential fault may lie with philosophy. . . . He may not be a potential participant in Hegelian spirit, but then he is not subhuman.[98]

Furthermore, Notabene states, "See, philosophy is so good in these latter days . . . [that] it makes every theologian into a philosopher."[99] If philosophy becomes the arbiter of doctrine, then salvation comes through one's exercise of reason. The stupid cannot be saved, yet Notabene wants with all of his heart to live a fulfilled life.

Prefaces indirectly communicates the inability of philosophy, culture, or the academy to provide a viable means of existence. If we define ourselves as "nobody" rather than an individual before God, we will never arrive at a place of true understanding or stability. We often view the surrounding authority structures as *the* truth, but they stand on shaky foundation.[100] As Ángel Vera illuminates,

> Neither does it seem reasonable, according to Kierkegaardian thought, to submit oneself to the tyranny of the needs of the times, marked by supposed academic or scientific authorities. The philosopher writes for the world, its needs and pains, and for his companions on the way, but he does not write according to how the world dictates. Writing is an ethical work, and it seems that the adequate temper is one of responsibility for both the truth and the good.[101]

For Kierkegaard, the truth lies in subjectivity, the *individual* relating to God. Nicolaus, for all his striving, falls flat on his face. In his attempt to

97. *P*, 64 / *SKS* 4, 523–24.

98. Crites, "Unfathomable Stupidity of Nicolaus Notabene," 37–38.

99. *P*, 50 / *SKS* 4, 511.

100. We will examine issues of truth and the larger "crowd" in chapter 5.

101. Vera, "Escribir filosofía," 440 (my translation).

become a part of the culture, he does not become a true self. He lives in despair, always seeking definition from an impotent source. In the end, Nicolaus Notabene chooses to be *nomen nescio*.

5. INDIRECT APOLOGETICS?

Apologetic method is important because it is concerned with how we *do* apologetics. There are varying perspectives on apologetic method. Peter Kreeft and Ronald Tacelli seek to return to a medieval-like love of reason, like Aquinas in the *Summa*, stating that "apologetics gets at the heart *through* the head. The head is important precisely because it is a gate to the heart. We can love only what we know."[102] Douglas Groothuis prefers "worldview hypothesis evaluation and verification through a cumulative-case method. That is, the apologist makes her case by using sound arguments from a variety of disciplines, each of which contributes to the rationality of the Christian worldview."[103] William Lane Craig endorses "offensive apologetics [that] seeks to present a positive case for Christian truth claims."[104] There are various starting points, from Presuppositionalism to Reformed epistemology to classical apologetics to Evidentialism.[105]

What all of these have in common is that they are direct and argument-based. They either tend to ignore or downplay nonrational aspects of our decisions or argue the best way to the nonrational is through the rational. James K. A. Smith argues, "We are essentially and ultimately desiring animals, which is simply to say that we are essentially and ultimately lovers. . . . To be a human is to be just such a lover—a creature whose orientation and form of life is most primordially shaped by what one loves as ultimate."[106] We all have an ultimate love in our life, and the Christian response, as Augustine puts it, is that "You [God] made us for yourself and our hearts find no peace until they rest in you."[107] While our current context is not an illusion of Hegelianism running rampant through Danish Christendom, we are surrounded by various and sundry

102. Kreeft and Tacelli, *Handbook of Christian Apologetics*, 21.
103. Groothuis, *Christian Apologetics*, 41–42.
104. Craig, *Reasonable Faith*, 23.
105. For an assessment of major methods, see Morley, *Mapping Apologetics*.
106. Smith, *Desiring the Kingdom*, 50–51.
107. Augustine, *Confessions*, 1.1.

illusions, these "ultimate loves" of which Smith speaks. Every song, movie, television show, novel, news article, etc. is trying to sell us a narrative, to capture our imagination. Karen Swallow Prior reminds us that "while the objective world in all its entirety exists all around us, our imagination draws only from what we perceive. And we primarily perceive what we attend to."[108] While the direct context between Kierkegaard and modern Western society has changed, what has not changed is the way in which we are all lulled to sleep by our surroundings; and we all need to wake up.

I recently listened to Rainn Wilson's podcast *Soul Boom*. Wilson interviewed staunch atheist Alex O'Connor. Wilson asks a poignant question to O'Connor: "What is the best argument you've ever heard in your infinite number of debates both online and in person for the existence of God?" O'Connor replies with the ontological argument put forth by Anselm. O'Connor then proceeds to correctly explain and demonstrate its brilliance to Wilson, yet O'Connor still does not believe in God. Wilson then asks, "What would it take for you to become a theist? Would it take increased understanding? Would it be an argument? Would it be some kind of scientific proof? . . . Or would it be some kind of lived experience?" O'Connor's reply is fascinating: "I think it would be the second. I think it would be an experience."[109]

Kierkegaard's pseudonymous works demonstrate lived experience. He takes characters from differing perspectives and says, "Let's see how they would live out their worldview to its ultimate conclusions." Kierkegaard leaves us with broken characters who do not realize their brokenness—but the reader *does* see the plight. When we see that our ultimate loves leave us lost, maybe we will start to become subjective. The idea enters our mind, and we note well that not all is well.

Apologetics needs to consider an indirect method. I am not saying we should dismiss direct argumentation, but the fact of the matter is that we are completely missing ways of impacting the people around us. The Enlightenment has seduced us into believing that a precise, logical argument will cause people to change their minds. Kierkegaard shows us we are ignoring that we are under an illusion of some sort, and direct argumentation is often screaming at a wall. An indirect method captures the imagination and causes us to confront how we live. It attempts to bring an *experience* to the apologetic enterprise. How do we effectively

108. Prior, *Evangelical Imagination*, 12.

109. Wilson, "Atheist Plays Devil's Advocate," 11:20.

communicate indirectly? Unfortunately, I have no clear paradigm to offer. What I can say is that I agree with Kierkegaard that we must know our audience and where they are at; but that is as varied as the people we encounter. Kierkegaard gives us tools to think about apologetics that "approach from behind," but we have the difficult task actually executing our ideas. Such necessary work must be done with great fear and trembling before God.

> Personally—also when I consider my own inner sufferings, which I personally may have deserved—personally, one thing absorbs me unconditionally, is more important to me and lies more upon my heart than the whole authorship: to express as honestly and as strongly as possible something for which I can never adequately give thanks and which I, when I at some time have forgotten the whole authorship, will eternally recollect unchanged—how infinitely much more Governance has done for me than I had ever expected, could have expected, or dared to have expected.[110]

110. *PV*, 12 / *SKS* 13, 18.

5

Time to Be a Gadfly

Critiquing the Present Age

I HAVE ALWAYS FELT like I do not fit in. I consider myself a classical evangelical—not the contemporary demographic/political movement in US politics—but I do not fit the standard mold: born in the South to Midwestern parents; attended seminary without a family legacy of ministry; having a father raised Catholic while me being raised in a fundamentalist-leaning Baptist church; listening to punk rock while everyone listens to "praise-worship" or country; preferring continental philosophy to analytic; a theologian who deeply cares for the church but *not* called to pastor. It is not like I seek to be different; I never want to be *that* guy who is different for different's sake. I have been accused of being overly critical, a contrarian, and a "grumpy cat" by friends and colleagues. I have been advised to get on staff at church to pad my resume so Christian colleges and universities will hire me. I've been told to tone down my opinions and questions because it may upset the apple cart. It is an odd situation; I am on the same team but feel like an opponent.

Now, I am not trying to write some "woe is me" story to garner sympathy or to shame anyone. I only mention this because we all tend toward monolithic uniformity. I often joke, "If I were in charge, there wouldn't be any problems." Like-minds congeal, transmogrifying opposing opinions into enemies for exile. Apologetics becomes "destroying the atheists." Theology turns into "owning the liberals/Pelagians/enemy du jour." Consequently, we lose sight of the *purpose* of theology and apologetics. Why do we set up systems or methods? Concerning theology, Rhyne Putman explains that systematic reflection "organizes the teaching of the whole Bible into categories and topics, answering critical questions about the contents of its teaching."[1] Concerning apologetics, William Lane Craig explains the purpose is "to answer the question, What rational warrant can be given for the Christian faith?"[2] Proper theology and apologetics serve as paradigms to assist us in our task as Christians. They are tools in our tool belts.

We cannot avoid systematic thinking, and systems are not bad per se. When a system becomes "The System" that must be defended at all costs, we have moved beyond a useful tool to an idol, an "elevation of a preliminary concern to ultimacy," as Paul Tillich puts it.[3] I do not know any apologist with his or her salt who seeks to set up his or her system as the be-all end-all, but unfortunately, an unintended consequence of endorsing a system or method is that we find our purpose in said method rather than God. As Shirley Guthrie comments, "The most dangerous heretics the creeds had to fight . . . are the people within the church . . . who are enthusiastically in favor of the Bible, religion, morality, and the church—but use them to lend authority and respectability to ideologies and methods they consciously or unconsciously want to enthrone *in place of* God in Christ."[4] Or as Augustine famously states, "Whoever, then, thinks that he understands the Holy Scriptures, or any part of them, but puts such an interpretation upon them as does not tend to build up this twofold love of God and our neighbor, does not yet understand them as he ought."[5] There is a real temptation to see arguments, creeds, and proofs as the *end* rather than the *means* to the end of the twofold love of God and neighbor.

An unfortunate recent example of this "defend-the-system" mindset is the scandal around apologist Ravi Zacharias. Zacharias's fall from grace was particularly troubling to me because I had a personal connection to his work. In my teenage doubting, my youth pastor handed me a copy of *Jesus Among Other Gods* by Zacharias. That book sparked my desire to study theology and philosophy at an academic level. I thought, "Wow, there are smart Christians with good answers!" Zacharias held a special

1. Putman, *Method of Christian Theology*, 18.
2. Craig, *Reasonable Faith*, 15.
3. Tillich, *Systematic Theology*, 1:13.
4. Guthrie, *Christian Doctrine*, 23.
5. Augustine, *On Christian Doctrine*, 1.36.40.

place in my heart, but in 2016, several bloggers posted details accusing Zacharias of grooming a married woman and soliciting sexual photos. I remember that when these rumblings first started, many faithful supporters backed Zacharias's story, blaming the accuser as a narcissist looking for a paycheck. Zacharias filed a lawsuit against his accuser, and he released a statement in 2017:

> In late 2016, she [the accuser] sent an email informing me [Zacharias] she planned to tell her husband about the inappropriate pictures she had sent and to claim that I had solicited them. In April 2017, together they sent me, through an attorney, a letter demanding money. I immediately notified members of my board, and as they advised, I personally engaged legal counsel. . . . Let me state categorically that I never met this woman alone, publicly or privately. The question is not whether I solicited or sent any illicit photos or messages to another woman—I did not, and there is no evidence to the contrary.[6]

Yet after Zacharias's death in 2020, the allegations resurfaced. His ministry platform, Ravi Zacharias International Ministries investigated the claims, and found them to be credible. I won't rehash all the sordid details here, but Daniel Silliman and Kate Shellnutt's article in *Christianity Today* summarizes the sentiment well:

> When [Zacharias] died in May, he was praised for his faithful witness, his commitment to the truth, and his personal integrity. Now it is clear that, offstage, the man so long admired by Christians around the world abused numerous women and manipulated those around him to turn a blind eye.[7]

Silliman also reports that "Ravi Zacharias International Ministries (RZIM) spent nearly $1 million to defend its founder and namesake against allegations of sexual misconduct in 2017 *and then lied about it*."[8] A world-renowned apologist sets up an organization, and when cracks started showing, Zacharias and his ministry circled the wagons, defaming the character of an abuse victim. The entire ordeal is a tragic example of protecting "The System" at all costs.

Such situations are by no means unique to apologetic ministries or churches. Whenever a movement—whether it be cultural or

6. Farley, "Ravi Zacharias Denies 'Grooming' Accusations."
7. Silliman and Shellnutt, "Ravi Zacharias Hid Hundreds," para. 9.
8. Silliman, "RZIM Spent Nearly $1M Suing," para. 1.

religious—gains a critical mass, it becomes a behemoth. Any targeted criticism of the behemoth becomes an enemy to destroy rather than an opportunity to take a breath and reflect on the situation. People within the movement will create all sorts of justifications for its behavior. Any behemoth can be slain, but it is a monumental task not for the faint of heart.

Søren Kierkegaard discusses the nature of these sorts of systems. While there was no physical adultery as the target of his criticism, Kierkegaard did believe Christendom was committing spiritual adultery:

> It is always that way when the established order has gone so far as to deify itself. Finally custom and usage become articles of faith; everything becomes equally important, or ordinances, usage, and custom become what is important. The single individual does not feel and acknowledge that he, and thus every individual, has a relationship with God that is to have absolute meaning for him. No, the relationship with God is abolished; custom, ordinance, and the like are deified. But that kind of fear of God is nothing but contempt for God; indeed, it does not fear God, it fears people.[9]

Christendom—the amalgamation of a state church and a national culture—was a behemoth Kierkegaard sought to slay. Kierkegaard comments in his personal journal that an awakening "is urgently needed in Denmark, since more than a generation of artistically perfect and secularly sagacious, skillful proclamation of Christianity has hexed us into a kind of esthetic spell." Kierkegaard continues, stating that "by the highest approval of divine governance" he will become "a vexing 'gadfly,' a quickening whip on all this spiritlessness."[10]

The issue with gadflies is that they beg to be swatted, and Kierkegaard was definitely swatted at many times in his career, by both the literary culture and the state church. When Kierkegaard critiqued, "The System" was not happy. We see this most readily in his interaction with *The Corsair*, a publication that walked the line between tabloid and literary journal. Howard and Edna Hong describe *The Corsair*: "With the largest circulation in the city and in the country, with talented anonymous writers and cartoonists of wit and malice, with a series of straw men as 'responsible editor,' with disdain for public position and personal privacy, *The Corsair* gathered and cleverly exploited fact, rumor, and gossip."[11] In an article published

9. *PC*, 92 / *SKS* 12, 100.

10. *JP* 6, 6943 / *Pap.* XI3 B 53.

11. Hong and Hong, "Historical Introduction," ix.

in *Fædrelandet*, Kierkegaard, via pseudonym Frater Taciturnus, snarkily comments, "Would that I might only get into *The Corsair* soon. It is really hard for a poor author to be so singled out in Danish literature that he (assuming that we pseudonyms are one) is the only one who is not abused there."[12] Kierkegaard's open invitation led to severe mockery by the paper, and as the Hongs note, "The character assassination by way of identification of Kierkegaard with Crazy Nathanson and the incessant ridicule of his clothes and physical features made [Kierkegaard] the object of curiosity and taunting on the streets."[13] The attack on Kierkegaard's appearance and personal life took place between January and February of 1846. In March of the same year, Kierkegaard published *Two Ages*, a literary review of a novel of the same name. Kierkegaard's review does indeed comment on the contents of the novel, but his analysis turns into an examination of his present moment, a moment of a blind following of Christendom, a system to be preserved at all costs.

The purpose of this chapter is to hear Kierkegaard's critique of an abstract crowd that seeks to level any form of opposition. This is particularly helpful for apologetics and theology for two reasons. First, if we seek to dismantle systems that are contra-Gospel, we *will* receive opposition. Kierkegaard's analysis is therefore helpful to anyone who opposes power structures. Second, we are unfortunately prone to setup and defend our own systems. We ought to consider Kierkegaard's warning so that we do not slide into idolatry. Although Kierkegaard talks about the "public" or the "crowd" throughout his writings, we will focus primarily on two works: *Two Ages* and *Practice in Christianity*. His cultural analysis in *Two Ages* of the pitfalls of nineteenth-century Denmark and its relation to Christendom are eerily similar to our current Western culture. Kierkegaard is an inadvertently forward thinker, and his assessment of culture, philosophy's impact on it, and our tendency to fall into a malaise of nominal Christianity is worth investigation. His direct critique of the state church in *Practice in Christianity* demonstrates how a calcified institution leads to mass deception.

We start with an investigation of Kierkegaard's culture and the basic plot of the novel *Two Ages*. Kierkegaard wrote during the Golden Age of Denmark, and understanding the zeitgeist sets the stage for Kierkegaard's critique of his age. Second, we discuss Kierkegaard's thoughts concerning

12. *COR*, 46 / *SKS* 14, 84.

13. Hong and Hong, "Historical Introduction," xxx.

"the public." Once people stop thinking of themselves as individuals before God, the "common sense" of the culture becomes the god they serve. It muddies the waters, deceiving people away from authenticity. Third, we observe what the crowd does when challenged: it *levels* individuality. While we can change public opinion, popular sentiment does not give up without a fight. Fourth, we examine Kierkegaard's contention with the Danish Evangelical Lutheran Church of his epoch. Lastly, we consider how Kierkegaard's analysis of group dynamics assists us in our theological and apologetic endeavors.

1. *TWO AGES* AND GOLDEN AGE DENMARK

The novel *Two Ages* was originally published anonymously in 1845, but the author was posthumously identified as Thomasine Gyllembourg, mother of the influential J. L. Heiberg, a colleague of Kierkegaard. As was unfortunately common in the nineteenth century, Gyllembourg remained anonymous because society did not approve of women as authors. Katalin Nun remarks that "[Gyllembourg's] stories concern everyday life of the Copenhagen middle-class of the Danish Golden Age. Thus, it is hardly an exaggeration to say that Thomasine Gyllembourg's novels and stories give a reliable picture of bourgeois culture and mentality of the Danish capital of the 1830's and 1840's."[14] *Two Ages* is Gyllembourg's final novel, and it follows a cast of characters from two different generations: the age of revolution and the present age.

Following these two ages helps us understand the mood of the Danish Golden Age. Denmark, like many European countries in the nineteenth century, was going through a political upheaval. Ideas of representative democracy clashed with monarchies. Feudal systems gave way to modern capitalism. Serfs were no longer subservient but equal in rights. A middle class started to grow, and seeds of modern industries were sown. In a relatively short time, the fundamentals of Danish society changed. As Bruce Kirmmse explains, "Since the latter part of the seventeenth century Denmark had been an absolute monarchy in which most political, social, and cultural power was concentrated in an oligarchical coalition of the crown and several hundred families."[15] The early nineteenth century went through various crises—Napoleonic wars

14. Nun, "Thomasine Gyllembourg's *Two Ages*," 276.

15. Kirmmse, "Out with It!," 16.

and the bankruptcy of Denmark as a few examples—yet a middle-class emerged with a penchant for the arts and maintaining the political status quo. As Kirmmse notes, "It is thus no surprise that the literature of the Golden Age is for the most part anti-bourgeois, stressing poetry at the expense of prose, and is essentially aristocratic and conservative in its social and political outlook, appealing to the standards of the absolutist *ancien régime*."[16]

During the Golden Age, Copenhagen had a veritable explosion of artistic talent, from literature to poetry to plays to paintings and more. Art was not done merely for art's sake, but there was a desire for Copenhagen to come into its own, like many other neighboring, German-speaking locales during the Romantic movement.[17] The goal was *Dannelse*, as Kirmmse comments:

> The [Golden Age] artist's task is to instruct, to serve as the catalyst who assists the uncultivated (*udannet*) individual in gaining the higher outlook called 'cultivation' (*Dannelse*), which will in turn enable the individual to find his appointed place in the differentiated and organic whole constituting society.[18]

Such a task of "cultivation" fueled the thinkers and poets of Copenhagen to develop a Danish culture that could stand against larger nation's outputs. The results speak for themselves: Hans Christian Andersen and Søren Kierkegaard are two prime examples of Golden Age authors still read to this day. Nun clarifies that *Dannelse* "means in short a harmonious and general education of human beings, the perfect development of the physical, intellectual, emotional and social competences which will result in an inner perfection and an outward beauty and grace."[19] *Dannelse* led to cultural tastemakers, gurus of art and philosophy. The public looked to this cadre for guidance and growth.[20] J. L. Heiberg, son of Gyllembourg, became the supreme cultural critic of the age. Thomas Millay explains the overall mood of the Golden Age: "In sum, the Golden Age believed in nobility; it believed in refinement; it believed in church as a

16. Kirmmse, *Kierkegaard in Golden Age Denmark*, 78.

17. For more on Romanticism's influence on Denmark and Kierkegaard, see McDonald, "Kierkegaard and Romanticism," 94–97.

18. Kirmmse, "Out with It!," 18.

19. Nun, "Thomasine Gyllembourg's *Two Ages*," 285.

20. As noted in chapter 4, Kierkegaard consistently satirizes the literary elite in *Prefaces*.

space in which God's good ordering of society was proclaimed; and it promulgated these beliefs in the splendid cultural artifacts it produced."[21]

By 1848, the monarchy relinquished absolute power and transitioned Denmark to a modern constitutional monarchy. As Henriette Steiner comments, "This shift from absolute to constitutional monarchy, however, comes to symbolise the end of the Golden Age."[22] With this shift, certain thinkers sought to disengage the Danish Lutheran Church from the state. For example, theologian, professor, and pastor Andreas Rudelbach was a key figure questioning the union of church and state. Rudelbach even tried to claim Kierkegaard as a compatriot because of the various themes in Kierkegaard's writings. In 1851, Kierkegaard wrote an article in *Fædrelandet* declining to join the movement.[23] Although, to this day, Denmark still has a state church, the fundamental way of viewing oneself as a part of the nation was forever changed. José Ortega y Gasset summarizes the mood of Europe during this epoch: "At the appearance in Europe of this psychological state of the average man, at the rising level of one's integral existence, the tone and manners of all aspects of European life suddenly acquired an appearance many have called: 'the Americanization of Europe.'"[24] America was founded—at least in theory—on the concept of intrinsic, personal rights rather than one's birth status. Such a radical, modern concept crossed the Atlantic: all are equal. Such leads to democracy, but it also leads to viewing humanity as an amorphous "common man" or "public."

Two Ages is a story about two groups of people during the age of revolution—that is, the years following the French Revolution and its surrounding turmoil—and the present age—Copenhagen in the 1840s, a time "in which bourgeois liberalism and aristocratic Hegelian conservatism were in fashion."[25] In the age of revolution, the young Claudine falls in love with the French Lusard. Upon Lusard's departure from Denmark, Claudine is found to be pregnant, and she delivers a healthy boy named Charles. After nine years of holding out hope, Claudine is finally reunited with Lusard, where they live out the rest of their days together. The present age follows Claudine and Lusard's son Charles, who is now fifty years old and heirless. He travels to Copenhagen to find a suitable

21. Millay, *Kierkegaard and the New Nationalism*, 22–23.

22. Steiner, *Emergence of a Modern City*, 19.

23. *COR*, 51–59 / *SKS* 14, 111–16.

24. Ortega y Gasset, *La rebelión de las masas*, 80–81 (my translation).

25. Kirmmse, *Kierkegaard in Golden Age Denmark*, 267.

heir, commenting on how the city has changed since his youth. He finds a young woman named Mariane who is engaged to Ferdinand, a distant relative of Charles. In the end, Mariane and Ferdinand marry, and Charles adopts the couple as his heirs. While this sounds like melodrama, Gyllembourg clearly presents the milieu of the world of her youth and the world of her present moment. Nun comments,

> This difference between the two ages is clearly demonstrated through Claudine's and Mariane's respective romantic affairs: Claudine and Lusard abandon themselves fully to their love, without hesitation or consideration of the fact that Lusard must leave Denmark and their future is completely uncertain. Mariane's fiancé Ferdinand Bergland, by contrast, is willing to give up his love because of the difficulties he anticipates he will have in earning a living for them.[26]

Kierkegaard comments that "the *difference* [of the two ages] essentially sums up the relation between *inwardness* and the malady of *exhibitionism*, and the present age is frequently accused of the latter."[27] With these preliminary marks on the Golden Age and *Two Ages*, we can now address Kierkegaard's assessment of the present age.

2. THE CROWD IN THE AGE OF REVOLUTION AND THE PRESENT AGE

Kierkegaard explains that "the age of revolution is essentially passionate and therefore essentially has *culture* [*Dannelse*]," while "the present age is essentially a *sensible, reflecting age, devoid of passion, flaring up in superficial, short-lived enthusiasm and prudentially relaxing indolence*."[28] What does Kierkegaard mean by passion? The word "passion" in English can be a substitute for "emotion," but Kierkegaard avers something more profound than emotions. We note that he critiques the present age's "short-lived enthusiasm" as a negative quality. Having strong feelings is not necessarily having *passion* about something. Robert Roberts explains Kierkegaard's use of passion, particularly in *Two Ages*: "A passion is a disposition of pathos." *Pathos* is a personality trait, something deeper to the formation of the self; it is Kierkegaardian subjectivity, a deep and lasting

26. Nun, "Thomasine Gyllembourg's *Two Ages*," 280.
27. *TA*, 35 / *SKS* 8, 35.
28. *TA*, 61, 68 / *SKS* 8, 60, 66 (emphasis original).

commitment to being oneself. Roberts comments that the present age is full of "people [who] lack sustained interests that are deep enough to shape consciousness and behavior decisively."[29]

"Superficial" is a good word to describe the present age. Kierkegaard notes that in the age of revolution, people bandied together to overthrow governments, yet this sort of crowd was not superficial: "When individuals (each one individually) are essentially and passionately related . . . to the same idea, the relation is optimal and normative."[30] In revolution, people have individual, passionate convictions that spill out into their behavior. These like-minds congregate, whether it be a political or cultural movement. We must remember that passion is not a mere sentiment of opinion but something that drives people to live a certain way. The present age, however, has "individuals [relating] to an idea merely *en masse*." The starting point for the present age is group identity *and then one adopts the ideas of the group*. Functionally, the crowd *is* the ideal. If I define myself first-and-foremost as a member of a group, then I will follow said group even if its stated ideals change. I forfeit my direct relationship to an ideal and replaced it with "popular opinion." As Ortega y Gasset correctly notes, "The mass is anyone who does not value himself as himself—for good or for bad—for special reasons, but rather he sees himself 'like the rest of the world,' yet he is not distressed—he feels good about understanding himself as identical to others."[31] I identify with the group *because I have no essential, passionate relation to anything eternal.* I may relate emotionally to something, but the whims of culture—Spirit/*Geist* moving through history—change frequently. Tomorrow brings a new crisis or fad.

Kierkegaard presciently proposes,

> Suppose that such an age has invented the swiftest means of transportation and communication, has unlimited combined financial resources: how ironic that the velocity of the transportation system and the speed of communication stand in an inverse relationship to the dilatoriness of irresolution.[32]

Kierkegaard foresees a day of instantaneous, global dissemination of ideas. In the hands of an amorphous crowd, the behemoth grows and

29. Roberts, "Passion and Reflection," 88.

30. *TA*, 62 / *SKS* 8, 61.

31. Ortega y Gasset, *La rebelión de las masas*, 69–70 (my translation).

32. *TA*, 64 / *SKS* 8, 62.

grows. Kierkegaard continues: "The present age is an age of publicity, the age of miscellaneous announcement: nothing happens but still there is instant publicity."[33] By "nothing happens," Kierkegaard does not mean that no events occur; he means that nothing *essentially* happens. While someone may signal a change, the status quo prevails. It is like in *The Office* when Toby has a weekly standing meeting with Dwight to log all of Dwight's complaints against Jim.[34] Toby puts the complaints in a box and stores them in the warehouse for no one to read. Something occurred but nothing essentially changed. Dwight is still Dwight, and Jim is still Jim.[35] Kierkegaard sees this "nothing happening" in religious life as well: "We are willing to keep Christian terminology but privately know that nothing decisive is supposed to be meant by it."[36] Values become labels, and as long as we sport the brand, we are virtuous. Paul Tyson comments, "Thus, the capacity merely to *do* things, and to do them always faster, better, cheaper, but without any high or intrinsic reason *to* do things, characterizes the frenetic activism of the options-open instrumental potency of our age."[37]

A passionless age forms "a monstrous abstraction, an all-encompassing something that is nothing, a mirage—and this phantom is *the public*."[38] Public opinion becomes the arbiter of good and evil, yet it has no concrete form. The public cannot be wrong. How could we even try the public in a court of law? We can try an individual, but the public can run roughshod over anything it wants with seeming immunity. Kierkegaard continues,

> Only when there is no strong communal life to give substance to the concretion will the press create this abstraction "the public," made up of unsubstantial individuals who are never united or never can be united in the simultaneity of any situation or organization and yet are claimed to be a whole. The public is a corps, outnumbering all the people together, but this corps can never be called up for inspection; indeed, it cannot even have so much as a single representative.[39]

33. *TA*, 70 / *SKS* 8, 68.
34. McDougall, *Office*.
35. And Toby is still the worst.
36. *TA*, 81 / *SKS* 8, 77.
37. Tyson, *Kierkegaard's Theological Sociology*, 25.
38. *TA*, 90 / *SKS* 8, 86.
39. *TA*, 91 / *SKS* 8, 87.

This "monstrous abstraction" increases at an alarming rate with impunity. David Lappano comments on the character of the public: "'A public' is really a commercial and political construction of mass media, which obstructs the kinds of communications and relationships that positively build up individuals and communities. That means, for Kierkegaard, a successful antidote to the alienated sociality of mass society must be able to communicate the personalism of the ethical-religious capability and subjective life."[40] Subjectivity is what, argues Kierkegaard, the age of revolution had, and subjectivity is the antidote against the public of the present age. Subjectivity—the individual existing in passionate inwardness—is, by definition, at odds with the public, and unfortunately, the public cannot abide subjectivity.

3. LEVELING

Kierkegaard's historical context in the waning days of the Danish Golden Age was educated and active but also vapid. As mentioned in other chapters, Hegelian philosophy made its way into all sorts of subjects. Kierkegaard abhors Hegelian reflection because it makes "everything . . . relative in the continuous process" of mediation.[41] If everything is relative in continual process, then there is no eternal idea to which one relates. No firm foundation means shifting sand. Kierkegaard explains,

> An age that is revolutionary but also reflecting and devoid of passion changes the expression of power into a *dialectical tour de force: it lets everything remain but subtly drains the meaning out of it; rather than culminating in an uprising, it exhausts the inner actuality of relations in a tension of whole existence into an equivocation that in its facticity is—while entirely privately a dialectical fraud interpolates a secret way of reading—that it is not.*[42]

Let us use an example of beauty. If Hegelian mediation is correct, then "beauty" is a *relative* opposite to "ugly"—meaning beauty is not an eternal standard by which we judge but only defined relative to its opposite. We ask, "Is a painting beautiful?" We respond, both "yes" and "no." In comparison to a child's drawing, "yes." In comparison to Rembrandt, "no." Beauty is not something fixed but merely relative to its surroundings, in

40. Lappano, "Coiled Spring," 785.

41. *CUP1*, 33 / *SKS* 7, 40.

42. *TA*, 77 / *SKS* 8, 74–75 (emphasis original).

the eye of the beholder. But if beauty truly is in the eye of the beholder, then there really is no such thing as "beautiful." It is a moniker of what Derrida calls *différance*, constantly deferred meaning. "Beautiful" is simply whatever I prefer. I can still use the word in public discourse, but it has no concrete foundation. I can write a treatise on beauty, clearly define it, and give examples, but all I am doing is giving an illusion of truth, an illusion that may unite the public in a tumultuous sea of meaninglessness.

When we have mass meaninglessness combined with a reflective culture and a task of *Dannelse*, then any individual who seeks to establish some form of bedrock foundation becomes a problem. Kierkegaard comments, "Ultimately the tension of reflection establishes itself as a principle, and just as *enthusiasm* is the unifying principle in a passionate age, so *envy* becomes the *negatively unifying principle* in a passionless and very reflective age."[43] Why is the crowd envious? Any sort of true excellence is a threat to their monopoly of mediocrity. Kierkegaard explains: "Envy in the process of *establishing* itself takes the form of *leveling*, and whereas a passionate age *accelerates, raises up and debases*, a reflective apathetic age does the opposite, it *stifles and impedes, it levels*."[44] Like playing whack-a-mole, the public seeks to squash any person who challenges its concept of popular opinion. Individuality is dangerous: it may mess up our finely ordered system, so the opposition must be leveled.

"The public," claims Kierkegaard, "is all and nothing, the most dangerous of all powers and the most meaningless."[45] The obvious danger is the public's power to rally a mob and punish contrarians, but another danger lies in its propagation of insipid chatter through media: "Together with the passionlessness and reflectiveness of the age, the abstraction 'the press' . . . gives rise to the abstraction's phantom, 'the public,' which is the real leveler."[46] By "the press," Kierkegaard means the media in general. Yi-Ping Ong remarks that "the references to seemingly innocuous aspects of our daily lives—newspapers, buses, the hours in a day—bring together the intangible and dehumanizing force of 'nothingness's public' with those aspects of our lives and environment that we find most familiar and reassuring."[47] Kierkegaard draws an analogy between the leveling

43. *TA*, 81 / *SKS* 8, 78.

44. *TA*, 84 / *SKS* 8, 80 (emphasis original).

45. *TA*, 93 / *SKS* 8, 89.

46. *TA*, 93 / *SKS* 8, 89.

47. Ong, "On Authenticity," 876.

of the media and a dog that attacks other people. Although lengthy, the quotation summarizes the sentiment well:

> The public keeps a dog for its amusement. This dog is the contemptible part of the literary world. If a superior person shows up, perhaps even a man of distinction, the dog is goaded to attack him, and then the fun begins. The nasty dog tears at his coattails, indulges in all sorts of rough tricks, until the public is tired of it all and says: That is enough now. So the public has done its leveling. The superior one, the stronger one, has been mistreated—and the dog, well, it remains a dog that even the public holds in contempt. In this way the leveling has been done by a third party; the public of nothingness has leveled through a third party that in and through its contemptibleness was already more than leveled and less than nothing. And the public is unrepentant, for after all it was not the public—in fact it was the dog, just as one tells children: It was the cat that did it. And the public is unrepentant because after all it was not really slander—it was just a bit of fun. . . . And the public will be unrepentant, for it actually does not keep the dog, it merely subscribes; neither did it directly goad the dog to attack nor whistle it back. . . . And if the dog is apprehended and sent . . . to be exterminated, the public could still say: It was really a good thing that the bad dog was exterminated; we all wanted it done—even the subscribers.[48]

Leveling turns into entertainment, and whenever someone points out the horrifying nature of what has taken place, the audience washes its hands, declaring itself a mere bystander. Merold Westphal explains that "for the amoral herd that fears boredom above all else, everything becomes entertainment. Sex and sports, politics and the arts are transformed into entertainment. Even religion will have to become show business if it is to survive."[49]

In the present age, we are inundated with meaningless information that poses as entertainment, and what we fear the most is silence. "Chattering," quips Kierkegaard, "dreads the moment of silence, which would reveal the emptiness."[50] We have to *do* something with silence. We can either ingest the chatter of the media, or we can look inward to become subjective. Kierkegaard comments, "The less ideality and the more externality, the more the conversation will tend to become a trivial rattling and

48. *TA*, 95 / *SKS* 8, 90–91.

49. Westphal, "Kierkegaard's Sociology," 143.

50. *TA*, 98 / *SKS* 8, 93.

name-dropping, references to persons with 'absolutely reliable' private information on what this one and that one, mentioned by name, have said, etc."[51] "Trivial" is the key to the present age. Chattering may have truth to it, but said truth in turn does nothing *for* the individual, has no essential relationship to the individual. Lappano notes that "according to Kierkegaard the press is not only happy to indulge the public, but it has an economic interest in doing so. . . . Therefore the titillating and *de jour* are elevated to public opinion."[52] The public, fueled by incessant drivel, deals out *soma* so that no transition to authentic religiousness occurs. Kierkegaard summarizes his present age: "The present age is basically sensible, perhaps knows more on the average than any previous generation, but it is devoid of passion. Everyone is well informed; we all know everything, every course to take and the alternative courses, but no one is willing to take it."[53]

4. THE DEIFIED CHURCH

Not only does the public become an amorphous blob of novel tastes and trends that levels any opposition, but unfortunately, any structure can level. *Practice in Christianity*, via pseudonym Anti-Climacus, concerns itself with "the requirement for being a Christian" in a monolithic culture of Christendom.[54] In part 2 of *Practice in Christianity*, Kierkegaard quotes Matt 15 where the Pharisees are offended by Jesus' disciples not following proper hand washing rituals when they eat. Christ declares, "It is not what goes into the mouth that defiles a person, but what comes out of the mouth; this defiles a person."[55] Kierkegaard remarks, "The established order, however, at that time insisted and always insist on being the objective, higher than each and every individual, than subjectivity."[56] The Pharisees want to be the intermediary between the individual and God. The religious elite become the standard bearers, the determiners of right and wrong.

Christ's chastisement of the religious leaders leads to *offense*. Who is this man from Nazareth to tell us what is righteous? Kierkegaard explains,

51. *TA*, 99 / *SKS* 8, 94.
52. Lappano, "Coiled Spring," 789.
53. *TA*, 104 / *SKS* 8, 99.
54. *PC*, 7 / *SKS* 12, 15.
55. Matt 15:11.
56. *PC*, 86 / *SKS* 12, 95.

"Every time a witness to the truth transforms truth into inwardness . . . every time a genius internalizes the true in an original way—then the established order will in fact be offended at him."[57] Christ does not *seek* to offend people. He outright declares, "Blessed is the one who is not offended by me."[58] Niels Cappelørn comments,

> It is not necessarily the case, however, that the individual aims to offend others by asserting that he or she is greater and truer than the establishment, the religious establishment. On the contrary, it is more often the case that it is the establishment which becomes offended *in order to protect its own self-divinization.*[59]

The Pharisees—and Kierkegaard's Christendom—elevate themselves in the place of God. "Being a Christian" simply means "following what the establishment declares."

When an establishment becomes the objective standard, one can never become truly subjective, for individuality is stifled by conformity. In the same way that the public cannot passionately relate to a citizen, a deified order cannot relate in the passion of subjectivity to a parishioner. An objective Christianity means following rules and cultural mores. Kierkegaard has a scathing critique:

> This deification of the established order is the perpetual revolt, the continual mutiny against God. . . . The deification of the established order . . . is the smug invention of the lazy, secular human mentality that wants to settle down and fancy that now there is total peace and security, now we have achieved the highest.[60]

Once the established order has deified itself, then it has "won" whatever war it conceived in its mind. All that needs to happen is for individuals to get with the program. Check the right boxes. Throw coins in the coffer. Participate in *Dannelse*. These activities—which may appear good—are rooted in objectivity rather than a place of authenticity. John Lippitt comments,

> *Can we afford to overlook the importance of character?* A person's ethical or religious character cannot be divorced from their passions: what they care about. The virtue-signaler cares about how they will be perceived by a particular in-group and is thus

57. *PC*, 87 / *SKS* 12, 96.

58. Matt 11:6.

59. Cappelørn, "Movements of Offense," 111 (my emphasis).

60. *PC*, 88 / *SKS* 12, 97.

> ultimately dependent upon what some analogue of "the public" thinks and cares about.[61]

Although many of Christendom's activities are morally good, if one does not *actually* believe in what he is doing, the act is immoral. These "good works" are merely glittering vices.

A deified church must maintain the status quo. Kierkegaard retorts, "What is meant by a triumphant Church? By this is meant a Church that assumes that the time of struggle is over, that the Church, although it is still in this world, has nothing more about or for which to struggle. But then, of course, the Church and this world have become synonymous."[62] The deified order is merely a reflection of the culture's values. Association with a religion becomes association with citizenship. As Lappano clarifies,

> The question before us is whether the doctrine of the Church tends towards professing a *national*, *nativist*, of *cultural* relationship to God over shared expressions of *existential* relationship to God. For Kierkegaard, no nation, race, or class received divine favor or salvation simply through membership in the nation, race, or class. Religious life and the God-relationship cannot bypass the individual. In Kierkegaard's view the church has allowed Christianity to become what it is not—a matter of national identity and a European historical-cultural achievement.[63]

One may argue that Kierkegaard's aversion to an established order combined with the supremacy of the individual envisions a solitary Christianity where no church is needed. Such thinking is conflating the source of authentic religiousness. The individual *becomes* a Christian through an individual leap to faith in the God-man. She is now relating to God—to the ideal—and she finds like minds who also relate to the ideal. They then congregate. This is the opposite of Christendom, where everyone directly relates to the church/culture, seeking one's definition in the hullabaloo of daily life. As Kierkegaard comments, "If everyone defines himself as being a Christian *just like* 'the others,' then no one, if it is looked at this way, is really confessing Christ."[64] In Christendom, individuals relate to the deified order. In Christianity, individuals relate to Christ.

61. Lippitt, "Kierkegaard, 'the Public,' and Vices," 17.

62. *PC*, 211–12 / *SKS* 12, 208.

63. Lappano, *Kierkegaard's Theology of Encounter*, 189.

64. *PC*, 219 / *SKS* 12, 214.

Authentic Christianity is a *danger* to the established order because is zaps it of power. Christendom will level individuals to maintain its status, but the act of leveling paradoxically decries the established order's true standing. In *Two Ages*, Kierkegaard explains,

> Only through a *suffering* act will the unrecognizable one dare to contribute to leveling and by the same suffering act will pass judgment on the instrument. He does not dare to defeat leveling outright . . . but in suffering he will defeat it and thereby experience in truth the law of his existence, which is not to rule, to guide, to lead but in suffering to serve, to help indirectly. Those who have not made the leap will interpret the suffering act of the unrecognizable one as his defeat, and those who have made the leap will have a vague idea that it was his victory.[65]

Christ Jesus defeated injustice through an act of suffering. The religious establishment *thought* it won. The prophet was crucified! Yet, as the apostle Paul reminds us, "We preach Christ crucified, a stumbling block to Jews and folly to Gentiles, but to those who are called, both Jews and Greeks, Christ the power of God and the wisdom of God. For the foolishness of God is wiser than men, and the weakness of God is stronger than men."[66] The visible act of Christendom leveling an individual *opens the door to real change, to subjectivity*. It is a gadfly, a buzzing reminder that all is not well. As Millay comments, "The purpose of *Practice in Christianity* is the maintenance of the status quo, with one important difference: *the status quo must admit that it is not equivalent to the ideal of Christianity*."[67]

5. CONCLUSIONS

Kierkegaard's reflection on his passionless age offers fertile ground for reflection on our contemporary age. Mass media is everywhere. We are awash in information throughout every moment of the day. The small devices in our pockets constantly buzz to remind us of what is new. Did you see what he said? I must respond immediately! Yet this buzzing is not a gadfly—it is the call of the public for us to participate in our own *Dannelse*. The question, then, is what are we building? Are we building "whatever is true, whatever is honorable, whatever is just, whatever is pure, whatever is lovely, whatever is commendable, if there is any excellence, if there is

65. *TA*, 109 / *SKS* 8, 103.

66. 1 Cor 1:23–25.

67. Millay, *Kierkegaard and the New Nationalism*, 2 (my emphasis).

anything worthy of praise," or are we constructing an abstract public, a deified order?[68] The applications of Kierkegaard's *Two Ages* are myriad, but two aspects come to my mind when thinking about apologetics.

First, whenever we are challenged, do we seek to level the opposition, pummel them into the ground? I am vexed by the attitude of certain Christians, seeing the lost as foes to vanquish. And if we mock them? Well, it was their fault for being so dumb. The truly intelligent will see that we are obviously correct! We create our deified order—idols of our own making. We start getting high on our own supply, buying into the deception of our own self-importance. We construct our own little kingdoms that cannot fall. We start granting ourselves exceptions, moving the goalposts whenever some inconvenience appears. Kierkegaard's analysis of Golden Age Denmark is a stark reminder for us to check our motives. Let us use an apologetic outreach event as an example. Why are we doing what we are doing? Is it to meet some quota? To fundraise? To get a certain level of likes or engagement? To sell our merch? To start a podcast network? To develop a curriculum to pitch to churches for a nominal fee? To remain so busy that we cannot sit in silent reflection? Or is it because we truly care about the mission of loving both God and our neighbor?

This is not to say that we cannot have programs, podcasts, and groups that sell merch. Kierkegaard's question is, "Are we creating objectivity, a program that hinders people from becoming subjective?" Remember, subjective individuality for Kierkegaard is not, "I do what I want," but rather it is an individual relating to God in *inwardness*. It is easy to fall into the trap of objectifying our own platforms. When our mission becomes routine, we are in dangerous waters of promoting *outwardness*. We risk deifying our parachurch groups and methods. When our consortiums and ministries become too big to fail, then we open the door to idolatry and the potential for abuse. Kierkegaard's analysis of crowd dynamics is a sobering reminder about *what* we are doing and *why* we are doing it.

Second, Kierkegaard's emphasis on suffering that comes from the leveling of the public should recall us to our crucified Lord. Immanuel, God with us, the perfect son of God came to seek and save that which was lost—the religious leaders, who should have embraced Jesus, turned him over to the authorities who strung him up on a tree and beat him to death. The Prince of Peace was *rejected* by the crowd. The crowd shouted,

68. Phil 4:8.

"Not this man, but Barabbas!"[69] We will take a murderer over the very Son of God. Paul reminds us that our task is to imitate Christ, including his sufferings: "The Spirit himself bears witness with our spirit that we are children of God, and if children, then heirs—heirs of God and fellow heirs with Christ, provided we suffer with him in order that we may also be glorified with him."[70] When we stand for truth, suffering will happen.

I had a professor who once said, "If you aren't seeing opposition, you probably aren't really following Jesus." We often think said opposition comes from "the world"—false religions and trends that actively attack Christianity. While the world does come into conflict with authentic Christianity, religious establishments with "correct" doctrine can be just as vicious. I need not relay examples from church history, both ancient and recent. We ought not seek out opposition, but if we identify with the crucified God, we will encounter suffering, from both the crowd and the deified religious establishment. As Peter charges us when facing persecution, "Humble yourselves, therefore, under the mighty hand of God so that at the proper time he may exalt you, casting all your anxieties on him, because he cares for you."[71] May we flee the temptation of enthroning ourselves as little lords of our own fiefdoms and chase after the Lord of all in passionate inwardness.

> And if I were a physician and someone asked me "What do you think should be done?" I would answer, "The first thing, the unconditional condition for anything to be done, consequently the very first thing that must be done is: create silence, bring about silence; God's Word cannot be heard, and if in order to be heard in the hullabaloo it must be shouted deafeningly with noisy instrumentation, then it is not God's Word; create silence! Ah, everything is noisy; and just as strong drink is said to stir the blood, so everything in our day, even the most insignificant project, even the most empty communication, is designed merely to jolt the sense or to stir up the masses, the crowd, the public, noise! And man, this clever fellow, seems to have become sleepless in order to invent ever new instruments to increase noise, to spread noise and insignificance with the greatest possible haste and on the greatest possible scale. . . . Oh, create silence!"[72]

69. John 18:40.

70. Rom 8:16–17.

71. 1 Pet 5:6–7.

72. *FSE* 47–48 / *SKS* 13, 73.

6

This Life of Care and Love

In the episode "End of the World" of the television show *Parks and Recreation*, Herb Scaifer, leader of the Reasonableists, claims that the world will end at dawn of the following day. Reasonableism teaches that Zorp is a "giant lizard god who will destroy the earth with his cleansing fire of judgment." Herb meets with Leslie Knope to reserve one of the parks in Pawnee, Indiana, for an all-night vigil, where Zorp will return and "your faces will be melted off and used as fuel." Leslie tells us that Herb's request is a common occurrence; the members of the cult incorrectly predict the end of the world every few years. Leslie comments, "It's super annoying. Turns out, when you think the world's ending, you don't aim so carefully in the port-a-potties." The episode juxtaposes the Zorpie vigil with Tom Haverford and Jean-Ralphio Saperstein's own party. Tom and Jean-Ralphio started a media conglomerate called Entertainment 720, which they quickly ran into the ground with their lack of business sense. With their remaining $10,000 after liquidating assets, Tom and Jean-Ralphio decide to celebrate the death of their company with an over-the-top "end of the world" celebration.

Reasonableism teaches reincarnation, as Herb explains to Chris Traeger: "From the universe, we emerge. Into the universe, we return. And there are infinite forms we can take in infinite universes. . . . This morning at dawn, you will take a new form, that of a fleshless, chattering skeleton, when Zorp the Surveyor arrives and burns your flesh off with his volcano mouth." Chris likes the idea of reincarnation, that his current life is not the only life that he will live. Ann Perkins has a poignant remark to Chris, "I think the danger in believing in reincarnation is that you spend so much time trying to figure out what you're going to be in the next lifetime that you forget to enjoy the one you're in now." Chris agrees, "Ann Perkins! That was beautiful! Let's go to that party Tom's having—have some fun in this life." The episode ends with the dawn of the following morning. After a successfully thrown party, Tom gets a kiss from a beautiful woman, while the Zorpies look foolish with their false prediction.[1]

While set in a zany scenario, the episode provides a critique of a certain type of religious belief that forgoes one's present, physical existence in order to find "true life" in a transcendent reality. Chris's interest in reincarnation almost caused him to miss out on *living* his present life, and, the critique goes, religion is detrimental because it fixes our attention on the hereafter rather than the right-here. This criticism is in no way unique to *Parks and Recreation*. Karl Marx famously states that "religion is the sigh of the oppressed creature, the sentiment of a heartless world, and the soul of soulless conditions. It is the *opium* of the people."[2] Friedrich Nietzsche states, "I beseech you, my brothers, *remain true to the earth*, and do not believe those who speak to you of otherworldly hopes! . . . Once the sin against God was the greatest sin, but God died, and those sinners died with him. To sin against the earth is now the most dreadful sin, and to esteem the entrails of the unknowable higher than the meaning of the earth!"[3] *Parks and Recreation* offers a similar, although informal, *existential* apologetic against an eternal-focused life, against the idea that true life only commences upon death.

Martin Hägglund is a recent example of one who critiques any form of supernaturalism, for he argues that belief in the eternal renders our earthly existence meaningless. In *This Life*, Hägglund states, "I do not want to die, since I want to sustain my life and the life of what I love. At the same time, I do not want my life to be eternal. An eternal life is not only unattainable but also undesirable, since it would eliminate the care and passion that animate my life."[4] Hägglund argues that eternal life is undesirable because a real threat of loss must be present for something to have meaning: "For anything to be intelligible *as mattering*—for anything

1. Holland, *Parks and Recreation*.
2. Marx, "Contribution to the Critique," 54.
3. Nietzsche, *Thus Spoke Zarathustra*, 10.
4. Hägglund, *This Life*, 4.

to be at stake—we have to believe in the irreplaceable value of someone or something that is finite."[5] Interestingly, Hägglund admits that his "critique of religious faith does not primarily appeal to scientific *knowledge*," but rather, Hägglund constructs an existential apologetic of atheism.[6] Hägglund argues for "secular" faith, a faith "devoted to a form of life that is bounded by time" rather than eternity.[7]

In this chapter, I address Hägglund's argument with the help of Søren Kierkegaard. Since Hägglund admits that his proposal is not primarily pinned to objective, scientific knowledge, Kierkegaard is an excellent resource to approach an existential argument for atheism. Furthermore, Hägglund devotes a chapter to Kierkegaard's *Fear and Trembling*, so Kierkegaard is a natural interlocutor for Hägglund's central thesis. Ultimately, I argue that Hägglund's secular faith breaks down as unintelligible and unlivable. To make my case, I start with Hägglund's primary argument for secular faith, looking particularly at his concepts of meaning, care, and love. Second, I critique Hägglund's central argument for secular faith. Third, we consider "The Cares of the Pagans" from Kierkegaard's *Christian Discourses* as a response to Hägglund's discourse on authentic care. Lastly, we look to Kierkegaard's *Works of Love* to assess what it means to be a truly loving person. Kierkegaard's wisdom concerning lived experience demonstrates a vibrant life of care and love for both God and neighbor.

1. SECULAR FAITH AND SPIRITUAL FREEDOM

Hägglund expounds his purpose in *This Life*: "I seek to show that an eternal life would not fulfill our desire to live on. The commitment to living on—rather than to eternal life—lies at the heart of secular faith."[8] If we have faith in any concept of eternal life—whether it be the Christian concept of heaven or the Buddhist concept of nirvana—then we do not truly *care* about our present circumstances. Hägglund explains that "the common denominator for what I call *religious* forms of faith is a devaluation of our finite lives as a lower form of being. . . . To be religious—or adopt a religious perspective on life—is to regard our finitude as a lack,

5. Hägglund, *This Life*, 49.

6. Hägglund, *This Life*, 13.

7. Hägglund, *This Life*, 6.

8. Hägglund, *This Life*, 28.

an illusion, or a fallen state of being."[9] If we see our present life as a prison or a temporary stop on the way to the "real" world, then we cannot truly *value* our present life as an end in itself. Since religious perspectives reverberate in all that we do—from politics to ethics to environmentalism—Hägglund argues that we need a *secular* faith, a faith committed to *this* life in order for humans to unlock their full potential—both as individuals and as a larger society.

Hägglund surprisingly uses the term "faith" in his atheistic project, for atheists usually view faith as a weakness, a closing of one's eyes to the brute facts of the world; but Hägglund wisely perceives science does not paint a proper portrait of our experience as existing individuals. He states, "I call it secular *faith*, since the object of devotion does not exist independently of those who believe in its importance and who keep it alive through their fidelity. The object of secular faith . . . is *inseparable* from what we do and how we do it."[10] The word "faith" illuminates the volitional nature of the commitments we make: "Caring about someone or something requires that we believe in its value, but it also requires that we believe that what is valued can cease to be."[11] The finite nature of everything—our lives, our goals, our loves—causes us to truly care, for we could lose any of these at any moment; such risk of loss makes things matter. Let us use the death of a loved one as an example. If I am eternal, meaning I will see my loved one again in heaven, then her death does not *ultimately* matter to me. I do not *care* that she is dead because I will see her again. Bringing it to individual purpose, if the life I toil to create—my passions, loves, accomplishments—is a temporary sojourn to the ultimate reality, then all of my striving is pointless; all my effort is moot once in the presence of God/nirvana/Brahman/Zorp/insert any form of transcendent paradise. Hägglund explains, "Being eternal is therefore *undesirable* and a standpoint of eternity is *unintelligible*, since it would remove any form of practical commitment that makes it possible to be engaged in the world."[12] Hägglund has a challenging explanation:

> The most fundamental form of secular faith is the faith that life is worth living, which is intrinsic in all forms of care. In caring about our own lives and the lives of others, we necessarily

9. Hägglund, *This Life*, 6.
10. Hägglund, *This Life*, 7.
11. Hägglund, *This Life*, 10.
12. Hägglund, *This Life*, 48.

> believe that life is worth living. This is a matter of faith because we cannot *prove* that life is worth living despite all the suffering it entails. That life is worth living cannot be demonstrated through logical deduction or rational calculation. Rather, the faith that life is worth living sustains us even when our lives seem unbearable or intolerable. Moreover, it is because we believe that life is worth living that our lives appear *as* unbearable or intolerable in the first place. If we did not believe that life is worth living, we could not experience our lives either as fulfilling or as unbearable, since we would be indifferent to the quality of our lives and unmoved by anything that happens.[13]

Let me illustrate Hägglund's perspective using our episode from *Parks and Recreation*. While the A and B storylines juxtapose the Zorpies against Tom and Jean-Ralphio, the C storyline follows the young married couple April and Andy. April finds out that Andy has a bucket list of things to do before he dies. Since the world may end that night, they decide to do as many items on the list as possible. Toward the end of the night, Andy attempts to throw in the towel. He wants to see the Grand Canyon, but it is a thirty-hour drive from Pawnee; furthermore, his car cannot handle the long trip. April replies: "So, I'll steal my dad's car! Look, this is a stupid idea, but right at this exact second, we have enough momentum to do something stupid before we realize how stupid it is!" Andy responds, "You are absolutely right. No thinking, just stupid!" The episode ends with Andy and April standing at the Grand Canyon in awe of its natural beauty. Their decision paid off in the end, although Andy is disappointed, asking, "Where's all the faces? Like the presidents." April and Andy have *secular* faith. Science cannot tell them the existential importance of seeing the Grand Canyon. All objectivity can do is provide data: how long it would take to travel, the average cost of gas, how many years of erosion formed the Grand Canyon, etc. What encourages April and Andy's adventure is the fact that someday, they will die, and they determine it would be a shame to not see the Grand Canyon before their death. They cannot *know* that seeing the Grand Canyon would be monumental until they experience it; they take it on faith that seeing the Grand Canyon is a goal worth having. They keep secular faith and achieved their goal, and they are rewarded with a meaningful experience they will remember for the rest of their lives. From Hägglund's perspective, religious faith would *prevent* April and Andy from truly living their

13. Hägglund, *This Life*, 49.

lives. They would have gone to the vigil to await Zorp's volcano mouth for their "real" life to begin.

Hägglund takes religious people to task, claiming that their religious faith is at odds with how they live their lives. Hägglund devotes a chapter on Saint Augustine and love. Augustine states that love of anything finite in and of itself is, as Hägglund puts it, "the 'wrong' kind of love since it makes us dependent on what we can lose."[14] Hägglund explains, "Hence, Augustine underlines that you should not enjoy (*frui*) anything in this life as an end in itself. Rather, you should use (*uti*) what you love as a means for devotion to the eternity of God."[15] If we do not love our family as ends in themselves, then they ultimately do not matter to us, argues Hägglund. Such a view is Stoicism repackaged, or ultimately, the Buddhist concept of nirvana, the death of individual personality. As Hägglund explicates,

> An endless existence would have no horizon of death and could therefore never be the life of a *person*. . . . Buddhism is remarkably honest about this implication of eternal life. Rather than promising that your life will continue, or that you will see you loved ones again, the goal of nirvana is to extinguish your life and your attachments.[16]

If, as Augustine posits, we use people as the means to love of God—the divine—then attachments to this world are ultimately an illusion. Christianity—and all forms of religious faith—collapses into the nonexistence of the individual: "The Buddhist standpoint [of nirvana] reveals the implication of all religious ideals of salvation."[17]

Hägglund offers a similar critique to Kierkegaard. Hägglund notes that while Kierkegaard focuses on the existential nature of *living* one's faith in the present, he is ultimately inconsistent. We recall from chapter 2 that *Fear and Trembling* is a poetic reflection on Abraham offering his son Isaac on Mount Moriah. God commanded Abraham to sacrifice Isaac, and Abraham did so without questioning. Kierkegaard—via Johannes de Silentio—states,

> Abraham makes two movements. He makes the infinite movement of resignation and gives up Isaac, which no one can understand because it is a private venture; but next, at every moment,

14. Hägglund, *This Life*, 78.
15. Hägglund, *This Life*, 79.
16. Hägglund, *This Life*, 204–5.
17. Hägglund, *This Life*, 211.

> he makes the movement of faith. This is his consolation. In other words, he is saying: But it will not happen, or if it does, the Lord will give me a new Isaac, that is, by virtue of the absurd.[18]

In Hägglund's reading of *Fear and Trembling*, he concludes,

> Thus, while Kierkegaard promotes a living religious faith as the highest of all, his own texts reveal why such faith must be completely *irresponsible* with regard to any other concern. Having religious faith means *not being responsive* to anything that calls your faith into question, even if it is the cry of your child as you are taking his life.[19]

Such religious faith Kierkegaard proposes is dangerous, shirking earthly responsibility by following an "absurd" divine command. Hägglund has a biting critique: "*Fear and Trembling* shows that . . . if there is a God for whom everything is possible, then anything can be permitted, even the killing of your own child for no reason other than God's command."[20]

Secular faith grants true freedom, according to Hägglund. Natural freedom is our ability to make our own choices—for example, April and Andy deciding to go to the Grand Canyon. Animals share in this natural freedom, like when a dog decides to run to the left instead of the right. What makes humans different from other animals is not an immaterial soul but what Hägglund calls *spiritual* freedom, "the ability to ask which imperatives to follow in light of our ends, as well as the ability to call into question, challenge, and transform our ends themselves."[21] We can question our beliefs, society, or upbringing, evaluating if we ought to follow them or not. We can "convert" to a new set of values or vocations. We are not "stuck" in some sort of naturalistic determinism. In fact, spiritual freedom allows us "the ability to ask [ourselves] what to do with [our] time."[22] Since this life is all there is, then *how* we spend our time is of the utmost importance. When April and Andy consider their mortality, they value the trip to the Grand Canyon rather than a boring night at the park with the Zorpies. Hägglund comments, "That you value your own finite time *renders intelligible the possibility of valuing anything at all*."[23] If we are

18. *FT*, 115 / *SKS* 4, 203.
19. Hägglund, *This Life*, 161.
20. Hägglund, *This Life*, 169.
21. Hägglund, *This Life*, 175.
22. Hägglund, *This Life*, 191.
23. Hägglund, *This Life*, 219 (emphasis original).

eternal beings, then what we do with our time on earth has no meaning. Once we achieve eternity, there is no past, present, or future, rendering no sense of the human self because we only understand ourselves *through* the prism of time. Hägglund notes that "the critique of religion . . . must therefore be an immanent critique,"[24] and Hägglund keeps his word. He does not challenge the historicity of the Bible or attempt to demonstrate logical contradictions in the Trinity. Hägglund's overall argument is that religious faith robs our present life of purpose and joy. Our immanent life is simply not worth living if religious faith is true; yet we all go about living. This, Hägglund argues, is proof that even religious people actually live by secular faith.

2. DOES IT EVEN MATTER ANYWAY?

Hägglund offers both a positive and negative apologetic for secular faith. He posits a way of living—secular faith focused on this life as an end in itself—and he criticizes religious faith because of its other-worldly focus. How can one respond? To start, any sort of objective formulation, like the cosmological or teleological argument, will get us nowhere, for Hägglund admits that his apologetic is not based on scientific data but an explanation of how humans best exist in the world.[25] In fact, Hägglund proclaims that the best argument religious faith may offer is the "existential value" it brings to the lives of believers.[26] Such admission is where Kierkegaard is of immense help to Christian apologetics.

Hägglund's key thesis is that what makes life worth living—what causes it to matter and have value—is its *finite* nature. If I can lose my loved ones, truly lose them, then I can truly *care* for them since their loss is an "irreplaceable value."[27] Such perspective makes sense at first glance. I used to play the *Star Wars Customizable Card Game* by Decipher, Inc. back in the mid-1990s. I love this game, but in 2001, Decipher lost the Star Wars license, ending its production. If I check the internet to purchase unopened packs of cards, the cost is outrageous because there is a finite limit to sealed cards. If I were allowed to print the cards on-demand, then there would be nothing special about them. The quantity

24. Hägglund, *This Life*, 332.
25. Hägglund, *This Life*, 13.
26. Hägglund, *This Life*, 54.
27. Hägglund, *This Life*, 49.

sets the value. In fact, I must handle my small collection with *care*, for if I destroy some of the cards, I may never get them back. The constant threat of loss, the constant "prospect of death," as Hägglund puts it, drives me to create meaning and purpose.[28]

Yet, there is something different between human lives and *Star Wars* cards. While finiteness does lead to scarcity, which determines value, we cannot distill down the unique nature of humanity to supply and demand. If Hägglund's thesis is true, then no life has purpose or meaning. For Hägglund, my life has meaning because someday I will lose it, driving me to *live* in the now with care: "The precarious existence of time is not only a negative peril but also the positive possibility of coming into being, living on, and being motivated to act."[29] Yet if this life is all that there is, then *I cannot lose my life in an existential sense*. In order to "lose" something I have to exist to experience its loss. Let me use sleep as an example. I am unconscious at night for eight hours. I will never know that eight hours have passed unless something transcends my unconsciousness. *I* wake up, *I* see the sun, and *I* look at the clock to realize that *I* lost time. The fact that something transcends my personal existence means that I can realize something is amiss. From a purely atheistic experience, *I cannot lose my life because "I" no longer exist after the neurons stop firing in my brain.* Hägglund admits as much: "No matter how long I live, I will never arrive at my death, since I cannot *be* dead."[30] If I cannot experience the loss of my life, then, according to Hägglund, my life does not really matter. If a finite life of secular faith does not really matter, then how, in good faith, can Hägglund levy an attack at religious faith on the same grounds, all the while declaring the superiority of secular faith? Hägglund may reply that the "horizon of my death" is what I *can* experience, and "in spatial terms, the horizon is the condition of possibility for anything to be visible at all."[31] Hägglund believes all religious faith collapses into Buddhistic nirvana, the erasure of individual existence in a timeless eternity. In Buddhism, personal attachments are illusions we should shed, and after many lives of reincarnation, we may cast off all care and achieve nirvana—a cosmic delete key. Illusion is what keeps us stuck in the cycle of *samsara*, a meaningless toil. But if I do not *lose* my life because I do not transcend to know that it is lost, then the "horizon of death" is similarly

28. Hägglund, *This Life*, 181.

29. Hägglund, *This Life*, 44.

30. Hägglund, *This Life*, 200.

31. Hägglund, *This Life*, 200.

an illusion. Death is not something "real" that one experiences, yet the illusion of the horizon is what drives Hägglund—an illusion that what he values matters, a similar *samsara*. While Hägglund argues that religious people are inconsistent in how they live, he steps into the same snare.

To leave the argument here would be a half response, a negative argument rather than a positive apologetic. The crux of Hägglund's argument, the sentiment behind secular faith, is that what we do *right now* matters, and people who say "God will sort it out in the end" are neglecting their responsibility to each other and the environment. "When we get to heaven" is the cry of either the lazy or those controlled by external forces, those who do not want to stand up and make change now. Hägglund's critique of religion is summarized by a few lines from the classic hymn "We're Marching to Zion" by Isaac Watts: "Then let our songs abound / And every tear by dry; / We're marching through Immanuel's ground / To fairer worlds on high." If we are marching through this world to the next, then why should I care for my neighbor? Why should I care about pollution? Why should I get married and have a family? To answer this, we will look at religious faith not as an *escape* from this world but as a *state of existence* of true life. Christian faith is neither Buddhism nor Platonism.

3. CARE

As Hägglund states, Kierkegaard emphasizes the need to live one's faith in the present. Kierkegaard loathes a Hegelian system that declares we can only know the abstract purpose of world history at the end—that is, once we die. For Kierkegaard, such a system gives no answer of how to *live* as an existing individual. Kierkegaard has many works on living the Christian life, and in *Christian Discourses*, he writes an extended section titled "The Cares of the Pagans," where he examines how pagans[32] have a heavy load of cares that Christians do not. Since the concept of "care" is vital to Hägglund's thesis, *Christian Discourses* is a natural place to turn when thinking about having religious faith in an uncertain world.

"The Cares of the Pagans" consists of eight reflections on Matt 6:24–34. In this famous passage from the Sermon on the Mount, Jesus teaches about worry, using the lilies and the birds as teachers:

32. The word "pagan" has a slightly different context in our modern world. "Pagan" sometimes conjures up images of Satanic Panic, Wicca, or sacrificing chickens in the dead of night. Kierkegaard uses "pagan" in the classical sense: non-Christian.

> No one can serve two masters. Either you will hate the one and love the other, or you will be devoted to the one and despise the other. You cannot serve both God and money.
>
> Therefore I tell you, do not worry about your life, what you will eat or drink; or about your body, what you will wear. Is not life more than food, and the body more than clothes? Look at the birds of the air; they do not sow or reap or store away in barns, and yet your heavenly Father feeds them. Are you not much more valuable than they? Can any one of you by worrying add a single hour to your life?
>
> And why do you worry about clothes? See how the flowers of the field grow. They do not labor or spin. Yet I tell you that not even Solomon in all his splendor was dressed like one of these. If that is how God clothes the grass of the field, which is here today and tomorrow is thrown into the fire, will he not much more clothe you—you of little faith? So do not worry, saying, "What shall we eat?" or "What shall we drink?" or "What shall we wear?" For the pagans run after all these things, and your heavenly Father knows that you need them. But seek first his kingdom and his righteousness, and all these things will be given to you as well. Therefore do not worry about tomorrow, for tomorrow will worry about itself. Each day has enough trouble of its own.[33]

Kierkegaard examines this passage numerous times in his writings. In chapter 3 we considered his treatment of Matt 6 from *Upbuilding Discourses in Various Spirits*. How Kierkegaard broaches the subject in *Christian Discourses* is unique because he seeks to demonstrate how the pagan lives *differently* from the authentic Christian. As Paul Carron remarks, "We can look at the people in Christian Denmark and see the kinds of cares they have. If the cares that the bird and the lily do not have exist among the people of Christian Denmark, then those Christians are actually pagan."[34] Such is Kierkegaard's continual strategy in his writing: what one is *in actuality* matters more than what one professes.

With what are pagans concerned? The first discourse discusses the care of poverty. The bird does not concern itself with poverty, but rather, it "lives on the *daily bread*, this heavenly food that is never stale."[35] The pagan, on the other hand, "is without God in the world and makes himself important . . . he becomes significant to himself by means of the

33. NIV.

34. Carron, "Turn Your Gaze Upward!," 326.

35. *CD*, 13 / *SKS* 9, 25.

thought that he is exclusively occupying himself with this life-question."[36] Such concern is warranted: we all exist in a world where we have needs that we must meet. My stomach grumbles, and I need food to live. The poor person worries because he does not have the means to buy food. But, to borrow Hägglund's categories, humans have "spiritual" freedom, the freedom to ponder how they will respond in the face of adversity. As Anne Strelis Söderquist puts it, "While *The Lily and the Bird* emphasizes our commonality with plants and animals as finite beings subject to 'necessity,' it also underlines that, unlike the lily and the bird, *we exercise our freedom in response to human embodiment*."[37] When we have possibility, we have anxiety. If we recall from our discussion on *The Concept of Anxiety* in chapter 3, we have two options in the face of anxiety. We can either hold onto our finiteness, or we can reach out to God for assistance. Sharon Krishek and Rick Furtak concisely demonstrate the predicament of worry:

> The state of "being worried" reflects at least three things: first, since we are worried about things we care about, it reflects our attachment to things which are dear and meaningful to us. Second, since "being worried" always regards the unknown (the "what will be"), it reflects our focus on the future—on the "tomorrow," as the Gospel puts it. . . . As a consequence of that, thirdly, "being worried" reflects our awareness of the vulnerability of the things we care about. That is, we know that there is nothing that can completely secure tomorrow: we have no way to ascertain the future security of what we care about.[38]

We are worried *because* we care. Hägglund would say such proves secular faith, for if we escape to transcendence then we do not have to care about the present. Yet do we have to have such an either/or? Kierkegaard comments, "The temptation is down on the earth. . . . It is to live *in order to slave*. . . . Yes, to slave! Instead of *working* for the daily bread, which every human being is commanded to do, to *slave* for it—and yet not be satisfied by it."[39] Kierkegaard juxtaposes slaving away and working. In Christianity, *work* is not something bad or ultimately an illusion. God

36. *CD*, 18 / *SKS* 9, 30.

37. Söderquist, "Finitude, Necessity, and Healing," 96 (my emphasis).

38. Krishek and Furtak, "Cure for Worry?," 160.

39. *CD*, 21 / *SKS* 10, 33.

created Adam and Eve to work.[40] The fall causes the work to become *toil*, opening the door for work to become slavery.

How does the worry of poverty become slavery? Would not the antidote be wealth? If I lack basic resources, then I am worried, a slave to my need. If I accrue more resources, then I will not have this concern. It seems apparent that I need to get myself out of poverty to set myself free. Kierkegaard responds, "A person thinks that wealth and abundance would keep him free from cares. . . . Wealth and abundance come hypocritically in sheep's clothing under the guise of safeguarding against cares and then themselves become the object of care, become *the care*."[41] God gives the bird *enough*, and enough is vital to keep us from worry. If I create my own definition of "enough," then there is no way to know if I *truly* have enough. I can redefine it at any moment. What if today, "enough" is $50, but tomorrow I think it $100? What if I am deceived in my assessment, letting my emotions get the best of me? What if I surmise I have enough but my neighbors have more, convincing me that I need to keep up with the Joneses?

Interestingly, the Danish term translated as "care" may also be translated as "worry." Carron explains, "First, *bekymring* sometimes refers to an emotion—worry. Second, *bekymring* sometimes refers to a care—a deeper concern or commitment. This dual usage *suggests a connection between emotions and concerns*: emotions are based on concerns and reveal important aspects of a person's character."[42] Our worries become our concerns, and our concerns become our worries. Such shows our propensity to spiral downward into worry whenever we do not have a solid foundation. Kierkegaard explains,

> When I have nothing in my hands, then I do not clutch anything either; but when I hold in my hands something that slips away through the fingers, something losable, what then am I clutching? Riches are indeed a possession, but actually or essentially to possess something of which the essential feature is losableness or that it can be lost is just as impossible as to sit down and yet walk—at least thought cannot get anything in its head except that this must be a delusion. . . . This matter of possessing is a delusion.[43]

40. Gen 2:15.

41. *CD*, 23 / *SKS* 10, 35.

42. Carron, "Turn Your Gaze Upward!," 326 (my emphasis).

43. *CD*, 27–28 / *SKS* 10, 39.

Wealth is a delusion, says Kierkegaard. We think we have wealth, but it can always be taken away. We think we have enough, but "just as there has never lived a bird that has ever taken more than *enough*, so there has never lived a rich pagan who has obtained *enough*."[44] The poor believe liberation comes through wealth. The rich believe liberation comes through maintaining wealth, but "the more wealth and abundance they acquire, the more knowledge they also acquire; and this knowledge, which is the care, does not satisfy the hunger, does not quench the thirst—no, it stimulates the hunger and intensifies the thirst."[45]

A common refrain appears in "The Care of the Pagans": slavery. As Kierkegaard expresses,

> Paganism is precisely doubleness, the two wills, masterlessness, or what amounts to the same thing, slavery. Paganism is a kingdom divided against itself, a kingdom in continual rebellion, where one tyrant succeeds another, but where there still is never any master. Paganism is a mind in rebellion; by the devil's help the devil of the moment is driven out, and seven worse ones come in.[46]

To kill God and to be true to the earth, as Nietzsche puts it, *sounds* like liberation, but one shackles himself to the fetters of constant anxiety. "Such a pagan," says Kierkegaard, "considers himself to be without care, especially without the many useless cares the God-fearing person has. But this is not true. . . . On the contrary, he is in the power of anxiety."[47] The weight of the world is figuratively on the shoulders of the pagan. She constructs her world—what she values, what she cares for, in what she places secular faith. She is responsible for these concerns; the impetus is on her to achieve the goals, but also the failure falls on her when she does not live up to her own standard. As Krishek and Furtak elucidate, "Thus, to compare oneself to God is, in effect, to want to depend on nothing other than oneself, or to do without God's help . . . and this ultimately means *refusing to come to terms with one's existential insecurity*. However, soon enough reality intervenes and proves that one is far from being self-sufficient—and one's worry only increases."[48] As Kierkegaard retorts, "Underlying the poet's life

44. *CD*, 34–35 / *SKS* 10, 46.
45. *CD*, 34 / *SKS* 10, 45.
46. *CD*, 87 / *SKS* 10, 95.
47. *CD*, 66 / *SKS* 10, 75.
48. Krishek and Furtak, "Cure for Worry?," 162 (my emphasis).

there is really the despair of being able to become what is wished, and this despair feeds *the wish*. . . . The poet is the child of eternity but lacks the earnestness of eternity."[49] To be without God in the world is slavery to oneself. It is wishing for something that cannot happen.

What, then, is Kierkegaard's response to our worries? Are we to ignore our present predicament and merely focus on the great beyond, to abstract ourselves out of earthly existence? Kierkegaard highlights the birds and lilies—parts of creation—as our teachers. If the physical is either something that does not matter or merely a shadow of the world to come, then why does Kierkegaard insist we learn from animals? G. P. Marcar offers insight on this dynamic:

> On Kierkegaard's reading, the birds and the lilies are not simply the *objects* of human stewardship; they are also the *teachers* through which this stewardship is *learned* (or relearned). In other words, the life and modus operandi of nonhuman animals are valuable not merely as means to human ends, but in and of themselves because from them, human beings learn how to properly relate to themselves, their circumstances, and these nonhuman creatures, before God.[50]

God uses his creation to teach us about living in the present world. Kierkegaard notes that "the Gospel itself is certainly the actual teacher, he *the Teacher*—and the Way and the Truth and the Life—as the instructor, but the bird and the lily are still there as a kind of assistant teachers."[51] Humans are a *part* of creation, and this is part of God's plan. True, we are made in the image of God, which separates us from the rest of nature in some sense, but our creatureliness, our limitations as creations of the Creator, is *not* something we are seeking to transcend. I concur with Krishek and Furtak's assessment: "Reflecting on a Biblical image from the Sermon on the Mount, Kierkegaard seeks to offer a 'cure' for worry: *not, we argue, advising his readers to become unconcerned about temporal existence*, but showing how the person of faith could live with his or her temporal concerns, without having to endure the torment of worry."[52] Christian faith does not *ignore* our finitude or treat it as something inherently evil. Sin is the issue, not our physical bodies. If we recall the end of the creation

49. *WA*, 8 / *SKS* 11, 14.

50. Marcar, "Godly Diversions and Gifted Teachers," 416.

51. *CD*, 9 / *SKS* 10, 21.

52. Krishek and Furtak, "Cure for Worry?," 158 (my emphasis).

narrative, "God saw everything that he had made, and behold, it was very good."[53] It is *good* to exist in this world. As Söderquist puts it, "Kierkegaard now brings attention to an accompanying gift embedded in our assignments: that we may also *take joy in our embodiment*."[54] Jesus' resurrected body was corporeal. He ate fish.[55] He even retained his scars.[56] I agree with N. T. Wright's frustrations: "The roots of the misunderstanding go very deep, not least into the *residual Platonism* that has infected whole swaths of Christian thinking and has misled people into supposing that Christians are meant to devalue this present world and our present bodies and regard them as shabby or shameful."[57] "Residual Platonism" improperly informs Hägglund's view of the Christian God.

There is joy in this life. Unfortunately, there are many sorrows. Right before Jesus is betrayed, he shares a final meal with his disciples. He says,

> Behold, the hour is coming, indeed it has come, when you will be scattered, each to his own home, and will leave me alone. Yet I am not alone, for the Father is with me. I have said these things to you, that in me you may have peace. In the world you will have tribulation. But take heart; I have overcome the world.[58]

What we see in Christianity is not a lack of care for the world *but a world in which God cares for us*. We are never alone, even when we face sorrow or worry. The bird needs to eat, but it is not alone; God cares for it. As humans we have numerous concerns in our lives. If, in anxiety, we "[lay] hold of finiteness to support [ourselves]," we entrap ourselves in a prison of our own making.[59] We seek to define right and wrong in our own eyes, a delusion that we can create our own meaning. We burden ourselves to be the source of both our meaning and our salvation. As Louise Keeley remarks,

> The seeking of the pagan originates and terminates in worry. Seeking fueled by worry exacerbates worry. Anxiety, left to itself, becomes its own best accelerant. . . . Worry demonstrates that what the pagan seeks—namely, control over one's own life and destiny, with no dependence whatsoever on Another—is doomed

53. Gen 1:31.
54. Söderquist, "Finitude, Necessity, and Healing," 109 (my emphasis).
55. Luke 24:36–42.
56. John 20:27.
57. Wright, *Surprised by Hope*, 18 (my emphasis).
58. John 16:32–33.
59. *CA*, 61 / *SKS* 4, 365.

> to fail. When worry takes action to secure its own future, its failure is constantly on display since no one is really independent.[60]

Secular faith severs us from any real anchor, casting us away to be marooned on our separate islands. Hägglund would fire back that secular faith "is not in opposition to sociality. . . . To 'own' your life is not to be independent but to be able to acknowledge your dependence."[61] In secular faith I may *acknowledge* my dependence on others, but I am truly alone in how I construct my values and purpose. *I* decide what *I* will believe about *my* surrounding community. Secular faith is playing solitaire in a room full of people playing solitaire. Even if we look to others for assistance, they are ultimately impotent to help. The life of the pagan is, as Kierkegaard relates, slavery to the created order.

4. LOVE

Hägglund contends that grounding love in transcendence leads to someone never loving a person as an end in him/herself but merely a means to an end. As Hägglund comments on Augustine's concept of love, "You should *neither* love yourself *nor* your neighbors in their own right. Neither your own self nor your neighbors have any value in themselves, but only by belonging to the eternity of God."[62] If we tightly grip onto an "earthly" love, then we are opening ourselves up to disappointment because "it makes us dependent on what we can lose."[63] As Hägglund posits, "What renders the world meaningless—or meaningful—is not an objective feature of what there is but proceeds from the degree of your attachment to what you see."[64] If our love is rooted in the eternal, then we have no real attachment to our loves on the earth. Religious people ought not to love anything or anyone other than God, yet so many supposedly devout people care about the world, demonstrating the hypocrisy of religious faith.

Can the Christian answer this charge? Are we inconsistent in loving our world and neighbor *and* God at the same time? We turn to Kierkegaard's *Works of Love* for assistance. In this book, Kierkegaard examines

60. Keeley, "Genius and the Saint," 63–64.
61. Hägglund, *This Life*, 23.
62. Hägglund, *This Life*, 79.
63. Hägglund, *This Life*, 78.
64. Hägglund, *This Life*, 97.

works of love, meaning how Christians ought to act lovingly in existence. Jesus declares that a summary of the Law and the Prophets is two simple, yet profound, commands: "You shall love the Lord your God with all your heart and with all your soul and with all your mind," and "you shall love your neighbor as yourself."[65] Kierkegaard declares that love is what "connects the temporal and eternity."[66] Love comes from God himself, who is love, the "source of all love in heaven and on earth."[67] If we profess love yet have not love in our actions, then we are merely a "noisy gong or a clanging cymbal," as the apostle Paul remind us.[68] A gong or a cymbal can force someone to pay attention to an action, but real love is known by its fruits.

Why are we commanded to love our neighbor as ourselves? It is easy to love people we like. Jesus says as much in the Sermon on the Mount: "If you love those who love you, what reward will you get? Are not even the tax collectors doing that? And if you greet only your own people, what are you doing more than others? Do not even pagans do that? Be perfect, therefore, as your heavenly Father is perfect."[69] Danish has several words for "love," which is problematic when talking about *Works of Love* in English. *Elskov* is "erotic" or "romantic" love; *Forkjerlighed* is "preferential love"; and Christian love is *Kjerlighed*. Kierkegaard states, "*Erotic love* [*Elskov*] *and friendship are preferential love* [*Forkjerlighed*] *and the passion of preferential love*; Christian love [*Kjerlighed*] is self-denial's love."[70] Michael Strawser explains the significance of different words for "love" in this passage: "Here Kierkegaard is arguing that *Elskov* is defined by an object, whereas *Kjerlighed* is defined by love, and thus he claims that *Elskov* and *Kjerlighed* are not essentially related."[71] *Elskov* must have an object: I have to romantically love some*one*. *Kjerlighed* has no object—no means to an end—which is why Kierkegaard declares "Christian love abides, and for that very reason it *is*."[72] Since love comes from God and God is eternal, love simply *is* because God *is*. *Kjerlighed* needs no object to exist in the same way God does not need any object to exist. Yet God

65. Matt 22:34–40.
66. *WL*, 6 / *SKS* 9, 14.
67. *WL*, 3 / *SKS* 9, 12.
68. 1 Cor 13:1.
69. Matt 5:46–48, NIV.
70. *WL*, 52 / *SKS* 9, 59 (emphasis original).
71. Strawser, *Kierkegaard and Philosophy of Love*, 116.
72. *WL*, 8 / *SKS* 9, 16.

did create the world, objects external to himself. Lee Barrett explains, "God's 'external' loving actions in creating, redeeming, and sustaining the cosmos *are outpourings of God's eternal life*. God is love in God's own self even apart from the existence of the universe."[73] If we love anyone, whether romantically or preferentially, because of what he or she does *for* us, then we are not *really* loving. We are using said person as an object of our own gratification rather than because he or she deserves to be loved. Notice, this is not how Hägglund thinks Christian love acts. In his reading of Augustine, Hägglund thinks we are to bypass the present person to get to God. To the contrary, Kierkegaard says God allows us to *truly* love the person in him or herself rather than a selfish form of preferential love, where value comes from what the person does for us.

When we consider that God is love and that he created, we see that the physical world is by no means something inferior, a lesser reality that distracts us from the true. God lovingly creates the world *because he is love*. The physical world only becomes an impediment whenever we enthrone it *as God* rather than experience it as the good *creation of God*. As Amber Bowen comments, "Rather than needing to control love, love appears phenomenologically as coming from 'elsewhere.' It is *a gift to be received*, not an object to be possessed or an unpredictable force to be corralled."[74] If we are called to love (*Kjerlighed*) our neighbor, then is preferential love (*Forkjerlighed*) evil? Kierkegaard does not believe so, but we are all too quick to jettison *true* love for our preferences. Krishek highlights the issue at hand:

> Distinguishing between preferential love . . . and neighborly love . . . [Kierkegaard] claims that the first is nothing but self-love, and that only the latter is genuine. Thus, Kierkegaard holds that in order to love genuinely, we need to love in the neighborly way. Essentially, this means that we need to shape our preferential loves (for our romantic beloveds and close friends, for example)—which Kierkegaard does take to be legitimate—in the image and nature of neighborly love.[75]

In my preferences, I must love in the way God loves: self-sacrificially and out of pure intentions. Let me illustrate. Let's say I surprise my wife with a bouquet of daisies (her favorite flower). I hand my wife the flowers,

73. Barrett, "Neighbor's Material and Social Well-Being," 146 (my emphasis).

74. Bowen, "Real Love," 594 (my emphasis).

75. Krishek, "Love as the End," 6.

and she says, "How sweet! What's the occasion?" There are a plethora of potential responses. Maybe I said something rude in the morning, and I am trying to get out of the doghouse. Maybe I need to convince her to do something I want, like spend money that we don't have on a TV we don't need. Maybe I feel guilty because I have not bought her flowers in a *really* long time, and I want to make myself feel like a good husband. The Christian answer is, "Because I love you and you deserve to be blessed"—no baggage, no ulterior motives, the same way God loves us. He loves us because he loves us. He loves us eternally, and he loved us in a very earthly way: "When the fullness of time had come, God sent forth his Son, born of woman, born under the law, to redeem those who were under the law, so that we might receive adoption as sons."[76] Did Christ put on flesh so that he might gain something from us? All he got from the world was rejection: "He was despised and rejected by men, a man of sorrows and acquainted with grief; and as one from whom men hide their faces he was despised, and we esteemed him not."[77] Knowing all of this, Christ willingly loved us. As Paul reminds us, "For while we were still weak, at the right time Christ died for the ungodly. For one will scarcely die for a righteous person—though perhaps for a good person one would dare even to die—but God shows his love for us in that while we were still sinners, Christ died for us."[78] *This* is *Kjerlighed*, the love of self-denial. Thomas Millay has an astute observation: "Thus the Christian ethic of *Works of Love* is . . . both *concrete and otherworldly*: it fully embraces actuality as it stands and chooses to work within it."[79] "Only by loving God above all else," writes Kierkegaard, "can one love the neighbor in the other human being."[80]

Still, one may protest, such self-denial is not *true* love if we are commanded to do it. Christ commands us to love our neighbor as ourselves. If God commands me to do it, then it is not authentic. Kierkegaard's response is that love is special in that it *redoubles*: "What love does, that it is; what it is, that it does—at one and the same moment. At the same moment it goes out of itself (the outward direction), it is in itself (the inward direction)."[81] When we choose to love, we become loving: "The

76. Gal 4:4–5.

77. Isa 53:3.

78. Rom 5:6–8.

79. Millay, "Concrete and Otherworldly," 37 (my emphasis).

80. *WL*, 58 / *SKS* 9, 64.

81. *WL*, 280 / *SKS* 9, 278.

one who loves is or becomes what he does."[82] Martin Andic describes the redoubling nature of love: "[The eternal] is present (says Kierkegaard) as one and the same thing both *out*wardly in what it is through you to others (when it goes 'beyond itself') and *in*wardly in what it is in you by whom it acts (when it 'turns back into itself') so that, in other words, what *you* outwardly do to others *it* inwardly does to you, and the other way around."[83] If I agree with God, that his ways are best and that I should love unconditionally, then when I follow the command of love, I become loving. I may "perform" a loving deed—say, donating to a charity—but *performance does not determine if the act is truly loving.* If I *do not* actually believe God, then when I donate to charity, I am not truly loving; if I donate for a tax write-off rather than out of Christian love (*Kjerlighed*), then I exercise preferential love (*Forkjerlighed*). If I love the neighbor because I am afraid God will punish me, then I, too, am exercising preferential love (*Forkjerlighed*) rather than Christian love (*Kjerlighed*). If fear of hell or attainment of reward is what drives my behavior, then I am merely attempting to serve my own ends, my own preferences. This selfishness redoubles, and although, from the outside perspective, I am loving, internally, I am not. Yet, truly loving the other is a positive redoubling, and as Kierkegaard notes, it inspires others to be loving as well: "When we say, 'Love gives bold confidence,' we are saying . . . wherever love is present, it spreads bold confidence."[84] As Robert Roberts explains, "Christian love, to the extent that it becomes a character trait, a deep personal quality *consequent on* intentionally undertaking to love the neighbor in response to the commandment, is a personal passion whose output *is* a spontaneous play of feelings about the neighbor."[85] Because God is the source of love, Kierkegaard explains, "*To love God is to love oneself truly; to help another person to love God is to love another person; to be helped by another person to love God is to be loved.*"[86] God's command to love is not a burden but an opportunity to change our hearts to be more loving. Since love redoubles in us we can be transformed into the loving people God desires us to be.

82. *WL*, 281 / *SKS* 9, 279.

83. Andic, "Love's Redoubling," 17.

84. *WL*, 280 / *SKS* 9, 278.

85. Roberts, *Recovering Christian Character*, 267.

86. *WL*, 107 / *SKS* 9, 111 (emphasis original).

5. CONCLUSION

Martin Hägglund's *This Life* is a well written and well-reasoned apologetic for atheism. Hägglund fears that religious faith leads to a lack of care for the world. Hägglund is right to be concerned. Plato's ghost lingers in the thoughts of many Christian theologians and philosophers. Hägglund's critique of Augustine has some weight to it. He cites Hannah Arendt a few times in his discussion on Augustine,[87] but I think Hägglund leaves out an important clarification from Arendt: "Undoubtedly, insofar as Augustine defines love as a kind of desire, he *hardly speaks as a Christian*. His starting point is not God who revealed himself to mankind, but the experience of the deplorable state of the human condition, and *whatever he has to say in this context is far from original in late antiquity*."[88] While I may not go as far as to say that Augustine was *un*christian, he is clearly affected by the Neoplatonic philosophy of his day, and as Rik Van Nieuwenhove comments, one "lasting influence upon Augustine . . . [was] the emphasis on the utter transcendence of the One."[89] Augustine is a titan in Western Christianity, and his Neoplatonic emphasis on an utterly transcendent God is still felt today. Jaroslav Pelikan rightly comments that "much of Western theology since [the council of] Orange . . . [is] 'a series of footnotes' to Augustine."[90] The "residual Platonism," as Wright puts it, is *not* an accurate portrayal of the God of Christianity.

Kierkegaard offers a vibrant picture of Christian existence. Christianity does not cause us to forego the physical in lieu of the spiritual. Christian living embraces the world with real care. Creation is good, although subject to travail because of sin. Humans are prone to idolatry, "[exchanging] the glory of the immortal God for images resembling mortal man and birds and animals and creeping things."[91] The only way to truly love—to truly care—for the world is through works of love. Christians are not burdened with the cares of the pagans, but not because we are seeking to escape the world. Since God cares for us, we know we are not abandoned in our time of need. Christians can truly love the world, but not because we are earning brownie points to escape to the "real" life of heaven. God does not despise his creation, for he sent Christ to defeat

87. Hägglund, *This Life*, 77, 79.

88. Arendt, *Love and Saint Augustine*, 21 (my emphasis).

89. Van Nieuwenhove, *Introduction to Medieval Theology*, 8.

90. Pelikan, *Emergence of the Catholic Tradition*, 330.

91. Rom 1:23.

sin and death, "the firstfruits of those who have fallen asleep." As Paul continues, "Thanks be to God, who gives us the victory through our Lord Jesus Christ. Therefore, my beloved brothers, be steadfast, immovable, always abounding in the work of the Lord, knowing that in the Lord your labor is not in vain."[92] Our work is not in vain because Christ has conquered the secular—not in a rejection of the world but in a redeeming of the world. True love, not preferential love, comes from the ultimate Love. True care, for anything to matter, comes from the ultimate Carer. As an existential apologetic, we must ask ourselves, which type of faith is more livable, more satisfactory? That answer is for each individual to decide. I concur with Kierkegaard: the life of the pagan is slavery.

> The abominable era of bond service is past, and so there is the aim of going further—by means of the abomination of abolishing the person's bond service in relation to God, to whom every human being, not by birth but by creation from nothing, belongs as a bond servant, and in such a way as no bond servant has ever belonged to an earthly master, who at least admits that thoughts and feelings are free; but he belongs to God in every thought, the most hidden; in every feeling, the most secret; in every movement, the most inward. Yet this bond service is found to be a burdensome encumbrance and therefore there is more or less open intent to depose God in order to install human beings—in the rights of humanity? No, that is not needed; God has already done that—in the rights of God. If God is dismissed, the place will indeed be vacant.
>
> As a reward for such presumption, all existence will in that way probably come closer and closer to being transformed into doubt or a vortex. . . . In this way human life transforms itself into one big excuse.[93]

92. 1 Cor 15:20, 57–58.

93. *WL*, 115–16 / *SKS* 9, 118–19.

Conclusion

As I sit down to write this conclusion, my mind is drawing a blank. My deadline looms ever closer, yet I am not sure how to start. My mind then starts racing: write something, anything! Then I start worrying that I will not have the right words or a pithy story. What if the book falls flat because the conclusion is terrible? Or what if I ink something subpar to get it across the finish line, but the reading audience eviscerates my work? Now my heart starts beating a little faster, and the worry redoubles in my mind. My predicament is the definition of ironic. I know, as a Christian, that God watches over me. We spent *a lot* of time in this book pondering how the bird and the lily teach us *not* to worry. I have continually stressed the need for more subjectivity—but here I am, being thoroughly *un*subjective. I know the objective truth, that my heavenly Father provides, that I should not worry—yet, the anxiety finds its way into my mind. We see how Kierkegaard's challenge is easy on paper but difficult in daily life.

But Kierkegaard's charge is needed. One of the best apologetic arguments Christians may offer is *how* they live. Do we really believe what we say? Our explanations and proofs are good; we ought to have rational responses to probing questions, but we must offer more than mere warrant. The apostle James poignantly remarks, "But someone will say, 'You have faith and I have works.' Show me your faith apart from your works, and I will show you my faith by my works."[1] Demonstrating our faith through our existence shows that we really buy in. Our faith is not just a good argument. The church is not just a social club. We believe in the resurrected Christ so much that we change how we act.

1. Jas 2:18.

Unfortunately, we all fail at perfectly living our faith. We hold onto objectivity without being subjective, like I exemplify in writing this conclusion. One of the most consistent lines from the non-Christian is that Christians are a bunch of hypocrites. *We are*, but we ought to respond to our own hypocrisy with an apology—that is, asking for forgiveness rather than demonstrating that we are right even when we are wrong. By admitting our frailty, our imperfection, our own struggles with anxiety and sin, we demonstrate that God is a God of grace, not of works. We walk in humility, for at the cross, we are all on level ground.

We have covered various topics on how Kierkegaard is an asset for apologetics. I sought to clear up some common misconceptions of his thought: his understanding of truth, the leap *to* faith, and his use of "absurd." I hope my work mollifies the concerns some apologists may hold so they view Kierkegaard as a legitimate resource, for he offers pertinent reminders for our current context. He emphasizes our human condition, the limitations of our knowledge, and our tendency toward distraction. We must remember that we are creations of the Creator. God created us to live in truth rather than simply possessing the truth, and our logical formulations do not capture all that there is of God. Subjectivity is needed in our world of labels, marketing, and catchy slogans. Apologetics deals with objective facts, but we cannot forget the subjective.

Kierkegaard reminds us that our audience is coming from some point of view, a sphere of existence. Considering the sphere assists us to present the gospel or apologetic defense in a manner that our audience understands. We are all prone to jargon: we become so steeped in our field that we forget what it was like to not be in the conversation. When doing apologetics, we must truly know our audience! Sometimes, we use our technical terms. Sometimes, we directly address ideas. Sometimes, an indirect approach is best. It depends on who we interact with. Indirect apologetics is something the church ought to take up. There are a variety of ways that we can present a defense of Christianity, and we need to think creatively on how to portray the truth of Christianity. Furthermore, Kierkegaard provides us a real-life example of what happens when we over-institutionalize something—whether it be an apologetic platform, a church, or a charismatic leader. We love to make idols, to define ourselves by a physical something rather than the ineffable God. An apologetic enterprise may start off as a good ministry, but it may also transform into a deified order that levels any form of opposition. We do well to heed Kierkegaard's call, avoiding a passionless, blind following of a program, "continually on the move[,] hunting for something to do 'on principle'" rather than passionate inwardness.[2]

For the one who wants to leap into reading Kierkegaard for him or herself, I have a few recommendations. I would start with some of his signed, upbuilding discourses. These will give the reader an introduction to Kierkegaard's writing style and serve as a first step to his more challenging works. Kierkegaard wrote the discourses for the average Christian, so the theological and philosophical jargon are at a minimum. I propose starting with either *Christian Discourses*, *Three Discourses on Imagined Occasions*, or *Works of Love*. After getting one's feet wet with the signed discourses, I would proceed to the pseudonymous works. I think *Philosophical Fragments* is a great place to start. It is relatively short, and the content of the book is about the nature of God's revelation to humanity. *The Sickness unto Death* is a fantastic starting point that holds a special place in my heart, but I proffer a warning: the first few pages are some of the toughest reading there is; but if one perseveres, the book gets significantly easier. I suggest Bruce Kirmmse's new translation. It has a robust historical introduction with a highly readable translation. If one wants some of Kierkegaard's more poetic works, *Either/Or* may be a starting point, with the caveat that it is exceedingly long. Some of the chapters go on for over one hundred pages, which may be daunting to some readers. *Stages on Life's Way* may be a better option instead, for it has similar themes and artistry with more digestible sections. I would advise against jumping into *Fear and Trembling* or *Concluding Unscientific Postscript* until reading a few of Kierkegaard's other pseudonymous works. These two works are easy to misinterpret, although I believe them to be brilliant works that Christians should read. Lastly, I suggest the oft-overlooked *Two Ages*. In our modern world of AI and instantaneous communication, Kierkegaard's short work is a gold mine of wisdom for our current age.

I end with the beginning. My personal experience with doubt led me to where I am today. I am thankful that I had godly people around me who were patient, who did not treat my questions as a burden. I am thankful that, as Kierkegaard says, "in heaven, my listener, there lives the God who is capable of all things."[3] Our Father watches over us, leading and guiding us as we work out our "salvation with fear and trembling."[4] We are never alone, and this is a great comfort in our time of need. The

2. *TA*, 101 / *SKS* 8, 96.

3. *EUD*, 309–10 / *SKS* 5, 302.

4. Phil 2:12.

love and acceptance, the mercy and grace, the conquering of death—the gospel "is the power of God for salvation to everyone who believes."[5] The gospel is *why* we do apologetics. We want others to "taste and see that the LORD is good."[6] The Christian will have doubts on life's way. The non-Christian, like Johannes de Silentio, will be befuddled by faith. Christians have the glorious opportunity to aid people in their faith journey. I cannot save anyone, but God partners with the church in growing the kingdom of God. As Paul reminds us, "I planted, Apollos watered, but God gave the growth. So neither he who plants nor he who waters is anything, but only God who gives the growth."[7] We have the privilege of being a part of God's kingdom. We get to help answer questions, as William Lane Craig puts it, about "what rational warrant can be given for the Christian faith."[8] We also have the opportunity to show that one "demonstrates the existence of God by worship—not by demonstrations."[9] Both sides of the coin—the objective and the subjective—are needed for a wholistic faith. I pray that we may both know the truth and live the truth, "for only the truth that builds up is truth for you."[10]

> Indeed, what more powerful expression of wonder is there than for the wonderer to become as if changed, than for the wisher to change color; what more powerful expression than this, that he *actually* becomes changed! And so it is with this wonder—it changes the seeker; and so it is with this change—it seeks to become something else, indeed, become the very opposite: to seek means that the seeker himself is changed. He is not to look for the place where the object of his seeking is, because it is right with him; he is not to look for the place where God is, he is not to strive to get there, because God is right there with him, very near, everywhere near, at every moment everywhere present, but the seeker must be changed so that he himself can become the place where God in truth is.[11]

5. Rom 1:16.
6. Ps 34:8.
7. 1 Cor 3:6–7.
8. Craig, *Reasonable Faith*, 15.
9. *CUP1*, 546 / *SKS* 7, 469.
10. *EO2*, 354 / *SKS* 3, 332.
11. *TD*, 23 / *SKS* 5, 403–4.

Bibliography

Adorno, Theodor W. *Hegel: Three Studies*. 2nd ed. Translated by Shierry Weber Nicholsen. Studies in Contemporary German Social Thought. Cambridge, MA: MIT Press, 1999.

Anderson, Tawa J., et al. *An Introduction to Christian Worldview: Pursuing God's Perspective in a Pluralistic World*. Downers Grove, IL: IVP Academic, 2017.

Andic, Martin. "Love's Redoubling and the Eternal Like for Like." In *Works of Love*, edited by Robert L. Perkins, 9–38. International Kierkegaard Commentary 16. Macon, GA: Mercer University Press, 1999.

Anselm. *Proslogion*. In *Anselm of Canterbury: The Major Works*, edited by Brian Davies and G. R. Evans, translated by M. J. Charlesworth, 82–104. Oxford: Oxford University Press, 1998.

Arendt, Hannah. *Love and Saint Augustine*. Edited by Joanna Vecchiarelli Scott and Judith Chelius Stark. Chicago: University of Chicago Press, 1996.

The Augsburg Confession. In *The Creeds of Christendom, with a History and Critical Notes: The Evangelical Protestant Creeds, with Translations*, edited by Philip Schaff, translated by Charles P. Krauth, 3:3–73. New York: Harper & Brothers, 1882.

Augustine. *Confessions*. Translated by R. S. Pine-Coffin. New York: Penguin, 1961.

———. *On Christian Doctrine*. In *St. Augustin's City of God and Christian Doctrine*, edited by Philip Schaff, translated by J. F. Shaw, 2:515–97. A Select Library of the Nicene and Post-Nicene Fathers of the Christian Church, First Series. Buffalo: Christian Literature, 1887.

———. *On the Trinity*. In *St. Augustin: On the Holy Trinity, Doctrinal Treatises, Moral Treatises*, edited by Philip Schaff, translated by Arthur West Haddan, 3:3–228. A Select Library of the Nicene and Post-Nicene Fathers of the Christian Church, First Series. Buffalo: Christian Literature, 1887.

Barrett, Lee C. "Kierkegaard's 'Anxiety' and the Augustinian Doctrine of Original Sin." In *The Concept of Anxiety*, edited by Robert L. Perkins, 35–61. International Kierkegaard Commentary 8. Macon, GA: Mercer University Press, 1985.

———. "Kierkegaard's Authorship and the Paradox of Divine and Human Agencies." In *The Point of View*, edited by Robert L. Perkins, 48–77. International Kierkegaard Commentary 22. Macon, GA: Macon University Press, 2010.

———. "The Neighbor's Material and Social Well-Being in Kierkegaard's *Works of Love*: Does It Matter?" In *Works of Love*, edited by Robert L. Perkins, 137–65. International Kierkegaard Commentary 16. Macon, GA: Mercer University Press, 1999.

———. "The Passion of Kierkegaard's Existential Method." In *The Kierkegaardian Mind*, edited by Adam Buben, et al., 17–27. The Routledge Philosophical Minds. London: Routledge, 2019.

Barth, Karl. *The Epistle to the Romans*. 6th ed. Translated by Edwyn C. Hoskyns. Oxford: Oxford University Press, 1968.

Berkhof, Louis. *Systematic Theology*. 4th ed. Grand Rapids: Eerdmans, 1938.

Berthold, Daniel. "Kierkegaard's Seductions: The Ethics of Authorship." *MLN* 120.5 (2005) 1044–65. https://doi.org/10.1353/mln.2006.0002.

Blackburn, Simon. *The Oxford Dictionary of Philosophy*. Oxford Paperback Reference. New York: Oxford University Press, 1996.

Bonhoeffer, Dietrich. *The Cost of Discipleship*. Translated by R. H. Fuller. New York: Simon & Schuster, 1995.

Bowen, Amber. "Real Love: Kierkegaard, the Seducer, the Judge, and the Altar." *Journal of Religious Ethics* 49.3 (2021) 577–95.

Brunner, Emil. *God and Man: Four Essays on the Nature of Personality*. Translated by David Cairns. London: Student Christian Movement, 1936.

Buber, Martin. *Eclipse of God: Studies in the Relation Between Religion and Philosophy*. New York: Harper, 1952.

Byrne, James M. *Religion and the Enlightenment: From Descartes to Kant*. Louisville: Westminster John Knox, 1996.

Calvin, John. *Institutes of the Christian Religion*. Translated by Henry Beveridge. Peabody, MA: Hendrickson, 2009.

Cappelørn, Niels Jørgen. "The Movements of Offense Toward, Away from, and Within Faith: 'Blessed Is He Who Is Not Offended at Me.'" In *Practice in Christianity*, translated by K. Brian Söderquist, 95–124. International Kierkegaard Commentary 20. Macon, GA: Mercer University Press, 2004.

———. "The Retrospective Understanding of Søren Kierkegaard's Total Production." In *Kierkegaard: Resources and Results*, edited by Alastair McKinnon, 18–38. Montreal: Wilfrid Laurier University Press, 1982.

Carron, Paul. "Turn Your Gaze Upward! Emotions, Concerns, and Regulatory Strategies in Kierkegaard's Christian Discourses." *International Journal for Philosophy of Religion* 84.3 (2018) 323–43.

Connell, George. "The Importance of Being Earnest: Coming to Terms with Judge William's Seriousness." In *Stages on Life's Way*, edited by Robert L. Perkins, 113–48. International Kierkegaard Commentary 11. Macon, GA: Mercer University Press, 2000.

Craig, William Lane. *Reasonable Faith: Christian Truth and Apologetics*. 3rd ed. Wheaton, IL: Crossway, 2008.

Crites, Stephen. "'The Blissful Security of the Moment': Recollection, Repetition, and Eternal Recurrence." In *Fear and Trembling and Repetition*, edited by Robert L. Perkins, 225–46. International Kierkegaard Commentary 6. Macon, GA: Mercer University Press, 1993.

———. "Pseudonymous Authorship as Art and as Act." In *Kierkegaard: A Collection of Critical Essays*, edited by Josiah Thompson, 183–229. Garden City, NY: Anchor, 1972.

———. "The Unfathomable Stupidity of Nicolaus Notabene." In *Prefaces and Writing Sample and Three Discourses on Imagined Occasions*, edited by Robert L. Perkins, 29–40. International Kierkegaard Commentary 9–10. Macon, GA: Mercer University Press, 2006.

Cuarón, Alfonso, dir. *Children of Men*. Universal City, CA: Universal, 2006.

Daise, Benjamin. *Kierkegaard's Socratic Art*. Macon, GA: Mercer University Press, 1999.

Davis, Melissa. "Sabbath as a Counter-Formational Practice in a Culture of Busyness." *Journal of the Evangelical Theological Society* 64.3 (2021) 563–81.

Deede, Kristen K. "The Infinite Qualitative Difference: Sin, the Self, and Revelation in the Thought of Søren Kierkegaard." *International Journal for Philosophy of Religion* 53.1 (2003) 25–48.

Descartes, René. *Discourse on Method and Meditations on the First Philosophy*. Translated by John Veitch. New York: Barnes & Noble, 2004.

Dew, James K., Jr., and Paul M. Gould. *Philosophy: A Christian Introduction*. Grand Rapids: Baker Academic, 2019.

Dewey, Bradley R. "Seven Seducers: A Typology of Interpretations of the Aesthetic Stage in Kierkegaard's 'The Seducer's Diary.'" In *Either/Or, Part I*, edited by Robert L. Perkins, 159–99. International Kierkegaard Commentary 3. Macon: Mercer University Press, 1995.

Dunning, Stephen N. "Transformed by the Gospel: What We Learn About the Stages from the Lillies and the Birds." In *Upbuilding Discourses in Various Spirits*, edited by Robert L. Perkins, 111–28. International Kierkegaard Commentary 15. Macon, GA: Mercer University Press, 2005.

Dupré, Louis K. "Of Time and Eternity." In *The Concept of Anxiety*, edited by Robert L. Perkins, 111–31. International Kierkegaard Commentary 8. Macon, GA: Mercer University Press, 1985.

Edwards, Aaron P. "Thrill of the Chaste: The Pursuit of 'Love' as the Perpetual Dialectic between the 'Real' and the 'Ideal Image' in Kierkegaard's *The Seducer's Diary*." *Literature and Theology* 30.1 (2016) 15–32. https://doi.org/10.1093/litthe/fru055.

Erickson, Millard. *Christian Theology*. 3rd ed. Grand Rapids: Baker Academic, 2013.

Evans, C. Stephen. "Faith as the *Telos* of Morality: A Reading of *Fear and Trembling*." In *Fear and Trembling and Repetition*, edited by Robert L. Perkins, 9–27. International Kierkegaard Commentary 6. Macon, GA: Mercer University Press, 1993.

———. *Kierkegaard: An Introduction*. Cambridge: Cambridge University Press, 2009.

Farley, Harry. "Ravi Zacharias Denies 'Grooming' Accusations: 'I Have Learned a Difficult and Painful Lesson.'" *Christian Today*, Dec. 4, 2017. https://www.christiantoday.com/news/ravi-zacharias-denies-grooming-accusations-i-have-learned-a-difficult-and-painful-lesson.

Ferreira, M. Jamie. "Faith and the Kierkegaardian Leap." In *The Cambridge Companion to Kierkegaard*, 207–34. Cambridge: Cambridge University Press, 1998.

Findlay, J. N. *Hegel: A Re-Examination*. Muirhead Library of Philosophy. New York: Routledge, 2013.

Gabriel, Merigala. *Subjectivity and Religious Truth in the Philosophy of Søren Kierkegaard*. Macon, GA: Mercer University Press, 2010.

Garff, Joakim. "The Eyes of Argus: *The Point of View* and Points of View on Kierkegaard's Work as an Author." In *Kierkegaard: A Critical Reader*, translated by Jane Chamberlain and Belinda Ioni Rasmussen, 75–102. Oxford: Blackwell, 1998.

———. *Søren Kierkegaard: A Biography*. Translated by Bruce H. Kirmmse. Princeton: Princeton University Press, 2005.

Garrett, James Leo, Jr. *Systematic Theology: Biblical, Historical, and Evangelical.* Vol. 1. Grand Rapids: Eerdmans, 1990.

Glenn, John D., Jr. "The Definition of the Self and the Structure of Kierkegaard's Work." In *The Sickness unto Death*, edited by Robert L. Perkins, 5–21. International Kierkegaard Commentary 19. Macon: Mercer University Press, 1987.

Gouwens, David Jay. *Kierkegaard as Religious Thinker.* Cambridge: Cambridge University Press, 1996.

Green, Ronald M. "'Developing' *Fear and Trembling*." In *The Cambridge Companion to Kierkegaard*, edited by Alastair Hannay and Gordon D. Marino, 257–81. Cambridge: Cambridge University Press, 1998.

———. "Enough Is Enough! *Fear and Trembling* Is *Not* About Ethics." *Journal of Religious Ethics* 21.2 (1993) 191–209.

Grøn, Arne. *The Concept of Anxiety in Søren Kierkegaard.* Translated by Jeanette B. L. Knox. Macon, GA: Mercer University Press, 2008.

———. "The Concept of Existence." In *Kierkegaard's Existential Approach*, edited by Arne Grøn, et al., 71–90. Kierkegaard Studies Monograph Series 35. Berlin: De Gruyter, 2017.

Groothuis, Douglas. *Christian Apologetics: A Comprehensive Case for Biblical Faith.* 2nd ed. Downers Grove, IL: InterVarsity, 2022.

Guthrie, Shirley C., Jr. *Christian Doctrine.* Revised ed. Louisville: Westminster John Knox, 1994.

Hägglund, Martin. *This Life: Secular Faith and Spiritual Freedom.* New York: Anchor, 2020.

Hall, Amy Laura. *Kierkegaard and the Treachery of Love.* Cambridge Studies in Religion and Critical Thought. Cambridge: Cambridge University Press, 2002.

Hannay, Alastair. "Having Lessing on One's Side." In *Concluding Unscientific Postscript to "Philosophical Fragments."* International Kierkegaard Commentary 12. Macon, GA: Mercer University Press, 1997.

———. *Kierkegaard: A Biography.* Cambridge: Cambridge University Press, 2001.

———. "Spirit and the Idea of the Self as a Reflexive Relation." In *The Sickness unto Death*, edited by Robert L. Perkins, 23–38. International Kierkegaard Commentary 19. Macon, GA: Mercer University Press, 1987.

Hanson, Jeffrey. *Kierkegaard and the Life of Faith: The Aesthetic, the Ethical, and the Religious in Fear and Trembling.* Indiana Series in the Philosophy of Religion. Bloomington: Indiana University Press, 2017.

Harwood, Adam. *The Spiritual Condition of Infants: A Biblical-Historical Survey and Systematic Proposal.* Eugene, OR: Wipf & Stock, 2011.

Hegel, Georg Wilhelm Friedrich. *Grundlinien Der Philosophie Des Rechts.* Leipzig: F. Meiner, 1911.

———. *Phenomenology of Spirit.* Translated by A. V. Miller. New York: Oxford University Press, 1977.

———. *Philosophy of Right.* Translated by S. W. Dyde. New York: Prometheus, 1996.

Hodge, Charles. *Systematic Theology.* Vol. 1. New York: Charles Scribner, 1872.

Holland, Dean, dir. *Parks and Recreation.* Season 4, episode 6, "End of the World." Aired Nov. 3, 2011, on NBC.

Hong, Howard V., and Edna H. Hong. "Historical Introduction." In *The Corsair Affair and Articles Related to the Writings*, translated by Howard V. Hong and Edna H. Hong, vii–xxxviii. Princeton: Princeton University Press, 1982.

Jensen, Kipton E. "The Principle of Protestantism: On Hegel's (Mis)Reading of Schleiermacher's Speeches." *Journal of the American Academy of Religion* 71.2 (2003) 405–22. https://doi.org/10.1093/jaar/71.2.405.

Jones, Terry, dir. *Monty Python's Life of Brian*. London: Cinema International, 1979.

Jones, W. T. *A History of Western Philosophy: Kant and the Nineteenth Century*. 2nd ed. Belmont, CA: Thomson Wadsworth, 1975.

Jordán, Nassim Bravo. "Nicolaus Notabene: Kierkegaard's Satirical Mask." In *Kierkegaard's Pseudonyms*, edited by Katalin Nun and Jon Stewart, 193–204. Kierkegaard Research: Sources, Reception and Resources 17. Burlington, VT: Ashgate, 2015.

Kain, Philip J. *Hegel and Right: A Study of the Philosophy of Right*. Albany, NY: SUNY Press, 2018.

Keeley, Louise Carroll. "The Genius and the Saint: The Spiritual Teaching of Kierkegaard in *Christian Discourses* and Thérèse of Lisieux in *Story of a Soul*." In *Christian Discourses and The Crisis and a Crisis in the Life of an Actress*, edited by Robert L. Perkins, 61–93. International Kierkegaard Commentary 17. Macon, GA: Mercer University Press, 2007.

Keller, Timothy. "The Sickness unto Death." Gospel in Life, Sept. 14, 2003. https://gospelinlife.com/sermon/the-sickness-unto-death/.

Kemp, Ryan. "Johannes de Silentio: Religious Poet or Faithless Aesthete?" In *Kierkegaard's Pseudonyms*, edited by Katalin Nun and Jon Stewart, 143–58. Kierkegaard Research: Sources, Reception and Resources 17. Burlington, VT: Ashgate, 2015

Kirmmse, Bruce H., ed. *Encounters with Kierkegaard: A Life as Seen by His Contemporaries*. Translated by Bruce H. Kirmmse and Virginia R. Laursen. Princeton: Princeton University Press, 1998.

———. *Kierkegaard in Golden Age Denmark*. Indiana Series in the Philosophy of Religion. Bloomington: Indiana University Press, 1990.

———. "'Out with It!': The Modern Breakthrough, Kierkegaard and Denmark." In *The Cambridge Companion to Kierkegaard*, edited by Alastair Hannay and Gordon D. Marino, 15–47. Cambridge: Cambridge University Press, 1998.

Kjældgaard, Lasse Horne. "The Age of Miscellaneous Announcements: Paratextualism in Kierkegaard's *Prefaces* and Contemporary Literary Culture." In *Prefaces and Writing Sample and Three Discourses on Imagined Occasions*, edited by Robert L. Perkins, 7–28. International Kierkegaard Commentary 9–10. Macon, GA: Mercer University Press, 2006.

Kline, Peter. "Imaging Nothing: Kierkegaard and the Imago Dei." *Anglican Theological Review* 100.4 (2018) 697–719.

Kramer, Nathaniel. "Johannes the Seducer: The Aesthete *Par Excellence* or on the Way to Ethics?" In *Kierkegaard's Pseudonyms*, edited by Katalin Nun and Jon Stewart, 159–76. Kierkegaard Research: Sources, Reception and Resources 17. Burlington, VT: Ashgate, 2015.

Kreeft, Peter, and Ronald L. Tacelli. *Handbook of Christian Apologetics: Hundreds of Answers to Crucial Questions*. Downers Grove, IL: IVP Academic, 1994.

Krishek, Sharon. "Love as the End of Human Existence." In *Kierkegaard's God and the Good Life*, edited by Stephen Minister et al., 3–15. Indiana Series in the Philosophy of Religion. Bloomington: Indiana University Press, 2017.

Krishek, Sharon, and Rick Anthony Furtak. "A Cure for Worry? Kierkegaardian Faith and the Insecurity of Human Existence." *International Journal for Philosophy of Religion* 72.3 (2012) 157–75. https://doi.org/10.1007/s11153-11-9322-25.

Lappano, David. "A Coiled Spring: Kierkegaard on the Press, the Public, and a Crisis of Communication." *Heythrop Journal* 55.5 (2014) 783–98. https://doi.org/10.1111/heyj.12220.

———. *Kierkegaard's Theology of Encounter: An Edifying and Polemical Life*. Oxford Theology and Religion Monographs. Oxford: Oxford University Press, 2017.

Law, David R. "A Cacophony of Voices: The Multiple Authors and Readers of Kierkegaard's *The Point of View for My Work as an Author*." In *The Point of View*, edited by Robert L. Perkins, 12–47. International Kierkegaard Commentary 22. Macon, GA: Macon University Press, 2010.

Léon, Céline. "The No Woman's Land of Kierkegaardian Seduction." In *Either/Or, Part I*, edited by Robert L. Perkins, 229–50. International Kierkegaard Commentary 3. Macon, GA: Mercer University Press, 1995.

Lessing, Gotthold Ephraim. "On the Proof of the Spirit and of Power." In *Lessing: Philosophical and Theological Writings*, edited and translated by H. B. Nisbet, 83–88. Cambridge Texts in the History of Philosophy. Cambridge: Cambridge University Press, 2005.

Lewis, C. S. *The Problem of Pain*. New York: HarperOne, 2001.

Lippitt, John. *Humour and Irony in Kierkegaard's Thought*. London: Macmillan, 2000.

———. "Kierkegaard, 'the Public', and the Vices of Virtue-Signaling: The Dangers of Social Comparison." *Religions* 14.11 (2023) 1370. https://doi.org/10.3390/rel14111370.

Lowrie, Walter. "Introduction." In *Stages on Life's Way*, translated by Walter Lowrie, 3–16. London: Oxford University Press, 1945.

Lucas, George, dir. *Star Wars*. Los Angeles: Twentieth Century-Fox, 1977.

———, dir. *Star Wars: Episode IV—A New Hope*. Special ed. Los Angeles: Twentieth Century-Fox, 1997.

MacMullen, Ramsay. *Christianizing the Roman Empire: A.D. 100–400*. New Haven, CT: Yale University Press, 1984.

Malantschuk, Gregor. *Kierkegaard's Way to the Truth: An Introduction to the Authorship of Søren Kierkegaard*. Translated by Mary Michelsen. Minneapolis: Augsburg, 1963.

Marcar, G. P. "Godly Diversions and Gifted Teachers: Learning Joyful Stewardship from the Birds and the Lilies with Søren Kierkegaard." *Theological Studies* 82.3 (2021) 400–417. https://doi.org/10.1177/00405639211032700.

Marsh, James L. "Kierkegaard's Double Dialectic of Despair and Sin." In *The Sickness unto Death*, edited by Robert L. Perkins, 67–83. International Kierkegaard Commentary 19. Macon, GA: Mercer University Press, 1987.

Marshall, Ronald F. "The Traversed Path: Kierkegaard's Complex Way to Religious Simplicity." In *The Point of View*, edited by Robert L. Perkins, 117–56. International Kierkegaard Commentary 22. Macon, GA: Macon University Press, 2010.

Marx, Karl. "Contribution to the Critique of Hegel's *Philosophy of Right*: Introduction." In *The Marx-Engels Reader*, 2nd ed., edited by Robert C. Tucker, 53–65. New York: Norton, 1978.

McCabe, Herbert. "God, Evil, and Divine Responsibility." In *Philosophy of Religion: A Guide and Anthology*, edited by Brian Davies, 614–24. Oxford: Oxford University Press, 2000.

McCall, Thomas H. *Against God and Nature: The Doctrine of Sin*. Foundations of Evangelical Theology, edited by John S. Feinberg. Wheaton, IL: Crossway, 2019.

———. *An Invitation to Analytic Christian Theology*. Downers Grove, IL: IVP Academic, 2015.

McDonald, William. "Kierkegaard and Romanticism." In *The Oxford Handbook of Kierkegaard*, edited by John Lippitt and George Pattison, 94–111. Oxford: Oxford University Press, 2013.

McDougall, Charles, dir. *The Office*. Season 2, episode 21, "Conflict Resolution." Aired May 4, 2006, on NBC.

Millay, Thomas J. "Concrete and Otherworldly: Reading Kierkegaard's *Works of Love* Alongside Hegel's *Philosophy of Right*." *Modern Theology* 34.1 (2018) 23–41. https://doi.org/10.1111/moth.12368.

———. *Kierkegaard and the New Nationalism: A Contemporary Reinterpretation of the Attack upon Christendom*. Lanham, MD: Lexington, 2022.

Morley, Brian K. *Mapping Apologetics: Comparing Contemporary Approaches*. Downers Grove, IL: IVP, 2015.

Morris, T. F. "Constantin Constantius's Search for an Acceptable Way of Life." In *Fear and Trembling and Repetition*, edited by Robert L. Perkins, 309–34. International Kierkegaard Commentary 6. Macon, GA: Mercer University Press, 1993.

Morris, Thomas V. *Our Idea of God: An Introduction to Philosophical Theology*. Vancouver: Regent College, 2002.

Nietzsche, Friedrich. *Thus Spoke Zarathustra*. Translated by Clancy Martin. New York: Barnes & Noble, 2005.

Nisbet, H. B. "Introduction." In *Gotthold Ephraim Lessing: Philosophical and Theological Writings*, 1–22. Cambridge Texts in the History of Philosophy. Cambridge: Cambridge University Press, 2005.

Nun, Katalin. "Thomasine Gyllembourg's *Two Ages* and Her Portrayal of Everyday Life." In *Kierkegaard and His Contemporaries: The Culture of Golden Age Denmark*, edited by Jon Stewart, 272–97. Kierkegaard Studies 10. New York: De Gruyter, 2003.

Ong, Yi-Ping. "On Authenticity and the Concept of the Public in Kierkegaard and Heidegger." *MLN* 137.5 (2022) 872–83. https://doi.org/10.1353/mln.2022.0065.

Origen. *Against Celsus*. In *Fathers of the Third Century: Tertullian, Part Fourth; Minucius Felix; Commodian; Origen, Parts First and Second*, edited by Alexander Roberts, et al., translated by Frederick Crombie, 4:395–669. The Ante-Nicene Fathers. Buffalo: Christian Literature, 1885.

Ortega y Gasset, José. *La rebelión de las masas y otros ensayos*. Madrid: Alianza Editorial, 2014.

Otto, Rudolph. *The Idea of the Holy: An Inquiry into the Non-Rational Factor in the Idea of the Divine and Its Relation to the Relational*. Translated by John W. Harvey. Oxford: Oxford University Press, 1958.

Pelikan, Jaroslav. *The Emergence of the Catholic Tradition (100–600)*. The Christian Tradition: A History of the Development of Doctrine. Chicago: University of Chicago Press, 1971.

Perkins, Robert L. "Introduction." In *Fear and Trembling and Repetition*, edited by Robert L. Perkins, 3–8. International Kierkegaard Commentary 6. Macon, GA: Mercer University Press, 1993.

———. "Reading Kierkegaard's *Prefaces* with 'Continual Reference to Socrates.'" In *Prefaces and Writing Sample and Three Discourses on Imagined Occasions*, edited by Robert L. Perkins, 111–38. International Kierkegaard Commentary 9–10. Macon, GA: Mercer University Press, 2006.

Peterson, Mark C. E. "Ringing Doorbells: Eleventh Books and Authentic Authorship in Preface VII." In *Prefaces and Writing Sample and Three Discourses on Imagined Occasions*, edited by Robert L. Perkins, 87–109. International Kierkegaard Commentary 9–10. Macon, GA: Mercer University Press, 2006.

Piety, M. G. "A Little Light Music: The Subversion of Objectivity in Kierkegaard's *Philosophical Fragments*." In *Philosophical Fragments and Johannes Climacus*, 47–62. International Kierkegaard Commentary, edited by Robert L. Perkins, vol. 7. Macon: Mercer University Press, 1994.

———. *Ways of Knowing: Kierkegaard's Pluralistic Epistemology*. Waco, TX: Baylor University Press, 2010.

Plantinga, Alvin. *God, Freedom, and Evil*. New York: Harper & Row, 1974.

Plato. *Phaedo*. In *Plato: Complete Works*, edited by John M. Cooper, translated by G. M. A. Grube, 49–100. Indianapolis: Hackett, 1997.

Pojman, Louis. *The Logic of Subjectivity: Kierkegaard's Philosophy of Religion*. Tuscaloosa: University of Alabama Press, 1984.

Poole, Roger. *Kierkegaard: The Indirect Communication*. Studies in Religion and Culture. Charlottesville: University of Virginia Press, 1993.

Prior, Karen Swallow. *The Evangelical Imagination: How Stories, Images, and Metaphors Created a Culture in Crisis*. Grand Rapids: Brazos, 2023.

Putman, Rhyne R. *The Method of Christian Theology: A Basic Introduction*. Nashville: B&H Academic, 2021.

Rae, Murray. *Kierkegaard and Theology*. Philosophy and Theology. London: T&T Clark, 2010.

Roberts, Robert C. "Passion and Reflection." In *Two Ages*, edited by Robert L. Perkins, 87–106. International Kierkegaard Commentary 14. Macon, GA: Mercer University Press, 1984.

———. *Recovering Christian Character: The Psychological Wisdom of Søren Kierkegaard*. Kierkegaard as a Christian Thinker, edited by C. Stephen Evans and Paul Martens. Grand Rapids: Eerdmans, 2022.

———. "Rhetoric and Understanding: Authorship as Christian Mission." In *Authorship and Authority in Kierkegaard's Writings*, edited by Joseph Westfall, 41–58. London: Bloomsbury Academic, 2019.

Rowe, William L. *Philosophy of Religion: An Introduction*. 3rd ed. Belmont, CA: Wadsworth/Thomson Learning, 2001.

Schaeffer, Francis A. *The God Who Is There*. 2nd ed. The Complete Works of Francis A. Schaeffer 1. Westerchester, IL: Crossway, 1982.

Schleiermacher, Friedrich. *The Christian Faith*. 3rd ed. Cornerstones. London: T&T Clark, 2016.

Schönbaumsfeld, Genia. "The Aesthetic as Mirror of Faith in Kierkegaard's Fear and Trembling." *European Journal of Philosophy* 27.3 (2019) 661–74. https://doi.org/10.1111/ejop.12444.

Silliman, Daniel. "RZIM Spent Nearly $1M Suing Ravi Zacharias Abuse Victim." *Christianity Today*, Feb. 23, 2022. https://www.christianitytoday.com/2022/02/rzim-board-donor-money-guidepost-report-ravi/.

Silliman, Daniel, and Kate Shellnutt. “Ravi Zacharias Hid Hundreds of Pictures of Women, Abuse During Massages, and a Rape Allegation.” *Christianity Today*, Feb. 11, 2021. https://www.christianitytoday.com/2021/02/ravi-zacharias-rzim-investigation-sexual-abuse-sexting-rape/.

Silverman, Allan. “Plato’s Middle Period Metaphysics and Epistemology.” In *The Stanford Encyclopedia of Philosophy*, Fall 2014, edited by Edward N. Zalta. Metaphysics Research Lab, Stanford University, 2014. https://plato.stanford.edu/archives/fall2014/entries/plato-metaphysics/.

Sire, James W. *Naming the Elephant: Worldview as a Concept*. 2nd ed. Downers Grove, IL: IVP Academic, 2015.

———. *The Universe Next Door: A Basic Worldview Catalog*. 4th ed. Downers Grove, IL: IVP Academic, 2004.

Smith, James K. A. *Desiring the Kingdom: Worship, Worldview, and Cultural Formation*. Cultural Liturgies 1. Grand Rapids: Baker Academic, 2009.

Stan, Leo. “Qualitative Difference.” In *Kierkegaard’s Concepts: Tome V: Objectivity to Sacrifice*, edited by Jon Stewart, 15:179–83. Kierkegaard Research: Sources, Reception and Resources. Burlington, VT: Ashgate, 2015.

Steiner, Henriette. *The Emergence of a Modern City: Golden Age Copenhagen 1800–1850*. New York: Routledge, 2014.

Steinmetz, Michael Nathan. *The Severed Self: The Doctrine of Sin in the Works of Søren Kierkegaard*. Kierkegaard Studies Monograph Series 38. Berlin: De Gruyter, 2021.

Stern, David S. “The Ties That Bind: The Limits of Aesthetic Reflection in Kierkegaard’s *Either/Or*.” In *Either/Or, I*, edited by Robert L. Perkins, 251–69. International Kierkegaard Commentary 3. Macon, GA: Mercer University Press, 1995.

Stewart, Jon. “Hegel’s *Phenomenology* as a Systematic Fragment.” In *The Cambridge Companion to Hegel*, edited by Frederick C. Beiser, 74–93. Cambridge: Cambridge University Press, 1993.

———. “Kierkegaard and Hegelianism in Golden Age Denmark.” In *Kierkegaard and His Contemporaries: The Culture of Golden Age Denmark*, 106–45. Kierkegaard Studies, edited by Jon Stewart, vol. 10. New York: De Gruyter, 2003.

———. “Kierkegaard’s View of Hegel, His Followers and Critics.” In *A Companion to Kierkegaard*, edited by Jon Stewart, 50–65. Blackwell Companions to Philosophy 58. Chichester, UK: Wiley Blackwell, 2015.

Strawser, Michael. *Kierkegaard and the Philosophy of Love*. Lanham, MD: Lexington, 2015.

Söderquist, Anna Louise Strelis. “Finitude, Necessity, and Healing from Despair in Kierkegaard’s *The Lily and the Bird*.” *Journal of Religious Ethics* 52.1 (2024) 95–113. https://doi.org/10.1111/jore.12448.

Taliaferro, Charles. *Contemporary Philosophy of Religion*. Malden, MA: Blackwell, 1998.

Taylor, Charles. *A Secular Age*. Cambridge, MA: Belknap, 2007.

Taylor, Mark C. *Journeys to Selfhood: Hegel and Kierkegaard*. Berkeley: University of California Press, 1980.

Thomas, J. Heywood. “Revelation, Knowledge, and Proof.” In *Philosophical Fragments and Johannes Climacus*, 147–68. International Kierkegaard Commentary 7. Macon, GA: Mercer University Press, 1994.

Tietjen, Mark A. *Kierkegaard: A Christian Missionary to Christians*. Downers Grove, IL: IVP Academic, 2016.

———. *Kierkegaard, Communication, and Virtue: Authorship as Edification.* Bloomington: Indiana University Press, 2013.

Tillich, Paul. *Systematic Theology.* Vol. 1. Chicago: University of Chicago Press, 1973.

Tolkien, J. R. R. *The Return of the King.* 2nd ed. Boston: Houghton Mifflin, 1993.

Turchin, Sean A., and Christian Kettering. "Søren Kierkegaard: Apologetic of Christianity for Christendom." In *The History of Apologetics*, edited by Benjamin K. Forrest, et al., 410–28. Grand Rapids: Zondervan, 2020.

Tyson, Paul. *Kierkegaard's Theological Sociology: Prophetic Fire for the Present Age.* Eugene, OR: Cascade, 2019.

Van Nieuwenhove, Rik. *An Introduction to Medieval Theology.* Cambridge: Cambridge University Press, 2012.

Vera, Ángel Viñas. "Escribir filosofía: Kierkegaard y su *Forord*." *Cuadernos salmantinos de filosofía* 48 (Dec. 2021) 421–41.

Walsh, Sylvia. "Echoes of Absurdity: The Offended Consciousness and the Absolute Paradox in Kierkegaard's *Philosophical Fragments*." In *Philosophical Fragments and Johannes Climacus*, 33–46. International Kierkegaard Commentary 7. Macon, GA: Mercer University Press, 1994.

———. "If the Lily Could Speak: On the Contentment and Glory of Being Human." In *Upbuilding Discourses in Various Spirits*, edited by Robert L. Perkins, 129–52. International Kierkegaard Commentary 15. Macon, GA: Mercer, 2005.

Waltke, Bruce K., and Cathi J. Fredricks. *Genesis: A Commentary.* Grand Rapids: Zondervan, 2001.

Watkin, Julia. "Judge William—A Christian?" In *Either/Or, Part II*, edited by Robert L. Perkins, 113–24. International Kierkegaard Commentary 4. Macon, GA: Mercer University Press, 1995.

Westfall, Joseph. "Introduction: On Kierkegaard's Work as an Author." In *Authorship and Authority in Kierkegaard's Writings*, edited by Joseph Westfall, 1–25. London: Bloomsbury Academic, 2019.

Westphal, Merold. "Abraham and Hegel." In *Kierkegaard's* Fear and Trembling: *Critical Appraisals*, edited by Robert L. Perkins, 62–80. Tuscaloosa: University of Alabama Press, 1981.

———. "Johannes and Johannes: Kierkegaard and Difference." In *Philosophical Fragments and Johannes Climacus*, edited by Robert L. Perkins, 53–71. International Kierkegaard Commentary 7. Macon, GA: Mercer University Press, 1994.

———. "Kierkegaard's Sociology." In *Two Ages*, edited by Robert L. Perkins, 133–54. International Kierkegaard Commentary 14. Macon, GA: Mercer University Press, 1984.

Wilson, Rainn. "Atheist Plays Devil's Advocate for God's Existence (w/ Alex O'Connor)." Soul Boom w/ Rainn Wilson, Feb. 2, 2025. https://youtu.be/T6YJWoceB6U?si=O5Piwf3CHdvgjpdM.

Wright, N. T. *Surprised by Hope: Rethinking Heaven, the Resurrection, and the Mission of the Church.* New York: HarperOne, 2008.

Zwingli, Ulrich. "The Declaration of Huldreich Zwingli Regarding Original Sin, Addressed to Urbanus Rhegius." In *Zwingli: On Providence and Other Essays*, edited by William John Hinke, translated by Henry Preble, 1–61. Durham, NC: Labyrinth, 1983.

Index

absurd, 9, 47, 65, 69, 70–72, 81, 88, 161, 179
  absurdity, 9, 78
Adorno, Theodor W., 24
aesthetic sphere/stage, 48–49, 51–57, 62, 71, 79, 114, 119–21, 123–26, 129
Anderson, Tawa J., 112
Andic, Martin, 175
Anselm, 44
anxiety, 74–75, 85, 89–94, 128, 166, 168, 170, 178–79
Arendt, Hannah, 176
Augustine, 3, 28, 82, 132, 136, 160, 171, 173, 176

Barrett, Lee C., 2, 101, 117, 173
Barth, Karl, 44
Berkhof, Louis, 39–40
Berthold, Daniel, 122
Blackburn, Simon, 69
Bonhoeffer, Dietrich, 48, 77
Bowen, Amber, 124, 173
Brunner, Emil, 33, 40
Buber, Martin, 47–48
Byrne, James M., 17, 35

Calvin, John, 83
Cappelørn, Niels Jørgen, 116–17, 120–21, 150
Carron, Paul, 165, 167
Christendom, 5–7, 48, 50, 78, 109–11, 119, 132, 138–39, 149–52
Connell, George, 60
Craig, William Lane, 4–5, 15, 132, 136, 181
Crites, Stephen, 52, 54–55, 114, 131
Cuarón, Alfonso, 80

Daise, Benjamin, 111–12
Davis, Melissa, 76
Deede, Kristen K., 97
Descartes, René, 7, 20, 33, 39, 76
Dew, James K., Jr., 5–6, 69–70
Dewey, Bradley R., 123–25
Dunning, Stephen N., 105
Dupré, Louis K., 87–88

Edwards, Aaron P., 122
Erickson, Millard, 38, 86
ethical sphere/stage, 48–50, 56–59, 61–63, 68, 71, 79, 119–21, 124–25, 129
  Sittlichkeit, 65–68, 72, 79
  teleological suspension, 47, 67–69, 72, 75
Evans, C. Stephen, 46, 51–52, 54, 63–64, 119

faith
  authentic, 6, 14, 62–64, 68–69, 75, 78
  leap of, 3–4, 14, 36, 69
  leap to/toward 16–17, 35–37, 56, 63–64, 70, 97, 101, 151
  objective, 42–43, 109, 150

faith (cont.)
    secular, 11, 157–59, 161–64, 166, 168, 171
    subjective, 14, 50, 77
Farley, Harry, 137
Ferreira, M. Jamie, 36
fideism, 5–6, 36, 69, 70, 78
    fideist, 6, 9, 36, 71
Findlay, J. N., 24, 66
Fredricks, Cathi J., 89
Furtak, Rick Anthony, 166, 168–69

Gabriel, Merigala, 15
Garff, Joakim, 73, 116
Garrett, James Leo, Jr., 85
Glenn, John D., Jr., 88
Gould, Paul M., 5–6, 69–70
Gouwens, David Jay, 2
Green, Ronald M., 46–47, 64
Grøn, Arne, 85, 90–91
Groothuis, Douglas, 6, 10, 132
Guthrie, Shirley C., Jr., 98–99, 136
Gyllembourg, Thomasine, 140–41, 143

Hägglund, Martin, 11, 156–64, 166, 170–71, 173, 176
Hall, Amy Luara, 60
Hannay, Alastair, 34–35, 74, 86
Hanson, Jeffrey, 55, 67–68, 72
Harwood, Adam, 100
Hegel, George Wilhelm Friedrich, 16–17, 21–25, 27, 32, 39, 65–68, 76, 86–87, 128
    Hegelian, 7, 23, 31–32, 34, 48–49, 65, 67–68, 70, 72, 75–76, 79, 131, 142, 146, 164
    Hegelianism, 32, 49, 68, 70, 72, 77–78, 129–30, 132
Heiberg, J. L., 21, 140–41
Hodge, Charles, 38–39
Holland, Dean, 156
Hong, Edna H., 138–39
Hong, Howard V., 138–39

Jenson, Kipton E., 22
Jones, Terry, 59
Jones, W. T., 21
Jordán, Nassim Bravo, 129

Kain, Philip J., 66
Keeley, Louise Carroll, 170–71
Keller, Timothy, 3
Kemp, Ryan, 49
Kirmmse, Bruce H., 73, 109, 140–42, 180
Kjældgaard, Lasse Horne, 126, 129–30
Kline, Peter, 102
Kramer, Nathaniel, 121, 123–24
Kreeft, Peter, 30, 132
Krishek, Sharon, 166, 168–69, 173

Lappano, David, 146, 149, 151
Law, David R., 116
leap, 9, 15, 20, 34–37, 50, 56, 93, 95, 98, 101, 106, 152
    of/to faith, see faith
Léon, Céline, 124
Lessing, Gotthold Ephraim, 16–22, 24–25, 27, 30–31, 33–35, 39, 41
    Lessing's ditch, 20, 29, 34–35, 40
Lewis, C. S., 81, 90
Lippitt, John, 56, 58, 65, 150–51
Lowrie, Walter, 57
Lucas, George, 19–20

MacMullen, Ramsay, 18
Malantschuk, Gregor, 49–50, 56–57, 60–61
Marcar, G. P., 169
Marsh, James L., 94
Marshall, Ronald F., 113
Marx, Karl, 156
McCabe, Herbert, 84
McCall, Thomas H., 40, 94
McDonald, William, 141
McDougall, Charles, 145
Millay, Thomas J., 141–42, 152, 174
Morley, Brian K., 6, 132
Morris, T. F., 55
Morris, Thomas V., 40

Nietzsche, Friedrich, 156, 168
Nisbet, H. B., 17
Nun, Katalin, 140–41, 143

objectivity, 9, 15, 32–33, 43–44, 116, 150, 153, 159, 179
    objective faith, see faith
    objective truth, see truth

Ong, Yi-Ping, 147
Origen, 18–19
Ortega y Gasset, José, 142, 144
Otto, Rudolph, 41

paradox, 9, 29, 47–48, 67–68, 129
  absolute, 28–29, 65, 72
  paradoxical 62, 72
Pelikan, Jaroslav, 176
Perkins, Robert L., 47, 52, 129
Peterson, Mark C. E., 130
Piety, M. G., 27–28, 30–31
Plantinga, Alvin, 82
Plato, 52–53, 176
Platonism, 164, 170, 176
Pojman, Louis, 69–70
Poole, Roger, 115–16
Prior, Karen Swallow, 133
pseudonym
  A, 51–52, 55, 58, 115, 118–19, 121
  Anti-Climacus, 61, 94, 118, 120
  Constantin Constantius, 52–57, 114, 118–19
  Frater Taciturnus, 51, 57, 61, 118, 120, 139
  H. H., 118, 120
  Hilarious Bookbinder, 118, 120
  Johannes Climacus, 14, 26–27, 30, 33–34, 39, 57, 118–20
  Johannes de Silentio, 9, 47–49, 63–70, 72, 75, 114, 118–19, 160, 181
  Johannes the Seducer, 51, 111, 115, 118–19, 121–26
  Judge William, 57–61, 115, 118–21
  Nicolaus Notabene, 73–74, 111, 118, 120–21, 126–32
  Pastor, 58, 115, 118–19
  Petrus Minor, 118, 120
  Victor Eremita, 115, 118–19, 121
  Vigilius Haufniensis, 86, 118, 120
  William Afham, 114, 118, 120
  Young Man, 51–53, 56–57, 118–19
Putman, Rhyne R., 136

qualitative
  abyss, 4
  category, 101, 106
  decision, 34
  difference, 3, 39, 41, 65, 93
  sphere, 98
  state, 88, 93, 95–96
  transition, 36
Rae, Murray, 2
religious sphere/stage, 48–50, 56, 58–59, 61–62, 67–68, 73–74, 79, 120
  Religiousness A, 61–63, 97, 114
  Religiousness B, 61–63
Roberts, Robert C., 113, 143–44, 175
Rowe, William L., 81–82, 84

Schaeffer, Francis, 3, 14–16, 36, 69
Schleiermacher, Friedrich, 21–22, 24–25, 27, 39, 41
Schönbaumsfeld, Genia, 53
Shellnutt, Kate, 137
Silliman, Daniel, 137
Sire, James W., 2, 112
Smith, James K. A., 7, 132–33
Socrates, 26, 28, 33, 52–53
Söderquist, Anne Louise Strelis, 166, 170
Stan, Leo, 93
Steiner, Henriette, 142
Stern, David S., 125
Stewart, Jon, 21, 23–24
Strawser, Michael, 172
subjectivity 9, 15, 32–36, 38, 42–44, 62, 113, 116, 143, 146, 149–50, 152, 178–79
  subjective faith, see faith
  subjective truth, see truth

Tacelli, Ronald L., 30, 132
Taliaferro, Charles, 83
Taylor, Charles, 39, 55
Taylor, Mark C., 58, 61
Thomas, J. Heywood, 34, 71
Tietjen, Mark A., 5, 15, 116–17
Tillich, Paul, 136
Tolkien, J. R. R., 105
truth, 7–9, 12, 14, 20–24, 26–28, 32, 34, 37, 40, 43, 70, 107, 109–10, 113–14, 179, 181
  as approximation, 31–33, 35
  objective, 4, 14–16, 30, 31, 33, 42, 178
  subjective/subjectivity, 9, 15, 17, 30, 31, 35, 77, 130, 131
Tyson, Paul, 109, 145

Van Nieuwenhove, Rik, 176
Vera, Ángel Viñas, 131

Walsh, Sylvia, 72, 104
Waltke, Bruce K., 89
Watkin, Julia, 58
Westfall, Joseph, 115
Westphal, Merold, 54, 59, 63, 65, 67–68, 148
Wilson, Rainn, 133
Wright, N. T., 170, 176

Zwingli, Ulrich, 100

www.ingramcontent.com/pod-product-compliance
Lightning Source LLC
LaVergne TN
LVHW050632100826
845148LV00011B/1839

* 9 7 9 8 3 8 5 2 3 7 1 4 2 *